The Channel to the Med

A Guide to the Main Routes Through the French Canals

by

Derek Bowskill

PREFACE

I hope my passionate enthusiasm for the Inland Waterways of France comes over. Five years of single-handed endeavour through thousands of locks with a wooden sea-going boat have done nothing but increase my determination to return. I hope I can help you reach similar gratification.

derek bowskill,
pool in wharfedale,
may 1995.

To Anthea: The Channel to the Med........or a

Printed in Great Britain by:
Redwood Books, Trowbridge, Wiltshire

Photography: Derek Bowskill
Front Cover:
Back cover:

First edition 1995

ISBN 1 898574 01 4

Copyright © Derek Bowskill
Opus Book Publishing Limited
Millhouse, Riseden Road, Wadhurst, East Sussex TN5 6NY.

CONTENTS

INTRODUCTION

This is a guide to the main French Inland Waterways that descend from the English Channel to the Mediterranean Sea. It aims to help you plan and navigate your route: choosing between numbers of locks; availability of facilities; scenic appeal; peace and quiet; possible problems with props, keels and draught - or just getting to the Mediterranean as fast as possible.

For those new to these waterways, it also provides much useful information to ease your way through what can at first appear to be daunting difficulties. For example: the many different ways of working locks (or even lock-keepers!) Once you have read the section on locking in the first chapter I hope any apprehension you may feel will have been allayed.

Chapters are arranged by waterway as shown in the Contents and each is prefaced by a full-page outline map. Chapter sections, where appropriate, are preceded by an 'over-view' map; while the detailed commentaries are accompanied by full-page maps covering each section of the waterway. Locks, marinas, good moorings and notable stopping places are indicated by the symbols on the maps (shewn on p.6). The main outline maps are orientated north/south, but the detailed maps are presented for the best convenience of those who are heading 'from the channel to the med'. When studying these maps it should be remembered that the terms 'left bank' and 'right bank' always refer to a passage downstream and towards the sea.

Readers may wish to know that the research for this guide covered the years 1991 to 1995, and was undertaken in my (now old) friend, the motor-sailer Valcon. She was built in 1964 at Aberdour, by Finlayson Marine; she has twin Parsons Pike 56HP diesels and 6 berths in 3 cabins; she carries 175 gallons of fuel and 175 gallons of water. Her vital statistics are:

LOA	33' x 31'	10.1m x 9.45m
Beam	12'	3.66m
Draught	5'	1.52m
Air Draught	11'	3.35m

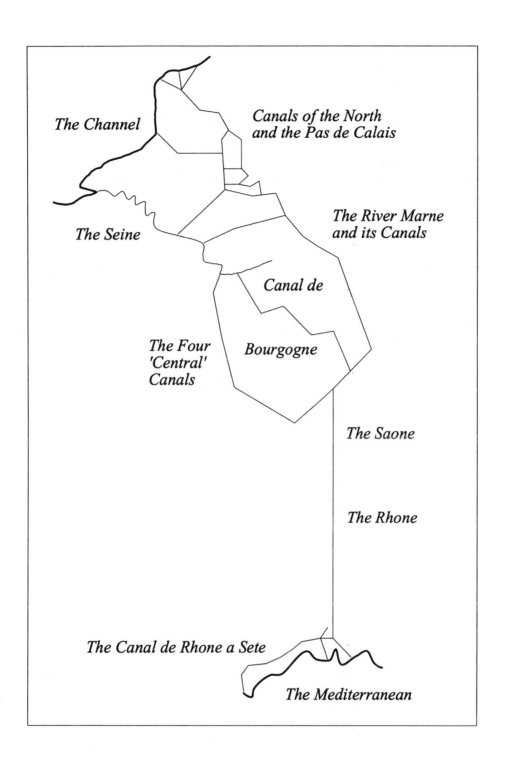

The Channel

Canals of the North
and the Pas de Calais

The Seine

The River Marne
and its Canals

Canal de

The Four
'Central'
Canals

Bourgogne

The Saone

The Rhone

The Canal de Rhone a Sete

The Mediterranean

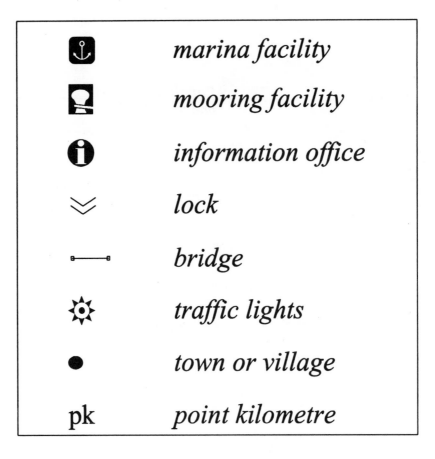

	marina facility
	mooring facility
	information office
	lock
	bridge
	traffic lights
●	*town or village*
pk	*point kilometre*

Glossary

Ancre	*anchor*	Hausse	*rising water (river)*
Bac	*ferry*	Haut-fonds	*impassable shoals*
Base Fluviale	*mooring with facilities*	L'Ecluse	*lock*
Bas-fonds	*shallows/shoals passable*	Largeur	*beam, width*
	for light draught vessels	Le Rouge	*red Diesel (illegal for yachts)*
Bateaux Mouches	*Paris trip boats*	Papiers/Cartes	*ship's papers*
Berge	*bank (of canal)*	Peniche	*barge*
Bief	*'pound' or reach of canal*	Plaisanciers	*leisure boat users*
Chomage	*lock closure or stoppage*	PK	*kilometre mark*
Darse	*tidal basin or dock*	Port de Plaisance	*leisure boat harbour*
Digue	*dyke, embankment*	Rive	*bank (of river)*
Essence	*petrol*	Sas	*lock chamber*
Feux-de-route	*navigation lights*	Souterrain	*tunnel*
Gas-oil	*diesel*	Vignette	*VNF Licence*
Halte Nautique	*stopping place*		

CHAPTER ONE

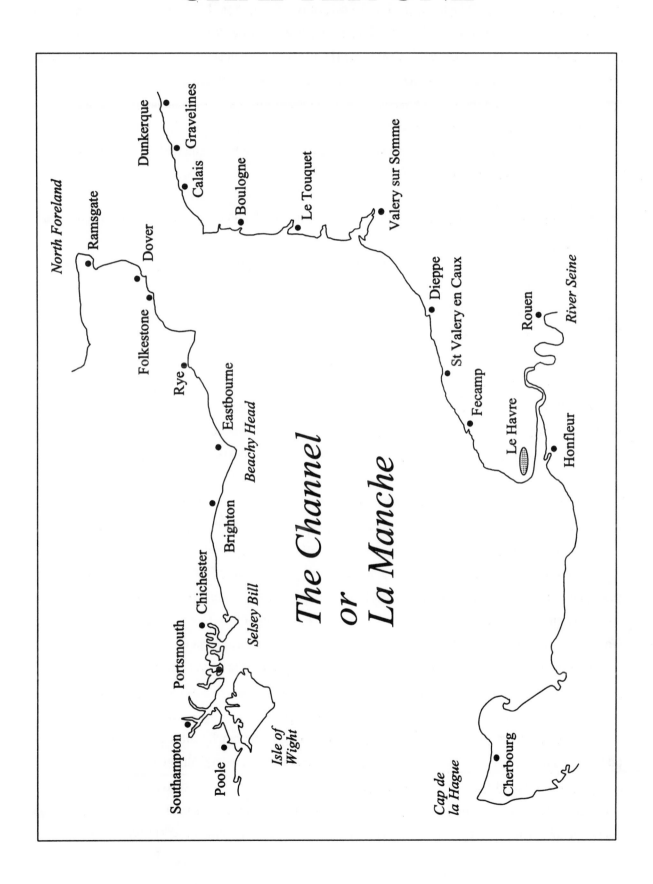

GETTING STARTED
PREPARATIONS

French Inland Waterways Requirements: for skippers of boats up to 15m LOA or capable of speeds not in excess of 20km/hr the requirement is as the French Certificate C: Coches de Plaisance; what the French call houseboats. For this, the UK equivalent is the Helmsman's Certificate of Competence (HOCC) or the International Certificate of Competence (ICC). For skippers of boats exceeding 15m LOA or capable of speeds in excess of 20km/hr the requirement is as the French Certificate PP: Peniches de Plaisance, namely barges converted into houseboats. For this, there is no exact UK equivalent, but in practice, the HOCC or the ICC are accepted. (It is also recommended to carry on board the CEVNI Rules: the European Code for Inland Waterways.)

In general, the permitted legal maximum dimensions for the rivers and canals between the Channel and the Mediterranean Sea are as follows:

Length	38.50m	126' 3"(converted down)
Beam	5.00m	16' 4"
Draught	1.80m	5' 10"
Air Draught	3.50m	11' 5"

This is not quite as straightforward as it might be, since the figures are all 'at best'. They take no account of the curves of bridges or the silted sides of canals; nor, of course, can they take into consideration the full width of the wheel-house at its maximum air draught, the type of hull or the position of the propeller(s). The need to bear all these factors in mind will come as no surprise to those skippers who have some experience of UK canals. But, as hinted above, most of the boats that get taken into the French system have been tried and tested very little in English rivers and seldom, if at all, in the canals. Most inveterate UK canal devotees are possessed of narrow boats and thus not equipped for a channel crossing. So, apparently, never the twain shall meet; which is unfortunate since the choice of the vessel is one of the most important factors in influencing your enjoyment of the French (or any other) canal system.

Many boats that would be quite suitable for cruising the smaller French canals cannot be described as being safely up to a full-blown channel crossing; although, in settled weather, small cruisers can easily and safely manage the Dover to Calais hop - especially if they travel in a group of four or five. However, there is the other side of the coin: some craft that would easily handle adverse weather conditions on even the longest of the crossings would not be suitable for the inland waterways once they got there. So the restrictions are twofold: a craft that is properly suited to a channel crossing and one that is also suited to the constraints of the canals and does not exceed the maximum permitted dimensions.

Two factors require serious thought before setting off on a French canals expedition: first, the position and protection of propellers; and second the problems associated with deep keel and bilge keel craft. One central propeller is in no danger, but is not of much help when manoeuvring in the tight circumstances that frequently prevail in the locks - and sometimes in the canals themselves. Twin propellers overcome the manoeuvring problems, but at the cost of vulnerability. Some locks (fortunately not many) have sloping sides - by design; and most of the waterways have sloping banks - by deterioration. Whatever the cause, this has the unfortunate result of making exposed propellers a liability, and bilge keels a really doubtful proposition. The sheer irritation of not being able to moor up easily and the risk of grounding when forced into the side by the (no more than proper) demands of a large barge in a narrow waterway can soon build into major aggravations and easily spoil everyone's enjoyment. You can arrange to have your propellers protected by seeking professional advice and attention in a boatyard; however, sad as it may be, there is no similar amelioration available for deep and bilge keeled boats.

Masts must come down everywhere except on the Seine up to Rouen. Many craft carry them on deck trestles without much inconvenience but if they exceed the length of the boat by more than a little, they will be a serious encumbrance. While it is true they can provide welcome support for a protective sun awning, they also offer a continuing and serious challenge to the skull. After my first year on the canals in Valcon, I arranged to stow them ashore and/or have them transported by land. It was much less expensive than I had thought, and the sense of freedom on deck was terrific. You may want to consider arranging for this at Calais, Dunkerque, Le Havre or Rouen.

A useful publication for general interest and up-to-date information is: FLUVIAL, a bi-monthly magazine published at 64, rue Jean Jacques Rousseau, 21000 DIJON. Tel: 00.33.80.73.39.39

PAPERWORK AND LICENCES

Voies Navigables de France - after much changing of minds and attitudes, VNF seem to have reached something of a compromise with the representatives of French leisure craft owners. Presently, the situation is as follows.

"*French Waterways (Voies Navigables de France - VNF) is the public body which takes responsibility for maintaining, running and developing most of the 8,500km of canals and canalised rivers which flow through our country. Over and above the main axes of waterborne transport, many different routes are now kept busy thanks to leisure users.*

So as to promote this activity VNF has set itself the priority of improving the service throughout the network which it looks after. The development of river-going tourism will require changes in the existing equipment to suit leisure boat travel. This is why VNF has decided to concentrate its efforts this year on installing equipment to make travel more comfortable. Water supply points and household waste containers will be provided. At the same time the leisure boat travellers will be consulted, making it possible to draw up a programme for equipping the river network with more elaborate services (toilets, washing and shower facilities, telephones etc.,) to which users would have access.

The network needs to be well maintained and well run to have an overall improvement in services. This is financed by contributions from all the users. For leisure boat users, this contribution will take the form of a statutory payment or toll.

The toll must be paid by all leisure boat owners. Light craft of 5 metres length and under with a motor of less than 9.9 CV in real terms (that is 7.29 kw) as well as all manually propelled boats are exempt from payment. The toll is due each time the boat travels on waterways entrusted to VNF; it gives the right to normal use of waterways in the public domain. By boat travel we understand boat movements, whether or not the boat passes through a lock.

The toll does not exempt the user from:

- payment for certain extra services such as going through underground passages in a tug convoy, use of lifts, sloping water sections ... or going through locks outside normal boating hours;

- mooring rights, especially in ports or for certain docking facilities which offer leisure users specialised services.

- the toll is not refundable.

When you pay the toll, you will receive a certificate of payment and a sticker which must be shown when required. The toll sticker must be placed at the front of the boat, on the starboard side so that it can been seen from outside, under all circumstances.

Checking-up operations may be carried out at any point in the network, either by official representatives from the VNF and the Services Navigation or by members of the police forces.

In the event of infringement, a police report will be drawn up. Those who contravene the regulations will be liable to pay a fine as laid down in the legislation and could in certain cases and after the agreement of the Chief Prosecutor of the French Republic pay a negotiated fine.

The toll sticker is available directly at one of the VNF centres, payable by cheque made out to Voies Navigables de France, in cash or by bank transfer, (VNF Bethune Siege, Bank code 10071. Code of cashier's desk: 62100 Bank, account Number 10003010 584 key 14.)

The simplest way is to pay the toll by post, sending it to the VNF centre of your choice. You must enclose the following with your payment

- the name of the owner and their address, the name of the boat,

- outside to outside length and width of the hull,

- the registration number, the enrolment number or at least the series number

- the type of toll desired and the dates of validity corresponding (for the "holiday" rate),

- a stamped envelope with your address,

If possible, produce or enclose a photocopy of the navigation permit, a sea card or a corresponding registration document, as well as proof of the motor's power. A receipt will be given on request.

In the case of the "leisure" rate, the user must date and sign one of the 30 spaces on the back of the toll card for each day of river travel. The back of the toll card must always be visible from the outside. The current rates are as follows: the prices are in French Francs:

	I	II	III	IV	V
	12m	12-25m	25-40m	40-60m	60+m
Yearly:	450	650	1300	2100	2600
Leisure: 30 days	250	450	800	1250	1550
Holiday: 15 days	100	200	300	400	500

The Waterbourne Tourism Bookshop specialises in "all that travels on water". You will find a wide selection of maps, books and guides at the VNF's bookshop to help you organise your stay and dis-

cover historical monuments, local cuisine - and special products. If you wish to prolong your holiday dream on water, art books, novels, travel books, posters and postcards are also available. To spread information about all the possibilities offered by waterways, VNF co-edits with Editions Danae the Fluvial Tourism Directory-Handbook. Where to rent a house-boat, what the most remarkable sites on the Canal de Bourgogne are, which lakes can be used for wind surfing, or where can one stop and fill up with fresh water or petrol? You will find all the answers to your questions as well as practical information and techniques and above all ideas for tourist itineraries, both picturesque and often little known. Price in 1995 149 FF. Orders and enquiries to La Librairie V.N.F., 18 quai d'Austerlitz 75684 PARIS Cedex 13. (Tel: 00.33.1.44.24.57.94. Fax: 00.33.1.45.84.58.46.)"

The relevant addresses and telephone numbers of the VNF Centres are given below. They can also provide a list of lock closures (chomages).

BOOKSHOP VNF	18, Quai d'Austerlitz. 75013 Paris Cedex 13	1.44.24.57.94
AGDE	Service de la Navigation de Toulouse	67.94.10.99
	Ecluse ronde d'Agde - 34304	67.94.23.09
ARLES	1, Quai Gare Maritime - 13637	90.96.00.85
BETHUNE	Chemin du halage - 62400	21.57.63.37
BETHUNE (Siege)	175, Rue Ludovic Boutleux - 62408	21.63.24.22
CALAIS	45, Quai de la Meuse - 62100	21.34.25.58
CHALON/SAONE	Port fluvial - 71100	85.43.20.10
CONFLANS	Cours de Chimay - 76700	1.39.72.73.09
DOUAI	319, Bd Paul Hayez	27.87.21.67
DUNKERQUE	Terre-plein du Jeu de Mail - 59140	28.25-30-78
LE HAVRE	La Citadelle Avenue Lucien Corbeaux - 76600	35.22.99.34
LYON	Quai Marechal Joffre - 69002	78.42.74.99
MARSEILLE/AUBIGNY	Ecluse d'Aubigny BP2 - 18320	48.76.41.95
PARIS	40, Quai de Grenelle - 75015	1.40.58-29.69
PARIS	18, Quai d'Austerlitz - 75013	1.45.84.85.69
PORT ST-LOUIS	Ecluse Maritime - 13230	42.48.41.94
REIMS	11, Bd Paul Doumer - 51084	26.85.75.95
ST JEAN DE LOSNE	17, Quai National BP 16 - 21170	80.29.01.37
SAINT MAMMES	11, Quai du Loing - 77670	60.70.53.65
SAINT QUENTIN	2, Avenue Leo Lagrange - 02100	23.62.60.21
SETE	1, Quai Philippe Regy - 34200	67.46.35.70
VALENCIENNES	24, Chemin du Halage - 59300	27.46.44.60
VITRY/FRANCOIS	La Citadelle BP 403 - 51308	26.74.60.94

GEAR

One subject frequently crops up first when boating folk discuss the French canals: the possibility of damage to the boat in a lock and its prevention by fenders. The written version of the French regulations is strict and strictly detailed. For example, *"Fenders must float. Tyres are only allowed if they have an inner tube, inflated so that they will float. Fix them in place with two crossed ropes tied to two different points on the boat."* The general and now almost customary understanding is not so rigid, and most visitors equip themselves with ordinary tyres, bind them thoroughly (mainly to protect the boat's hull) and secure them well. They then manage to proceed without let or hindrance from lock-keepers, inspectors or others.

In addition to fenders (if not, indeed, perhaps even instead of a whole host of fenders) a sturdy rubbing strake in heavy rubber, oak or rope will make life much easier when negotiating locks. It doesn't move; doesn't wear out; doesn't snag or catch; and can be cleaned without a lot of time, trouble or energy having to be expended. It costs a whole lot more than cast-off tyres and while it doesn't completely do away with the need for fenders, once the initial expense has been made, the rest is restful and relaxing.

In addition, and for all kinds of purposes, fendering included, a plank is a boon. In particular, it will enable you to get ashore even when you cannot moor up close enough to the side to be comfortable without it. Into this area come the other mooring necessities: four stout ropes of at least 20m, with a collection of (equally strong) shorter ones. At least two sound boat-hooks are needed; they are so easily broken or dropped overboard and lost and gone forever. Take strong wooden ones fitted with blunt metal double hook-ends.

Land anchors are also essential. The strong rounded heavy metal jobs are good in dryish conditions. In really wet muddy weather, metre-long wooden stakes in 2"x 2" are much more reliable. It is possible to get hold of long, strong 'corkscrew' anchors of which two have always been man enough to hold Valcon when the 'holding ground' has been good enough. Strong sharp axes and heavy hammers should accompany this gear; and there should always be two strong sharp knives to hand.

A reasonably powerful engine is essential and it must be able to run at slow speeds for a long time without getting aggrieved. For example, many is the time that I have had to cut one of Valcon's 56HP Parsons Pike diesels completely and run only at tick-over for hours at a time, simply to prevent causing damaging wash in narrow, shallow canals. It is important to have the engine well serviced in advance of the canal cruise, and a good idea to be able to have a few trips in hand to try it out before leaving. In addition, a full set of spares and all appropriate handbooks are essential.

Water intake filters can only too easily get blocked, from weed or the verge cuttings which are usually indiscriminately strewn over the length and breadth of the canal. The filters need to be really efficient and very easy of access, since when in one of the monitored convoys it is a difficult matter to convince the French supervisor that you have a sufficient and necessary reason for him to be put out of schedule - and of sorts.

The use of sea toilets is supposed to be illegal in France, and chemical ones necessary. However, no-one seems to comment at the discreet use of a sea toilet and I have never come across anyone who has been checked. One of the problems with chemical loos is the shortage of pump-out points. Promises have been made that this will be improved in the near future.

Petrol (essence) is simple and straightforward: you pay the going rate wherever you happen to be, and that is that; and there are always plenty of accessible points for you to pick up whatever you need in large or small measure. But diesel (gas-oil) is another matter. The inland waterways are not littered with diesel fuel points, so it is always a good idea to fill up whenever you have the chance.

The price of diesel is a controversial subject. I have had to pay as much as 50FF a litre for 'white' diesel, and with our rate of exchange continuing to drop, it works out extremely expensive. Skippers of commercial craft, barges and fishing boats are allowed to use 'red' diesel. This is much less taxed and is also used for domestic heating. Dependent upon who you are, where you are and how many litres you want, the price can be as low as 15FF per litre. However, 'le Rouge', is illegal for yachts, and the penalties are not worth the risk of the spot checks that can be made by the police, anywhere, anytime. There are those who will tell you with a sly nod and wink, "All you have to do is to say you have just come from the UK and brought it with you; and in any case plead ignorance. You're bound to get away with it." Like those individuals who creep out of French canal marinas at first light (not an immensely exacting achievement due to famous Gallic Indifference) later to boast about not having been charged, such Brits get us all a bad name.

This is the official position as outlined by VNF: *"Fuel: A 1976 law forbids the use of certain types of fuel, considered harmful to the environment, in the motors of pleasure craft. Fuel in the internal fuel tanks of boats entering France from another country is not subject to customs duty."*

Another kind of fuel is the bottled gas that is now almost universally used for cooking, water heating (god bless the boat shower) and refrigeration. Many people who use Calor gas on their boats in the UK seem to turn automatically to Camping Gaz when going to France. True, Camping Gaz is easily obtainable, but it is also true that it is neither inexpensive nor available in really man-size bottles. Perhaps I am more indulgent than most in my use of gas, but I find anything less than a 13kg bottle not really worth piping aboard. However, the problem is easily remedied, since both Butane and Propane are readily available at many fuel barges, garages and supermarkets. There are four or five main suppliers, and their bottles are recognisably coloured overall accordingly. The price is little different from Calor in the UK. You need a special pressure adapter, usually obtainable at the point of sale of the gas, then if not, at the local hardware shop or supermarket.

At most marinas and haltes there are mains electricity points. Since it is often a free source of power, it is silly not to be equipped with a set of continental and/or universal adapters so that you can exploit the service. After five years in France and the Med, I have come back with seven different power plugs and four water tap converters. Unfortunately, it is impossible to get all you need in England, but the basic French mains 2-3 pin plugs can be obtained. All others, as well as hose connections, must be obtained as and when needed. Two 20m lengths of water hose fitted with 'universal' adapters will see you through most of the time. Although there is no shortage of water points throughout the inland waterway system and improvements are being made all the time, you can still find yourself a long way from the tap.

On the essential non-navigational list comes a bicycle. Many folk buy 'marine specials': special in that they fold up, come in Designer Style, and cost the earth. A sound second-hand lady's miniature shopping bike is all that is needed and comes at literally a tenth of the price of one of the specials. Also essential are binoculars to con locks, bridges, bread shops and wine cellars - as well as to search out errant keepers. Even better for this, is a loud ship's whistle (or genuine klaxon) to alert them of your impending arrival. To be realistic, however, many of them actively dislike this practice - and, in addition, many actually spot you before you see them ... or if they don't, they will have been warned off already for the canal-bush-telegraph system is extremely efficient.

On the highly desirable list comes a good radio for BBC (Home and World Services) from the UK. If you want French TV, you can get 12/240v world-wide compatible sets for about £300; models exclusive to France come at well under £100. Handbooks giving the frequencies of all French radio stations are available free of charge at many newsagents-cum-tobacconists.

RADIO TELEPHONES

It is possible to have on board your boat a radio-telephone system that, thanks to a special service, allows you to connect with the national and international phone network either manually or automatically, according to the type of system you opt for.

To install a radio-telephone on board your boat, you must contact an authorized installer (a list of whom is available from FRANCE TELECOM in Saint Lys; tel: 61.19.36.36). Operating licences and all official certificates necessary for carrying an on-board radio-telephone can be obtained from FRANCE TELECOM inspectors, marine radio sector.

To call a boat with a phone aboard, dial first the area code in which the boat is located, followed by the boat's private five-digit number. Calling from Paris, it is necessary to first dial 16, then the three digit area code, then the five-digit boat number. It is possible that you will have problems getting through to your party, if he is not within range of a relay station, or if his boat phone is not on standby.

Regional area codes:

021: Nord

009: Ile de France,Normandy, Champagne, Alsace Lorraine

019: Rhone Valley, Canal du Midi

039: Aquitaine (Canal Lateral a la Garonne)

029: Ouest

It is possible to call a boat (assuming the phone is on standby) through the intermediary of several public relay services :

BOULOGNE RADIO: 21 33 25 26 (Nord, Ile de France, Normandy, Est, Alsace)

MARSEILLE RADIO: 91 73 11 14 (Rhone Valley, Midi)

ARCACHON RADIO: 56 83 40 50 (Gironde)

SAINT NAZAIRE RADIO: 40 91 04 00 (Ouest)

Boats equipped with radio-telephones are listed in the "Official Directory of Boats Partaking of Waterways Services," which is available at the Centre de Repartition et de Vente des Annuaire, 5, rue Emile Baudot, 91308, MASSY; tel: 60. 11. 52. 00.

In the event of technical problems, contact the Renseignements Radiomaritimes at 31470 SAINTLYS; tel: 61 19 36 00, or dial toll free: 05. 19. 20. 21.

THE ROUTES

All routes lead to Chalon sur Saone, and then have a common course until the Petit Rhone diverges just before Arles. Before that, there are two major choices: the first comes itself in two parts - the Seine to Paris or the Pas de Calais to Paris or the Marne; the second concerns what might be called The Inner Circle: the Marne, to the east and the Bourgogne, or what has become known as the Bourbonnais, to the west.

For those in a hurry, the quickest route is via the Seine to Paris and then down the central canals of the Bourbonnais. If you want to explore more canals before you actually set off full steam ahead, downstream for the Med, then the entry point will be further to the north. When it comes to choosing one of the three central canal routes, there are two major considerations. First comes speed, and there is little doubt that the Bourbonnais is the best for this. There is still a fair amount of commercial barge and hotel traffic so the route is in good repair and used to business. The Bourgogne is next fastest and generally less likely to run out of water at the summit than the Marne. With peace and quiet in mind, the Marne wins hands down, with Bourgogne coming second. With picturesque views and grandeur in mind, they all have their good points and their moments, but the Bourgogne must come first and the Marne second. Which leaves the Bourbonnais apparently the loser; but it has many advocates insofar as it leads when it comes to shoresides facilities and ease of access, with the Bourgogne second and the Marne a poor third. The following table shows this in brief:

	Bourbonnais	Bourgogne	Marne
Speed	***	**	*
Peace & Quiet	*	**	***
Scenery	*	***	**
Facilities & Access	***	**	*

Details of the lengths of the various stretches and numbers of locks are given on each of the detailed maps. Overleaf they are set out in a brief table to help with planning.

WATERWAY	DISTANCE kms	LOCKS number	DEEP metres	HEAD metres	LONG metres	WIDE metres
CANALS OF THE NORTH AND THE PAS DE CALAIS						
Aa - Gravelines to Watten	18	1	1.80	4.45	38.80	5.20
Canal de Bourbourg from Dunkerque to Grand Gabarit	10	1	2.20	3.50	110.00	12.00
Canal de Calais	29	1	2.00	3.47	92.00	8.00
Canal Grand Gabarit	143	8	3.00	4.50	144.60	12.00
Canal du Nord	95	19	2.40	3.70	91.90	6.00
Canal de St Quentin	92	35	2.20	3.58	39.40	5.13
Canal de la Sensee	4	0	1.80	4.10		
Canal de la Somme	156	25	1.80	3.50	39.00	6.00
Canal de l'Oise a l'Aisne	48	13	2.00	3.50	40.50	6.00
Canal Lateral a l'Aisne	51	8	1.80	3.70	38.50	5.20
l'Aisne Canalisee	57	7	2.00	3.70	46.00	7.95
THE RIVERS SEINE AND OISE						
The River Seine						
Le Havre to Rouen: tidal seaway navigation	105	0				
Rouen to Paris	233	6	3.50	6.90	180.00	11.40
Paris to Marcilly	174	19				
Paris to to La Grande Bosse			2.80	5.50	180.00	11.40
La Grande Bosse to Bray			2.20	5.50	90.00	11.40
Bray to Nogent			1.80	4.35	45.00	7.50
Nogent to Marcilly			1.40	3.75	38.50	7.50
Canal de Tancarville	25	1	3.50	7.00	185.00	23.00
Canal St Denis	7	7	4.60	2.60	61.50	8.00
Canal St Martin	5	9	4.37	1.90	40.70	7.70
Canal and River l'Ourcq	108	10				
Paris to Pavillons sur Bois			4.07	2.60		
Pavillons sur Bois to Port aux Peches			2.40	0.80		
Locks 1 - 4					62.00	5.20
Locks 5 - 10					58.80	3.20
Canal Lateral a l'Oise: Janville to the Canal du Nord	15	2	2.40	3.50	100.00	12.00
Canal Lateral a l'Oise: Canal du Nord to Chauny only	19	2	2.20	3.50	39.00	6.00
River Oise	104	7	2.50	5.25	180.00	11.40
THE MARNE: ITS RIVERS AND CANALS						
The River Marne	178	18				
Epernay to Meaux			1.80	5.22	45.00	7.60
Meaux to Neuilly			1.80	4.43	45.00	7.60
Neuilly to St Maur			2.80	7.08	100.00	11.00
Bonneuil to River Seine			3.00	6.40	125.00	11.40
Canal Lateral a la Marne	66	15	1.80	3.50	38.50	5.00
Canal de la Marne a la Saone	224	114	1.80	3.50	38.50	5.20
Canal de l'Aisne a la Marne	58	24	1.80	3.50	38.50	5.20
THE CANAL DE BOURGOGNE						
The River Yonne	108	26	1.80	4.40	96.00	8.30
Canal de Bourgogne	242	190	1.80	3.40	39.00	5.20
THE CENTRAL CANALS						
Canal du Loing	49	19	1.80	3.50	39.10	5.20
Canal de Briare	56	36	1.80	3.50	38.50	5.20
Canal Lateral a La Loire	197	38	1.80	3.50	38.50	5.20
Canal du Centre	112	61	1.80	3.50	39.50	5.10
THE SAONE						
Corre to St Symphorien	159	19	1.80	3.50	40.20	5.20
St Symphorien to Chalon sur Saone	60	2	1.80	6.00	185.00	12.00
Chalon sur Saone to Macon	63	1	2.00	6.00	185.00	12.00
Macon to Lyon	80	2	3.00	6.00	185.00	12.00
THE RHONE						
The River Rhone from Lyon to Port St Louis	310	12	3.00	6.06	190.00	11.40
The Petit Rhone						
the Rhone to St Gilles	21	1	2.70	4.70	195.00	12.00
St Gilles to the sea	36	0	0.70	2.50		
THE CANAL DU RHONE A SETE						
Canal du Rhone a Sete	71	1	1.80	5.15	120.00	8.00
Canal du Rhone a Sete-Beaucaire branch	29	1	1.80	5.00	70.00	8.00
Canal du Midi: Etang du Thau to Toulouse	240	63	1.60	3.30	40.50	6.00

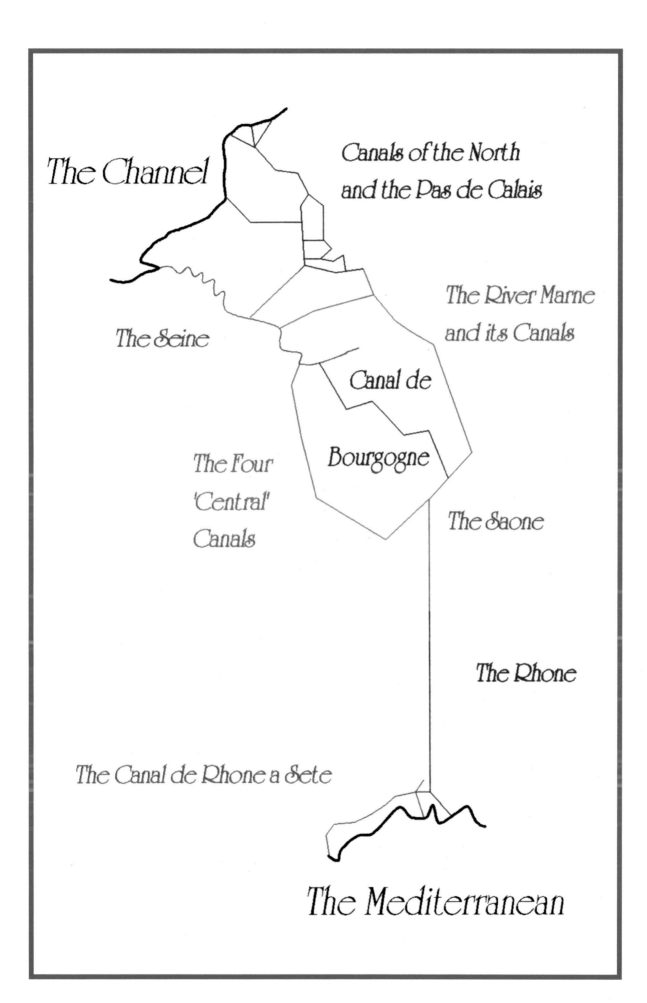

The Channel

Canals of the North
and the Pas de Calais

The River Marne
and its Canals

The Seine

Canal de

Bourgogne

The Four
'Central'
Canals

The Saone

The Rhone

The Canal de Rhone a Sete

The Mediterranean

MAIN SIGNALS ON FRENCH WATERWAYS

SOUND SIGNALS:

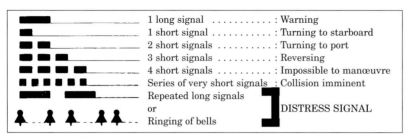

1 long signal	: Warning
1 short signal	: Turning to starboard
2 short signals	: Turning to port
3 short signals	: Reversing
4 short signals	: Impossible to manœuvre
Series of very short signals	: Collision imminent
Repeated long signals	
or	} DISTRESS SIGNAL
Ringing of bells	

VHF 11

Must contact the waterways staff on VHF radio (on the example using the eleven channel)

PROHIBITED:

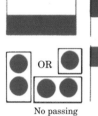

OR

No passing

No passing or only small non-powered craft allowed

No overtaking

No overtaking for push-tows

No passing or overtaking

No waiting

No anchoring

Do not proceed but get ready

Keep out of port and tributary

No mooring

No U-turns

Do not cause wash

OR

Keep within limits

No powered craft

No pleasure boats

No water-skiing

No sailing boats

No rowing boats

OBLIGATORY:

Follow the direction indicated

Head for the left-hand side of the waterway

Head for the right-hand side of the waterway

Keep on the left-hand side of the canal

Keep on the right-hand side of the canal

Cross to the left-hand side of the waterway

Cross to the right-hand side of the waterway

Stop under certain conditions

Do not exceed speed limit

Sound horn

Extra vigilance required

RESTRICTIONS:

Depth limited

Headroom limited

Width limited

Navigation partially restricted

The channel is 40m from the right bank

BUOYS

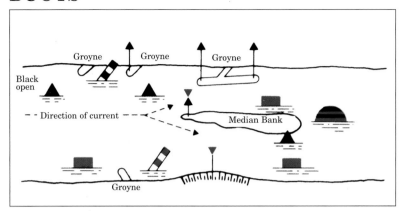

Black open

Groyne Groyne Groyne

Direction of current

Median Bank

Groyne

INDICATIONS:

Passing allowed

Electric cable

Cable ferry

End of restrictions

Outgoing boats

Waiting allowed

Anchoring allowed

Mooring allowed

Bend ahead

Water ski-ing area

Junctions or crossing of secondary waterways

Priority waterway ahead (junction or crossing)

Potable water

Phone box

ALLOWED:

Powered craft allowed

Pleasure boats allowed

Sailing boats allowed

Rowing boats allowed

RECOMMENDATION:

Passing permitted in both directions

Passing is permitted only in the direction indicated

Keep within limits

Follow the arrow

Head from fixed light in direction of flashing light

Unusual stream, cross on portside

Two locks and bridges operated in harness at Montceau Les Mines,
Canal du Centre

Lock control post - blue operate; red
emergency stop

Visitors disturbing lockkeeper and showing paddle gear

Converted Dutch barge in lock on Canal du Centre

Bureau de Declarations, Marolles,
Canal du Centre, typical lock office

LOCKS EQUIPPED WITH VHF

SEINE, OISE, PICARDIE	Channel		NORD / PAS DE CALAIS	Channel
Ablon	22		Courchelettes	18
Amfreville	18		Douai	22
Andresy	22		Flandres Saint Omer	18
Boran sur Oise	18		Folien Valenciennes	22
Bougival	22		Fontinettes	22
Champagne	18		Fresnes sur Escaut	22
Chatou	18		Guinchy	18
Coudray	22		Watten	22
Evry	18			
Grande Bosse	22		RHONE/SAONE	
Janville	22		Avignon	22
La Cave	22		Beauchastel	20
L'Isle Adam	22		Bollene	22
Marolles	18		Bourg les Valence	22
Mericourt	18		Caderousse	20
Notre Dame de la Garenne	22		Chateauneuf	20
Pontoise	18		Couzon	22
Port a l'Anglais	18		D'Ormes	22
Suresnes	22		Drace	22
Tancarville	18		Ecuelles	20
Varenne	22		Gervans	20
Venette	18		Logis Neuf	22
Vives Eaux	18		Pierre Benite	22
			Reventin Vaugris	20
			Sablons	22
			Seurre	22
			Vallabregues	20

CROSSINGS

Points of Departure for the French Inland Waterways will be influenced by where you live, the where-abouts of your home port and your chosen point of entry into the system. Possible crossings are many. Dover to Calais, is no more than a short 22nm while Poole to Le Havre is 110nm. The most popular come in clusters, twinned with their destinations on the other side. The easterly trio comprises Ramsgate, Dover and Folkestone with Rye making up a somewhat stretched out quarter. Their traditional opposite numbers are Dunkerque and Calais. The westerlies are Newhaven, Brighton, Shoreham and Littlehampton; together with the conglomerate of the Solent harbours from Selsey Bill to the Needles; and, slightly out on a limb, Poole and Weymouth, their usual target being Le Havre.

The main distances, rounded off to 5nm are:

Ramsgate	to	Dunkerque	35
Dover	to	Calais	20
Nab Tower	to	Le Havre	85
Needles	to	Le Havre	100

Calais harbour is accessible at all times and in all conditions, but the marina basin is locked and entry can be achieved only between one and a half hours before High Water to half an hour after (except at week-ends and public holidays when the gates open two hours before HW). However, there are buoys in the next-door basin for craft waiting entry, and they may be used free of charge for up to 24 hours.

Dunkerque is accessible at all times and in all conditions. Le Havre harbour is accessible at all times and in all conditions; with the proviso that wind against tide causes a most unpleasant sea in the area of the LHA Lanby that marks the beginning of the buoyed channel into the port. This is the area of the Grand Rade and the Estuaire de la Seine; and it can be just as lumpy a proposition as the Thames Estuary, with its 'short sharp little bastards' coming at you from every angle.

THE LAW
... and the 'right' side of the road

Keeping to the letter of the law is one thing; observing its spirit with courtesy is another - and practice of the latter enables (indeed almost ensures) skippers of light leisure craft an easy passage alongside the commercial traffic that still uses the French Inland Waterways in more substantial numbers than is current in the UK. Barges in France are Peniches, and they, their names and their skippers will accompany you throughout the waterways. Apart from the fact that most of them are fresh, they are the salt of the earth. To err is human - but to be friendly and co-operative seems to be the basic nature of French bargees.

The essence of the situation is straightforward and based on common sense: leisure and pleasure give way to hard labour. In practical terms, this means avoiding all working machinery afloat or ashore: dredging, maintenance, bridge building, bank piling and lock renovation and improvements; passing such works without causing wash; keeping out of the way of all barges (plush floating hotels included), ferries, trip boats and the like; giving way in narrow or shallow stretches, at tight bends and bridges and deferring at the entrance to locks. In spite of perhaps having arrived first at a lock, when there is commercial traffic on the move it is not a case of first come, first served - but for leisure craft, in Matthew's words: "But many that are first shall be last; and the last shall be first." Leisure craft should always permit commercial traffic to enter and leave the lock first - unless they are invited by the keeper or the bargee to do otherwise.

In general, the Rule of the Road is: Keep Right, passing to port. It is important to know it is frequent for barges steaming upriver/stream to retain the inside of channel to keep out of the stronger flow. Those going down respect this by tending to the middle/left. This intention is indicated by showing a blue flag/board on the right of the wheel-house. At night, a flashing white light is used. Boats going downstream respond by showing the same. Barge skippers may make such responses, but I have never observed it; and it would seem by general consent that 'small' leisure craft are not expected to do anything other than keep out of the way.

In terms of general navigation and negotiation, boats going downstream have right of way over those going up: the internationally accepted mode dictated by common sense, since those going against the stream have more control than those who are being carried by it. Overtaking is 'permitted' only when the channel is wide enough, and it is appropriate to do so. Except in the largest open waterways, leisure craft should always wait for a barge skipper to invite them to overtake since the operation can be difficult and requires the barge skipper's full co-operation. Except in the bigger waterways and with a high differential in speed, there is little point in overtaking, since the chances are that you will only have to wait at the next lock for the overtaken barge to arrive and go in first.

Whether overtaking or passing whenever there is any chance of difficulty it is essential to be cautious, and wise to be on the qui vive; use the ship's whistle freely when it seems sensible; and listen to the working barge channels. Speaking French is of course a great help in this since the VHF can be brought into full and useful play. Most commercial traffic uses channel 10. Lock-keepers will inform of local habits.

Once away from the major waterways (mainly the central canals) you can expect to achieve 6km/hr at best without causing comment or deterioration to the banks; and should be prepared to take an average of 15 minutes to pass through each lock. My longest delay through a single lock was two and a half hours and my speediest passage 4 minutes.

Navigation lights and signals are in accord with standard international regulations.

Right Bank and Left Bank always refer to going downstream: towards the sea.

LOCKING

Their first encounter with the French canals can come to many UK boaters as something of a shock. The chances are that the cause of the shock lies not in the Frenchness of the canals, but in the very essence of canals as such. The chances are that it is, in fact, their first encounter with a canal of any kind. There can be little doubt that most skippers, crews and boats would benefit from a short encounter with the British Inland Waterways before 'going foreign'. However, I have found it intriguing that many UK skippers who adamantly refuse even to consider cruising English canals seem to lose their critical factors when afloat on the French waterways. It would seem that ceremony, custom, culture and climate are all against such prior experimentation. In the event, there is no problem in locking - if you can handle your craft properly. Most of the disaster tales are rooted in the annals of inexperienced skippers and crews - often those who have hired a boat for a fortnight, never having been on the water before.

While there are many differences in locks and locking techniques, they are all apparent and obvious once you approach the gates. There is in fact nothing to fear; and even if there were, there is always your keeper ('minder' even) not far away.

The locks are generally linked by telephone, enabling the keepers to follow boats' progress and thus prepare the locks in advance. Accordingly, if you are planning to stop anywhere, have the courtesy to inform the last lock-keeper and advise him if possible of your intended time of departure.

Some keepers may say, "Don't bother to use your ropes, just use your engine" but most take the view that skippers of leisure craft are not capable of using their engines to steady the boat against a turbulent rise or fall, and get very uptight about it.

with the lower
gates open,
craft move
into the lock
on the lower
water level

the gates are closed
and water flows in
from the upper level
through sluice gates

with the upper
gates open,
craft move
out of the lock
on the upper
water level

open gates

closed gates

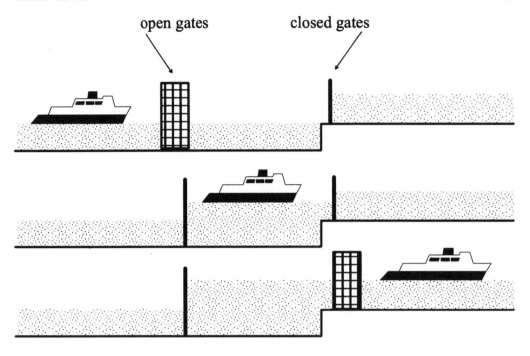

with the lower
gates open,
craft move
out of the lock
on the lower
water level

the gates are closed
and water flows out
from the upper level
through the sluice gates

with the upper
gates open,
craft move
into the lock
on the upper
water level

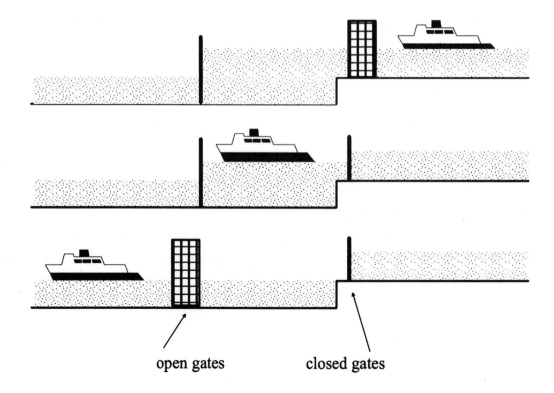

open gates

closed gates

Craft can negotiate against the natural flow of water by means of locked chambers.

At the summit, vessels either go right over the top:

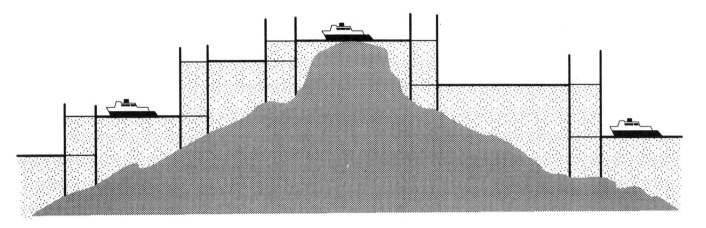

... or go right through the middle by means of a tunnel.

There are various kinds of lock and methods of operating them. The very largest are on the Saone and the Rhone. These have floating bollards and are as smooth as silk. Many of the smaller ones are now automatic, semi-automatic, boater-operated or semi-boater-operated. Some of this is by design and some by default: a stretch may be overseen by a peripatetic keeper or team of keepers, looking after two to twenty locks. They may assist; they may not. They may do it all; they may do nothing. These locks will have lights: red = do not enter; red & green = lock being prepared for you; green = enter.

Some locks are completely automated. They will also have traffic control lights. These may be controlled automatically by radar or photo-electric cells; or manually by the boater pulling or turning a tube, lever or cord hanging from a wire above the waterway or sited on the bankside. Not all the radars easily detect wooden or fibre-glass boats, and it is a good idea to have some really solid metal utensil to 'wave' at the sensor. One regular lady user I know has an iron cassoulet. Watch for the lights changing before you move on from the sensor; you may need to return and pass them again. Radar can be spotted by its grey sphere atop a small post but photo-electric cells are usually at water-line and difficult to see. There are also photo-electric cells at the exits/entrances to the locks: these detect the movements of boats in and out. They should be passed slowly to ensure they register, otherwise the lock ahead may be prepared for the wrong direction.

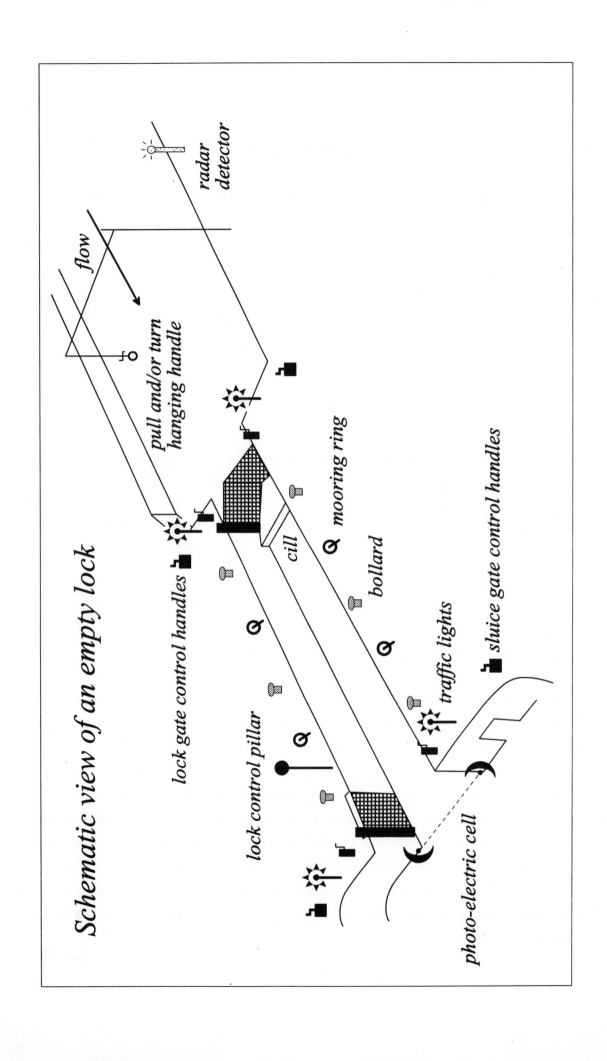

Schematic view of an empty lock

radar detector

flow

pull and/or turn hanging handle

lock gate control handles

mooring ring

cill

bollard

lock control pillar

traffic lights

sluice gate control handles

photo-electric cell

Once inside the lock, you are required to close and open the gates by using the metal rods or strong ropes on the lock side. They are hardly ever positioned in the same place, so it is difficult for a single-handed boater to work out a standard modus operandi. Such skippers must take them as they come, but with a crew it is of no concern. There are two rods or ropes: one blue and one red. The blue is for the boater to start the locking process and the red is for an emergency stop - and will alert the supervising officer. All ropes and some rods are worked by being pulled down, and this is easy. Some rods however are worked by being pushed upwards. A short delicate push is not likely to work. My experience has been that a very strong push/lift, ensuring a firm contact in the mechanism, held for at least five seconds is the best way to get them to work first time - and that is no guarantee.

NB: when your exit gates are open, don't delay in moving out, especially if in convoy. The last one on the move could have a hairy time - especially when a loud warning klaxon goes off.

The rest, and there are still many of them, are manually operated; mostly by one keeper per lock, although some have two to look after. A few tips regarding them: in my experience, keepers are very much more appreciative of your sensitive and sensible co-operation than of any monetary or liquid tips. The days of doling out cash for forelock touching are long gone. Look out for the position of the road bridge (if any) at the lock because that is where it is easier for the lock keeper to do it by himself. Help at the other end is more useful. Before entering, notice on which side he is working, and moor opposite so that you can get out quickly to assist with the gates. However, always check that the keeper approves of what you have in mind; some have had unhappy experiences at the hands of 'plaisanciers' and prefer to do it all themselves. Most are jolly thankful. Watch out for nicks and niches in walls, stone walls or steel buffer lined walls in locks; they can trap ropes disastrously, like a vice. Have a knife and an axe at the ready.

TIME AND TIDE

Flooding and ice - in general, the swelling of rivers is limited to the season between November and March. During exceptionally cold winters, it is possible that some canals freeze over, especially in the North, between December and February.

Dry spells - during periods of drought, the depths of some canals can be reduced, often to the point of making navigation impossible, in cases of extremely dry weather.

On some stretches leisure craft are permitted to navigate at night, but this impossible if you have to pass through locks that are closed. My personal experience is that it is best for leisure craft not to navigate either at night or in fog or other serious weather conditions. In times of flood, the authorities can close down the navigation, and that settles any personal decision making. But in times of high winds, for example, protected stretches can be quiet and tempting; after which you need only to negotiate a ninety degree bend to find you are in short sharp shockers that test your stowage and skills more than somewhat - especially where there is little room to move out of a narrow channel. My advice is, if necessary, sweat it out - but certainly wait it out.

FISHING IN FRESHWATER

Before trying to hook any fish, sportsmen must mandatorily:

- become members of an A.A.P.P. Association Agreee de Peche et de Pisciculture (official anglers' club) and have the required membership card, which is personal and annual;

- pay one of the above for a licence corresponding to the type of fishing he intends to do.

Certain local fishing associations have made with neighbouring A.A.P.P.'s reciprocity agreements whereby fishing possibilities would be increased (inquire locally). When a fisherman belongs to many associations, the fishing fee is due only once. Until 16 years of age, minors are not obliged to pay the fishing tax, as long as they use only one line with a maximum of two hooks (casting excluded);

What you have to know:

- in order to ensure healthful reproduction of the fish population, fishing is forbidden during certain periods of the year;

- specific laws make it forbidden to fish certain types of fish, also in order to protect certain species;

- rules for catch, minimum lengths for certain species and forbidden types of fishing are established by and published in an official decree;

- during fishing season, fishing is permitted starting 30 minutes before sunrise and 30 after sunset.

The tourist fisherman is advised to find out beforehand the specifics of fishing regulations in the waters he intends to fish by calling on:

- local police authorities;

- agriculture and forest authorities (Directions Departementales de l'Agriculture et de la Foret);

- waterways authorities (Directions Departementales de l'Equipment et aux Services de Navigation);

- local town halls (official decrees are posted there);

- local branches of the A.A.P.P.;

- official fishing organizations and bait and tackle shop owners.

USEFUL ADDRESSES

BASSIN DU RHONE

Comite Regional du Tourisme Vallee du Rhone
78, route de Paris
69260 CHARBONNIERES LES BAINS
72 38 40 00

Comite Departemental du Tourisme du Rhone
B. P. 3033, 69396 LYON Cedex 03
72 61 78 90

Comite Departemental du Tourisme de Loire Forez
5, place Jean Jaures, 42000 SAINT ETIENNE
77 33 15 39

Comite Departemental du Tourisme de la Drome
1, avenue Romans, 26000 VALENCE
75 43 27 12

Comite Departemental du Tourisme de l'Ardeche
4, cours Palais, 07000 PRIVAS
75 64 04 66

Chambre Departementale du Tourisme du Vaucluse
B. P. 147, 84000 AVIGNON
90 86 43 42 F

Comite Departemental du Tourisme des Bouches du
Rhone
6, rue Jeune Anacharsis, 13001 MARSEILLE
91 54 92 66

BOURGOGNE FRANCHE COMTE

Comite Regional du Tourisme de Bourgogne
12, boulevard Brosses, 21000 DIJON
80 50 10 20

Comite Departemental du Tourisme de Cote d'Or
53 bis, rue de la Prefecture, 21000 DIJON
80 63 66 00

Comite Departemental du Tourisme de la Nievre
3, rue du Sort, 58000 NEVERS
86 36 39 80

Comite Departemental du Tourisme de Saone et Loire
389, avenue de Lattre de Tassigny, 71000 MACON
85 38 27 92

Comite Departemental du Tourisme de l'Yonne
1, quai de la Republique, 89000 AUXERRE
86 52 26 27

Groupement du Tourisme Fluvial de Franche Comte
18, rue Ampere, 25000 BESANCON
81 88 71 38

CHAMPAGNE ARDENNES

Comite Regional du Tourisme de Champagne Ardennes
5, rue de Jericho
51037 CHALONS SUR MARNE Cedex
26 64 35 92

Comite Departemental du Tourisme de la Marne
2 bis, boulevard Vaubecourt,
51000 CHALONS SUR MARNE
26 68 37 52

SEINE

Comite Regional de Tourisme d'Ile de France
73-75, rue Cambronne 75015 PARIS
45 67 89 41

Comite Departemental de Tourisme de Seine-Maritime
2 bis, rue Petit Salut B. P. 680
76000 ROUEN Cedex
35 88 61 32

Comite Departemental du Tourisme et des Loisirs
Hotel du Departement
2, Le Campus, 95032 CERGY-PONTOISE Cedex
34 25 32 53

Office de Tourisme de Paris
127, avenue des Champs Elysees, 75008 PARIS
49 52 53 54

Comite Deportemental de Tourisme de Seine Saint
Denis
2 rue de la Legion d'Honneur,
93200 SAINT DENIS
42 43 33 55

CHAPTER TWO

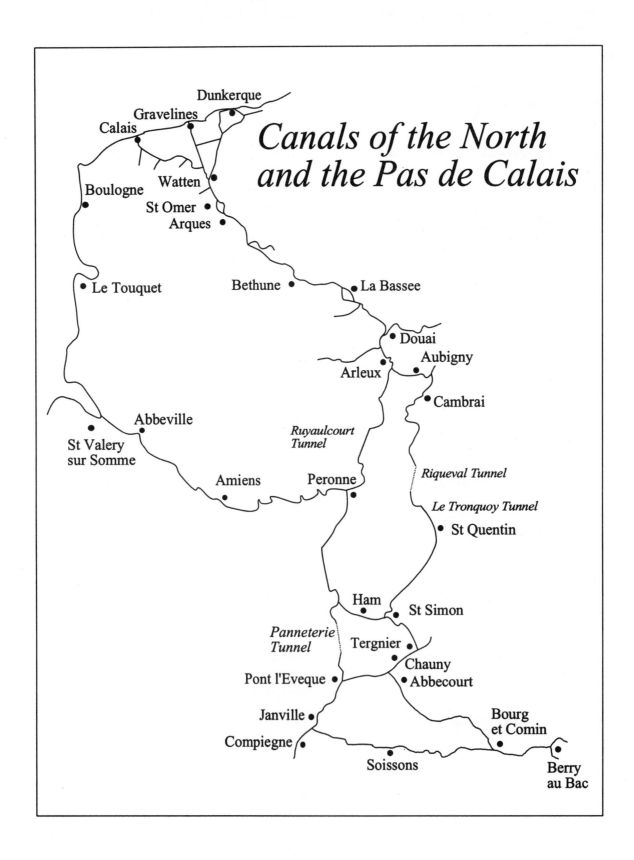

Canals of the North and the Pas de Calais

PART ONE: CANALS OF THE NORTH TO ARLEUX

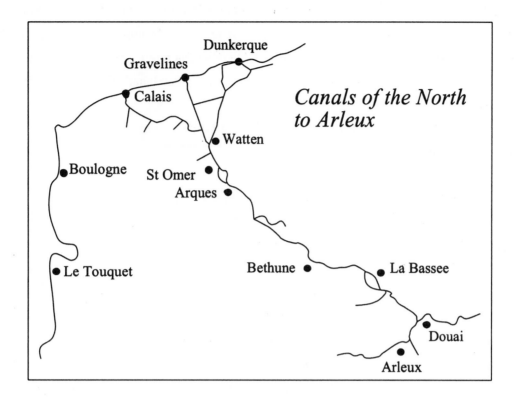

Canals of the North to Arleux

Picardie and Flanders have long been evocative names - unfortunately for many conjuring up only memories of wars and rumours of wars. Now, in happier days, they have become increasingly associated with inland waterway cruising and attract many enthusiasts from the UK. These waterways of the Pas de Calais and northern France can be reached through four ports of entry: Dunkerque, Gravelines, Calais and St Valery sur Somme. In terms of ease of access from the Channel, the small harbours of Gravelines and St Valery have pilotage and tidal problems that do not affect the major ports of Calais and Dunkerque. For those however, who wish to make their crossing an essentially vital and enjoyable part of their cruising a navigation from Burnham or Harwich to Dunkerque or the two previously mentioned smaller harbours will be an appealing proposition: but not for most devotees of inland waterways. Most dedicated inland waterway enthusiasts want to spend as little time as possible on a sea crossing, investing all their time and efforts into the different pleasures of rivers and canals. Thus, the thing for them is to get their craft to Ramsgate, Dover or Folkestone and sure as an arrow make for Calais.

However, whichever route and entry port you opt for, your first objective will be Watten: the unassuming community with a small well-kept halte nautique and a large not-very-well kept lock that is the key to the gateway to the northern inland waterways of France. There are various ways of getting there.

CALAIS TO WATTEN

Offering, as it does, a completely non-tidal route to Paris, and an easy, mainly effortless trip, Calais must put Le Havre fully in the shadow and cast at least a mild shade over Dunkerque. Once in the Calais outer basin two choices are available to the skipper: to lock into the Bassin Ouest marina for a day or so; or to move straight into the Canal de Calais. The marina gates and the Henri Henon road bridge open between 2hrs before and 30 minutes after High Water. Generally there are three openings: at 90 minutes before; at High Water and at 30 minutes after. There are usually plenty of vacant mooring buoys in the outer basin, but the Channel's swell, the wash from the ferries and the antics of some lunatic Gallic fishermen can make it unpleasant.

The following comes directly from the Calais Harbour Office's hand-out.

Notice to Yachtsmen and Users

Observe the signal station.

Once allowed to pass in or out negotiate the fairway as quickly as possible with engine assistance.

Be alert for any instructions given by loud hailer and on VHF channel 12.

Opening hours of the Pont Henri Henon - Rules and safety measures when leaving or entering the western Docks (Bassin Ouest).

Wishing to avoid misunderstandings that never fail to occur every season, we would like to remind all users of the following rules as far as the openings of the Bassin Ouest are concerned.

1.   The opening hours of the swing-bridge can be checked on the board outside the lock-keepers' station situated at the entrance of the Bassin Ouest. The bridge is opened three times at high tide. Special care is required if leaving at the last opening, a further opening is no longer possible after the lock-keepers have completed their shift.

2.   An orange light will come on 15 minutes before each opening. Vessels intending to leave must clearly show their purpose and move away from the quays. Yachtsmen intending to remain moored until the last minute must inform the lock-keepers, before going on board. Should they fail to do so, the lock-keepers on duty will assume no movement will take place and will not open bridge. In the case of the last opening, the doors will be shut, the stays wedged, and the lock-keepers will leave their posts. Special requests for the opening of the bridge, preferably for several vessels leaving together, may be made by contacting the Harbour Office at least 10 minutes before intended departure time. The H.O. can be contacted on VHF channel 12 or by telephone (21.96.31.20).

The times of opening are subject to alteration without notice due to movement of general traffic in the outer harbour. Any alteration to opening times will always involve their being put back and not their being brought forward. The H.O. accepts no liability for such alterations.

Outgoing traffic has generally right of way over incoming traffic when going through the lock.

Signal No 2 and 5 (red/red/red and green/white/green respectively) showing on the tower indicate movements, imminent or under way, of car ferries or cargo ships. Smaller vessels (less than 19.8 m. in length), yachts and fishing boats are strictly forbidden access to the inner fairway. They must stay on the roads (at entry) or must remain in the outer harbour (at departure) until the signal 4 (green/green/white) is shown indicating that the inner fairway is again clear for them. Navigation under sail is strictly forbidden in the inner fairway. In the area under harbour control, car ferries and cargo ships always have right of way over smaller sailing or motor boats.

With its well-equipped, friendly and inexpensive marina, and the almost ever-open doors of its well-used Yacht Club, Calais, just for its own sake, has been a favourite with UK channel hoppers for many a year. Since there are now plans to extend, expand and improve space and facilities, there seems every chance that its popularity will continue to grow - even in the wake of the Chunnel. The usual ploy is to make for the pontoons on the quayside just by the yacht club: these are to starboard on entering. They are immensely popular, being so close to the loos, the showers, the clubhouse and the main exit to the town. There are also pontoons along the whole of the starboard side, but those after the raft of visitors' berths are all permanently occupied and are not to be used without the prior permission of the marina staff. Their office is on the ground floor of the yacht club building. It is usually open - especially in the morning - but if there is no one in attendance, it is usually possible to find someone with authority if not responsibility by the small hoist and fuel station, halfway along the basin. All these berths have mains water and electricity.

It is also possible to moor alongside the wall on the port hand, from immediately inside the basin right to the end. Wall ladders are not much in evidence, and there is a tidal rise and fall because the system suffers from water loss. Attention to ropes is therefore necessary through the first tide and if you tie up at a blank stretch of wall and are without a ladder of your own, some agility will be called for if you are to get ashore at low water.

If you miss a gate opening and have a long wait before the next, you may be inclined to move straight into the transit Bassin Carnot. Normally, passage for leisure craft is available from 3hrs before High Water to 1hr after. It may be necessary to search out the Carnot bridge controller and lock-keeper - although dependent upon time of day, tide and air draught, it may be possible to steam through without negotiation, let or hindrance. A listening watch on VHF and a keen look-out are essential in case you are required to turn back.

Contacting the keeper 'person to person' is not always an easy task, as he does not always respond on VHF 12, but Calais Harbour Office are usually quite efficient in getting you put in touch. Considering their work and traffic load, they are extremely courteous with such demands from leisure craft.

If you have not already got your licence (see Chapter One) you can use any delay to obtain one from VNF (Voies Navigables de France) at the offices of the Bureau d'Affretement not far away at 45 Quai de la Meuse (office hours only).

Once through Carnot, you may have a second search: this time for the keeper of the Batellerie lock. The lock-keeper is by no means conspicuous by his presence and more use of VHF may be necessary, although in general, if you have successfully organised the passage through Carnot, he is likely to appear without too long a wait. The VNF office is just across the road and this might be a boon since the lock-keeper will probably demand to see your licence before letting you pass. Although in the past there were theoretical days of grace, the habit now seems to have been lost.

The keeper's office is immediately next to the lock: both suffer from apparent decay and lack of use, affording a disquieting impression of what is in store. If anything, conditions deteriorate once

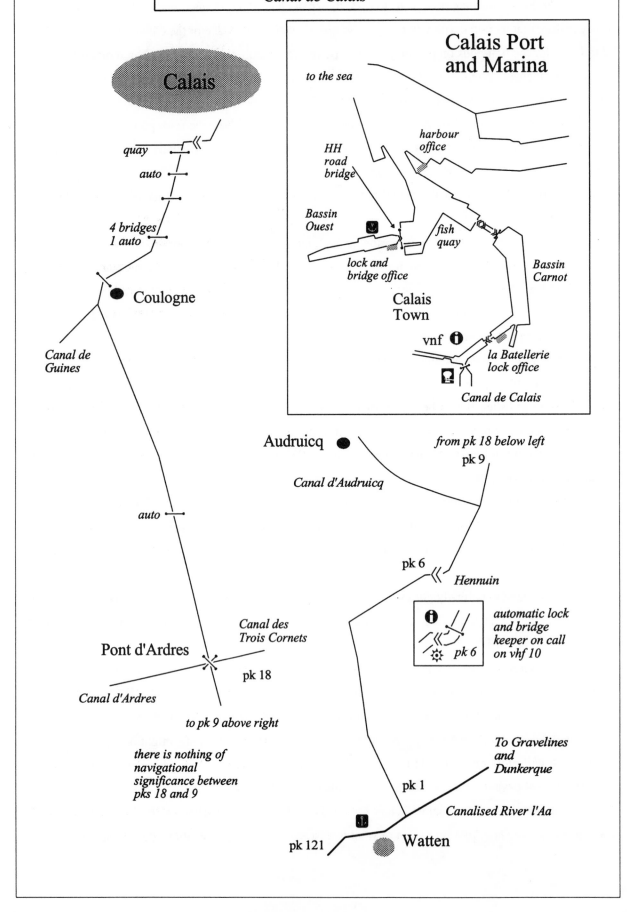

Calais to Watten: 30 km ... 2 locks
Canal de Calais

Calais

quay

auto

4 bridges
1 auto

Coulogne

Canal de
Guines

auto

Pont d'Ardres

Canal des
Trois Cornets

Canal d'Ardres

pk 18

to pk 9 above right

there is nothing of
navigational
significance between
pks 18 and 9

Calais Port
and Marina

to the sea

harbour
office

HH
road
bridge

Bassin
Ouest

fish
quay

lock and
bridge office

Bassin
Carnot

Calais
Town

vnf ⓘ

la Batellerie
lock office

Canal de Calais

Audruicq

from pk 18 below left

pk 9

Canal d'Audruicq

pk 6

Hennuin

ⓘ

automatic lock
and bridge
keeper on call
on vhf 10

pk 6

To Gravelines
and
Dunkerque

pk 1

Canalised River l'Aa

pk 121

Watten

through the lock gates, where there is usually a collection of particularly disgusting detritus - and in the summer months weed, weed and more weed.

One of the benefits of moving directly into the canal system, is that the first halte nautique is only just around the corner from the Batellerie. Mains electricity is not always available, but there is water. Mooring is free and gives easy access not only to the surrounding shops but also to Calais town centre. The area is neither a slum nor prone to vandalism, but it is still wise to leave a look-out on board although the nearby parking ground is much used by holidaymakers with camping cars, caravanettes and such. It is unlikely that you will be asked to move on from the pontoon, for it is usually quiet on the boating front. So: if you are not dedicated to yacht club life, want all the amenities of Calais and a berth entirely gratis, what could be better?

There are four specials worth seeking out in Calais. Actually, only three need to be sought out, since the fourth, the famous 'moules et frites' are to be found everywhere. Every morning, there is a fish market across the water from the marina. Each stall 'belongs' to its own boats, and you can buy what comes up the wall straight from the boat - and straight from that day's fishing. The central market place houses shops of most kinds, including an excellent hardware shop and twice a week it plays host to a genuine 'market town' type open-air market. This old man comes in to sell a few potatoes, tomatoes, carrots and uncooked earthy beetroot, this old lady brings in her own-made goat's cheese and a few bunches of herbs and this small boy offers four dozen eggs. Finally, across the road from the market, in a small square, there is a splendid cheese shop where the proprietor (who speaks modest English) will, upon request, advise you loquaciously after first having quizzed you about your preferences for fresh French fromages. He is a member of the Masters' Guild and more than a past master at both chat and cheese.

Sooner or later it will be time to move on. Shortly after the halte there are two automatic lifting bridges, each controlled by traffic lights, after which the built-up district slowly fades away as you move into more or less open country that tends to the flat and featureless. The canal is not the narrowest in France, but the green chick-weed-cum-algae, the decaying state of many of the banks and the presence of so many fishermen make it appear that there is only a thin red line of ribbon for UK boats to use - right in the centre and at dead slow speed. It is vital to keep a water-filter watch and it may be necessary to clean them more than once before reaching the end of the 30km stretch.

A special word of warning about the fishermen. They are as troubled by the weed as are skippers. Unfortunately, one of their ways of dealing with the problem is to string out at least one length of plastic pipe across the canal to prevent the drift of weed into their patch. They are as backward in moving their pipe lines as they are forward in vociferous complaint. For those of a sensitive nature, their body language is equally compelling: they are best avoided and ignored.

The canal has three branches: Audruicq, Ardres and Guines. They suffer even more than the main canal from silting and general degradation and only the shallowest of shoal craft should venture into their backwoods. The Ardres junction is noteworthy for its eye-catching criss-cross bridges: things not of beauty nor a joy forever, but of brutal concrete built to last. Some commercial traffic still uses the main canal but there is insufficient to keep it fully 'dredged' and free from small, irritating obstructions. The only lock on the canal is at Hennuin (PK 6) with a drop of no more than a metre. It is automatic and works in harness with the nearby automatic bridge. In the event of system failure (not unknown) it is possible to contact the lock/bridge keeper on VHF Channel 10. It should be noted that he wears all kinds of hats in his work (one of which is possibly freelance). In other words, he must not to be expected to turn up at the drop of a hat - or even the bleep of the VHF. Fortunately, the surroundings hereabouts are not without appeal and food and drink are available.

Although there are plenty of quiet places to tie up along the banks if your draught is modest, not many are particularly attractive or offer special shoreside features; so the best plan is perhaps to make for the first properly maintained halte nautique which is to be found at Watten, just under 35km from Calais.

CANAL DE BOURBOURG - DUNKERQUE TO WATTEN

The large industrial harbour of Dunkerque is, like Calais, open at all states of the tide. There is an important difference insofar as there is a much larger acreage of commercial dockland to be negotiated before you can rest at the first canal pontoon or proceed on the inland waterways.

Once in the port of Dunkerque, you follow the East jetty and then turn to starboard for Trystram lock and the two bridges that work in conjunction with it. This leads to the Bassin de Commerce. The lock and bridges operate between 0800 and 1930 on demand. In addition, there is a swing bridge to port after which you can choose the marina facility run by the Yacht Club de Dunkerque, by passing through the Pertuis Amont swing bridge. The alternative is to pass through Darse 1 or 2 and make for the base fluviale on the canal system. This is well situated near the centre of the town and is very convenient for all holiday requirements: from victuals to late-night revelling. The pontoon, which is equipped with mains water and electricity is popular with live-aboards; not surprisingly since its pleasant surroundings consist of well-kept lawns and gardens, with the noise from the town traffic (which in itself can be gruesome) not at all intrusive.

From Dunkerque to Watten there are two choices: both start with a passage through the Jeu de Mail lock where your papers will most likely be inspected. (Only once have I passed through without a full inspection - but that was perhaps because I was 'known' by then). You continue for about 10km until you pass the junction with the commercial arm of the Canal de Bourbourg/Grand Gabarit. After that, the Liaison Grand Gabarit leads straight ahead directly to Watten - at a distance of 14km with only one more lock; while the 'deviation' via the Canal de Bourbourg-Gabarit Freycinet is a distance of 33km with three more locks. The Bourbourg offers a quieter, slower and slightly more rural trip. There is a good mooring wall at the small community of Coppenaxfort, and I prefer it to the advertised halte nautique at Bourbourg, where there is much filth and little facility. In addition, there are some new small finger pontoons on the left bank just before the junction with the Grand Gabarit at Watten, but they are in an isolated position and without services. All in all, there is much to be said for enjoying Dunkerque to the full and then making straight for Watten.

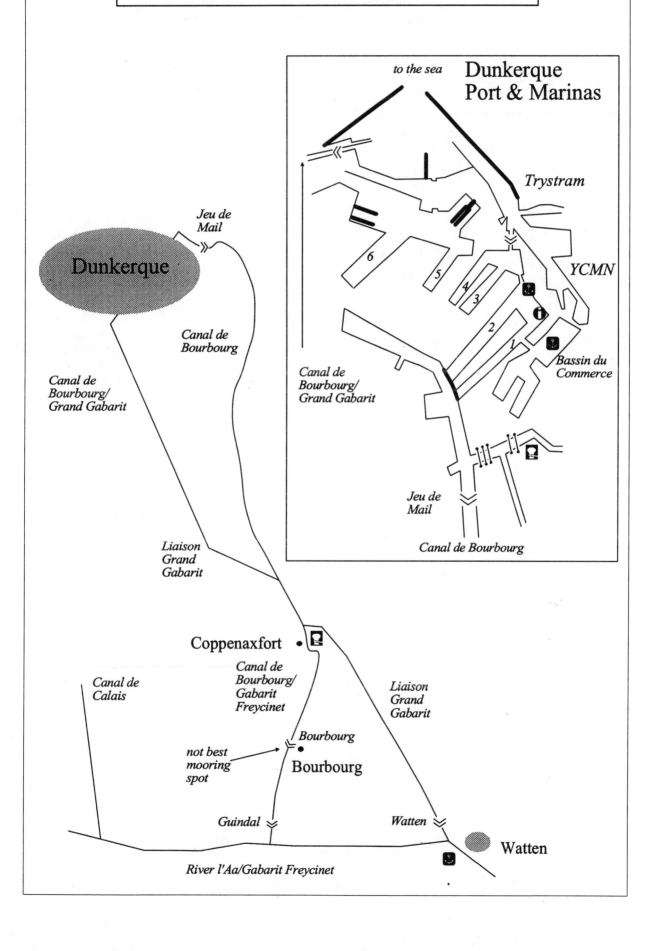

Dunkerque to Watten: 14/33 km ... 2/4 locks
Canal de Bourbourg (Gabarit Freycinet & Liaison)

to the sea

Dunkerque Port & Marinas

Trystram

Jeu de Mail

Dunkerque

6

5

4

3

2

1

YCMN

Bassin du Commerce

Canal de Bourbourg

Canal de Bourbourg/ Grand Gabarit

Canal de Bourbourg/ Grand Gabarit

Jeu de Mail

Canal de Bourbourg

Liaison Grand Gabarit

Coppenaxfort

Canal de Bourbourg/ Gabarit Freycinet

Liaison Grand Gabarit

Canal de Calais

not best mooring spot

Bourbourg

Bourbourg

Guindal

Watten

Watten

River l'Aa/Gabarit Freycinet

Gravelines to Watten: 18 km ... 2 locks
L'Aa (Gabarit Freycinet)

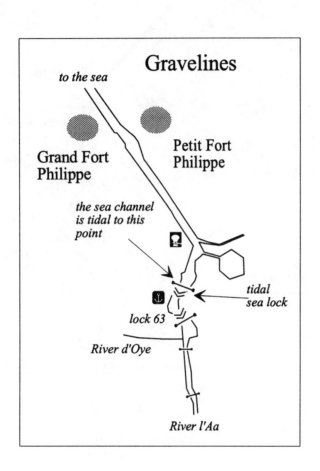

Gravelines

to the sea

Grand Fort Philippe

Petit Fort Philippe

the sea channel is tidal to this point

tidal sea lock

lock 63

River d'Oye

River l'Aa

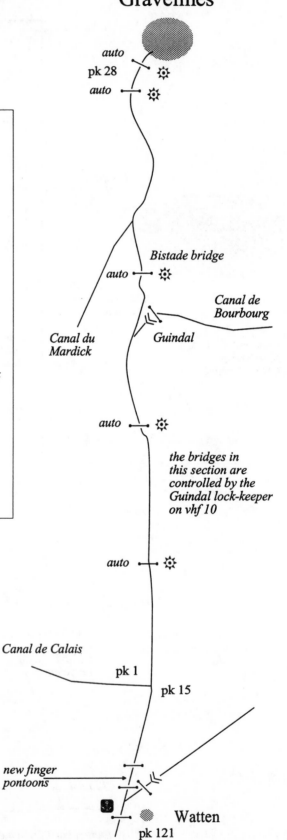

Gravelines

auto

pk 28

auto

Bistade bridge

auto

Canal de Bourbourg

Canal du Mardick

Guindal

auto

the bridges in this section are controlled by the Guindal lock-keeper on vhf 10

auto

Canal de Calais

pk 1

pk 15

new finger pontoons

Watten

pk 121

AA- GRAVELINES TO WATTEN

Gravelines offers a much shorter Channel crossing than St Valery sur Somme, but possesses the same tidal restrictions. The entrance dries at half-tide, and is best not tackled by strangers at night and not at all in poor weather. The training walls offer a straight course to the bridge and the lock gates that open between 90 mins before and after HWS and 45 mins either side of HWN. It must be noted that the bridge does not operate at all in strong winds, but Gravelines is no place for cruising under such conditions anyway. There are plenty of drying pontoon moorings just before and in the vicinity of the lock to wait for opening time. In addition, there is a large marina facility in the shallow basin, with nearly 500 berths. Shallow it may be, but craft up to 1.5m usually stay just afloat, unless the sluicing is particularly fierce when they may encounter the soft mud bottom.

This drainage, to prevent flooding of the surrounding fields and marshes, is an important feature of this stretch of the Aa waterway and can cause a strong flow towards the sea and a general lowering of water in the canal system.When they are working, flashing lights operate at the Guindal lock and the Bistade bridge (controlled by the Guindal keeper, who is available on VHF 10).

The Audomarois marshland is a huge area of ponds and small lakes in a verdant landscape. Market gardening country in the main, it also possesses old peat bogs: some set aside for fishing and hunting, and some as bird sanctuaries.

Gravelines is a welcoming spot, but the locks and bridges on the little-used narrow gauge system, while operated by very friendly keepers, are prone to relapse, backsliding and general degradation. Although in theory it affords a short route inland, locks and bridges can stall, bind and completely seize up (closed, of course) so it is by no means a reliable route to the Canal de Bourbourg, the Canal de Calais or straight down to Watten. Facilities are minimal before Watten on the main Grand Gabarit waterway. Although the place itself is indeed charming, there are pitfalls from inward and hazards from seaward, so overall it must be reckoned a port of call only for those who must visit every last, lost haven.

CANAL GRAND GABARIT (DUNKERQUE A L'ESCAUT) - WATTEN TO LA BASSEE

Superficially, Watten is not an attractive water hole but its halte nautique, tucked away from the main drag, is an open space with good depth and up-to-date facilities, mains power and water. It is approached via a small cut which can be easily missed on the left bank by PK120 just after the junction with the Canal de Calais and mooring is free. Close by, there is a modern family-business bar/restaurant where each and all contribute to the welcome that is offered to visitors - especially those on boats. In addition, there is a sports centre with a heavy committment to riding: horses and bicycles.

There are two small services worthy of note before the next main attraction. The first is the outboard motor garage near PK115 which offers emergency repairs and the second is the Clairmarais halte-fluvial at PK111, which is extremely pretty, but also extremely shallow. It is a fun place if you can get into it and worth a visit even if you have to moor to the banks outside. Between the two, by the St Omer Canal junction is a boat park in extremely secluded surroundings. In the past it was much used by barges, but now there is ample space - and you will never be moved on. Bikes are needed for water and victuals.

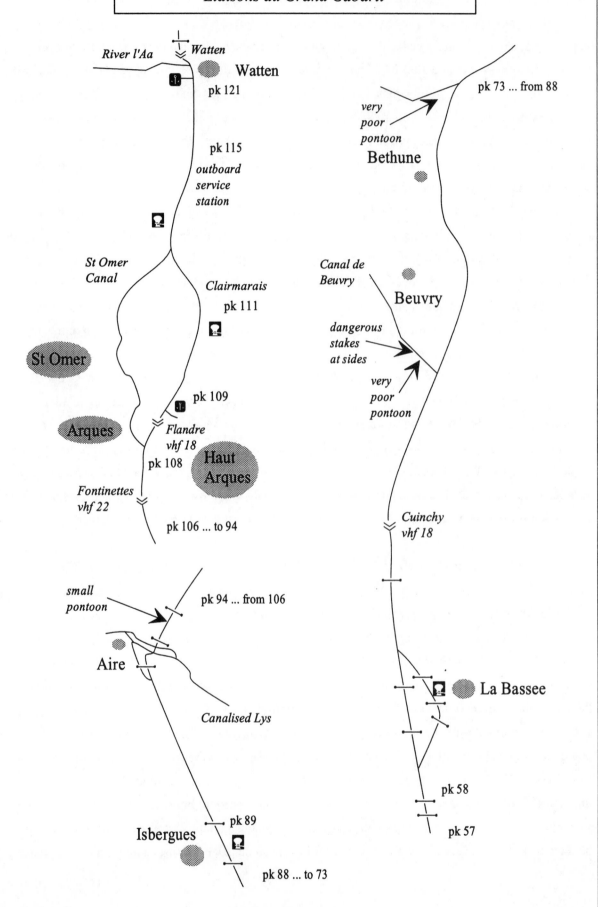

Watten to La Bassee: 60 km ... 3 locks
Liaisons au Grand Gabarit

River l'Aa

Watten

Watten

pk 121

pk 115

outboard service station

St Omer Canal

Clairmarais

pk 111

St Omer

pk 109

Arques

Flandre vhf 18

pk 108

Haut Arques

Fontinettes vhf 22

pk 106 ... to 94

small pontoon

pk 94 ... from 106

Aire

Canalised Lys

Isbergues

pk 89

pk 88 ... to 73

pk 73 ... from 88

Bethune

very poor pontoon

Canal de Beuvry

Beuvry

dangerous stakes at sides

very poor pontoon

Cuinchy vhf 18

La Bassee

pk 58

pk 57

The next excellent resting place with good space and depth is to be found between PKs 109 and 108. There is a small channel entrance on the right bank that leads past the new house and marina office on the left into a small inland 'lake', now converted into a base nautique, and the quietest marina facility coming down from the coast so far. Reception is friendly and pleasantly informal. In all probability you will be hailed and met by Madame Martine, a young and happy soul who does not look as capable or as strong as she is when it comes to hauling heavy boats about. Berths have mains water and electricity, and there are showers and a telephone; but for shopping you need to make a visit to nearby Arques, Haut Arques or St Omer. Martine and her husband are continuing with building and upgrading. Different from Watten, the marina is privately run and charges are levied: for mooring, water and electricity.

St Omer is nearby but its attractions do not justify the long telephone calls and even longer waits for the bridge and lock openings: waits that have now become almost obligatory before you can get in or out of the town. For anyone with a longish journey southward in mind, St Omer is best put out of mind.

Just past the second St Omer Canal junction, at Arques, is the famous barge lift of Fontinettes. It is now a relic, but still a technical masterpiece. In the 18th and 19th centuries, the Neuffossee canal (which was the old name for this stretch) climbed 13m in five successive locks; when opened, the Fontinettes lift did the same job in one move, using the simple principle of checks and balances with water in two huge chambers. It was replaced by the present lock , which is an equally vast affair. The lock-keepers here are not at all enthusiastic either about responding to VHF calls from leisure craft or about actually permitting passage - unless there is commercial traffic as well. Happily this is not the norm.

For the next 45km there are plenty of places where it is possible to moor, provided you choose your stretch of bank with care - for increasingly there are shortages of water at the sides as they fall not only into disrepair but also into the canal. There is little of charm in this stretch: the relais fluvial at Aire has a very small pontoon; Isbergues has a turning circle where it is just possible to tie up; the base fluviale at Bethune also suffers from a deficient pontoon and all other official or even semi-offical mooring places are either completely taken by barges (many in permanent occupation because of redundancy) or are seriously damaged. The first worthwhile stop comes at the halte nautique at La Bassee.

The mainstream continues dead ahead. It is the backwater on the right bank that goes to the town. The pontoon is generally quiet, with only the out-of-work barges that fill the stretch showing signs of life, (except just after school, that is, when students regularly occupy the whole pontoon for a couple of hours courting.) It affords easy access to the town including a nearby supermarket and filling station. In 1992 the halte was in excellent order with all services functioning, but in 1993 the services had been vandalised and the pontoon seriously damaged. Provided the pontoon and services meet your needs, the town offers an excellent range of shops - especially for food.

LA BASSEE TO ARLEUX

Between La Bassee and Douai, both moorings and scenery improve. Just down the road at the large junction for Lille, you can buy delicious fresh butter by the village of Berclau. The 25km to Douai offer plen-

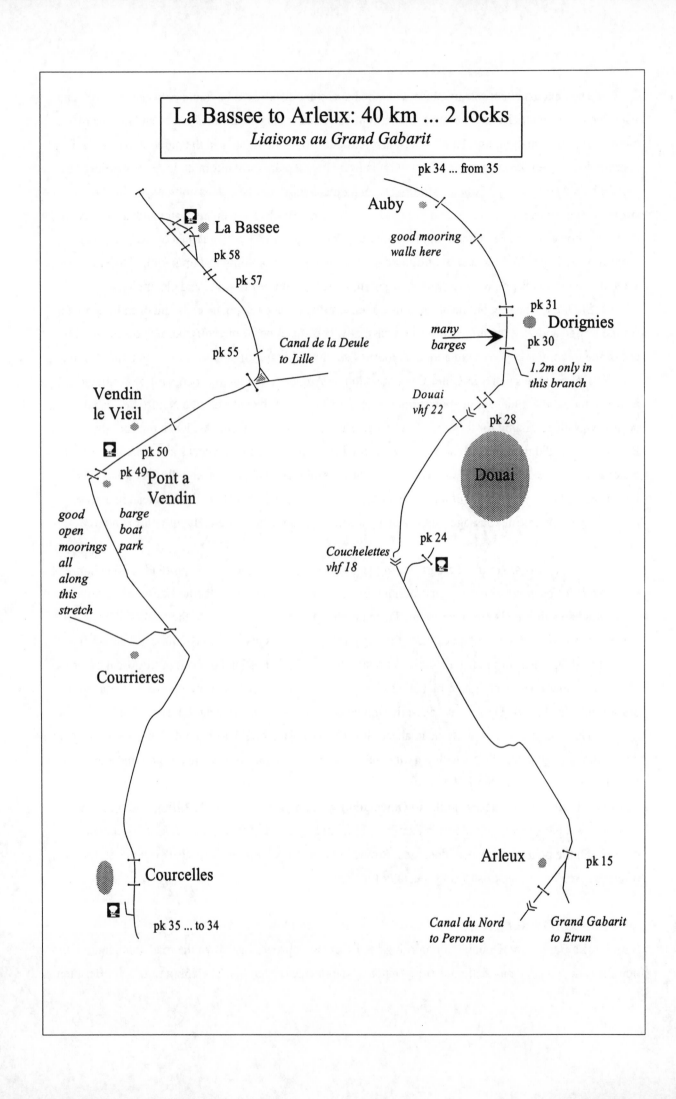

La Bassee to Arleux: 40 km ... 2 locks
Liaisons au Grand Gabarit

pk 34 ... from 35

Auby

*good mooring
walls here*

La Bassee

pk 58

pk 57

pk 55

*Canal de la Deule
to Lille*

Vendin
le Vieil

pk 50

pk 49 Pont a
Vendin

*good
open
moorings
all
along
this
stretch*

*barge
boat
park*

Courrieres

Courcelles

pk 35 ... to 34

pk 31

Dorignies

pk 30

*1.2m only in
this branch*

*many
barges*

*Douai
vhf 22*

pk 28

Douai

pk 24

*Couchelettes
vhf 18*

Arleux

pk 15

*Canal du Nord
to Peronne*

*Grand Gabarit
to Etrun*

ty of stopping places. The basin at Vendin le Vieil, the relais fluvial at Pont a Vendin and that at Courcelles are all well maintained; while the mooring walls and quaysides at Auby and Dorignies are all in good order. However, the supposedly first rate services at Courrieres are very poor.

At Douai itself, an industrial centre, there are two choices. First, the entry to the town's small branch canal at PK30, where empty barges crowd together in water that is foul with a depth hardly better than a metre. Second, the cutting just after Courchelettes lock, where, a short way up, there is a new and well-ordered pontoon at a pretty, quiet spot. Take care when entering, for there are many parked barges on the starboard hand and very little room to manoeuvre. It is worth searching out - especially if you have fishermen on board for there is an excellent and well-stocked dealer here.

PART TWO: CANALS DU NORD AND ST QUENTIN
CANAL DU NORD - ARLEUX TO ETRUN

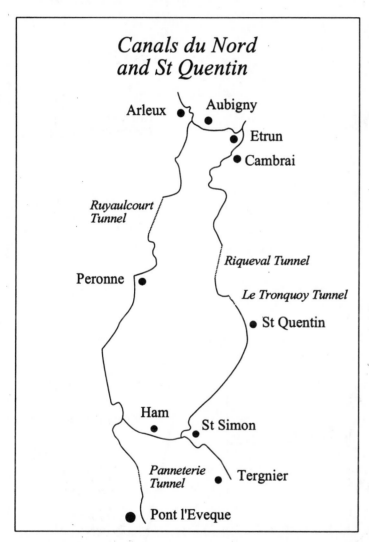

Arleux, 12km from Douai, marks the junction with the Grand Gabarit and the Canal du Nord, where 'All Change' is the order of the day. Staying on the Grand Gabarit takes you to Etrun and the junction with the St Quentin Canal. There is no port de plaisance or halte near Arleux (although the signposts carry legends that suggest there is honey still for tea) but there are very good banksides. Dependent upon your draught, you may need to use a plank or ladder. Arleux itself is a charming spot, and has two special features: the garlic festival held on the first Sunday in September and the navigation museum housed in a barge.

The villages of Aubigny and Fechain also have slightly better than basic services. At Etrun, the other side of le Bassin Rond island, a turn to port leads to l'Escaut, Valenciennes and Belgium; while starboard is for Cambrai, not far along the Canal St Quentin. The Canal du Nord route is the quicker, but some skippers prefer the eccentricities of the longer St Quentin route with the famous 5670km Grand Macquincourt-Riqueval Souterrain. We'll look at the regular du Nord route first.

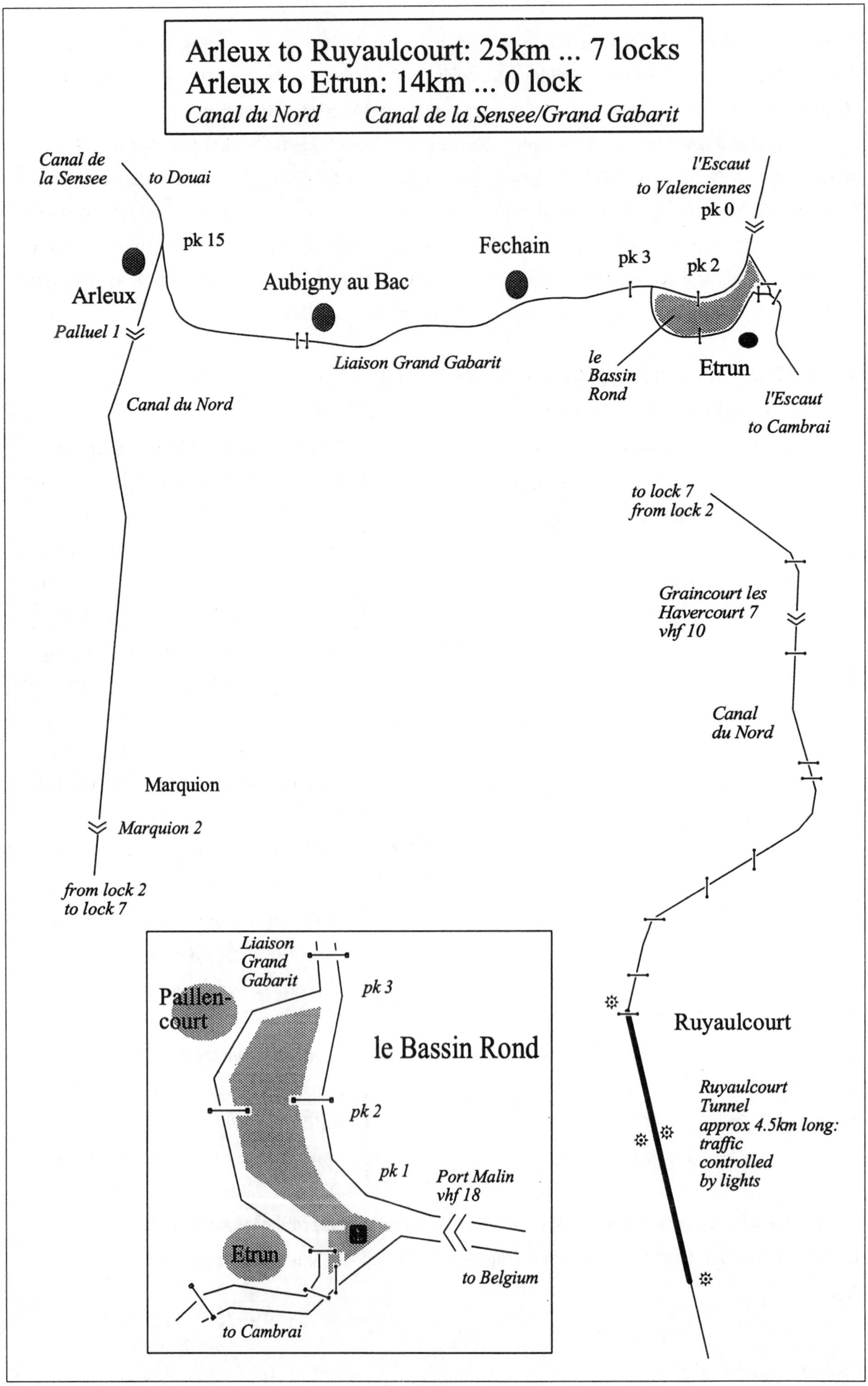

Arleux to Ruyaulcourt: 25km ... 7 locks
Arleux to Etrun: 14km ... 0 lock
Canal du Nord   Canal de la Sensee/Grand Gabarit

Canal de la Sensee

to Douai

pk 15

Arleux

Palluel 1

Canal du Nord

Aubigny au Bac

Liaison Grand Gabarit

Fechain

pk 3   pk 2

le Bassin Rond

Etrun

l'Escaut to Valenciennes pk 0

l'Escaut to Cambrai

to lock 7 from lock 2

Graincourt les Havercourt 7 vhf 10

Canal du Nord

Marquion

Marquion 2

from lock 2 to lock 7

Ruyaulcourt

Ruyaulcourt Tunnel approx 4.5km long: traffic controlled by lights

Liaison Grand Gabarit

pk 3

Paillen- court

le Bassin Rond

pk 2

pk 1   *Port Malin vhf 18*

Etrun

to Belgium

to Cambrai

ARLEUX TO PONT L'EVEQUE

From Arleux, the canal is completely man-made and runs a fairly straight course with locks that have gates at one end and guillotines at the other. Most of the canal is excellently well-marked by red-and-white panels in the side walls indicating the PK number - some of them more frequent than 1km apart. Many of the lock-keepers on the bief sell eggs, rabbits, flowers, fruit and veg - and lock-keeping characters abound. It is truly joyful. The Souterrain de Ruyaulcourt, at nearly 4.50km long, is an important feature. Like most French canal tunnels, Ruyaulcourt is controlled by lights; but uncommonly, it has a central passing station, also controlled by lights. I have heard many stories about skippers who have had to wait hours for the lights to change in their favour, but that has not been my experience. The lack of waiting is entirely due to the double-width passing place in the centre, so that any one craft need wait only for others to navigate half the system - and not, as in many cases, all of it, plus the extra time added by the controllers for safety. It is one of the most intriguing of the French waterway tunnels. Barge skippers do not like leisure craft using searchlights and for most of the time the lighting is good, but at times it is somewhat dingy, and is often made more so by the barges' dense exhaust fumes.

The small town of Moislains offers a public quay and good shopping halfway to Peronne, where there is a well-promulgated port de plaisance. It is possible that by 1996, the marina may have plentiful facilities and a good depth, but as recently as the end of 1993 it was unsafe for a boat of much more than a metre even to try to enter. There is a general shortage of depth in the surrounding area and the small headland is heavily silted for many metres out; in addition, services seemed virtually non-existent. The port legend reads, "Port Taxies To Be Paid" and that seems to sum up its essence. Don't count upon getting a berth for the night.

Peronne is an industrial centre, but with visible remains of its greater and grander past. For example, the remains of the 13th century castle, and the Four (rebuilt) Round Towers where Charles the Bold, Duke of Burgundy, held Louis XI prisoner.

About 20km after Peronne comes the miniature Souterrain de Panneterie. It is no more than a kilometre in length and since it is quite straight its exit is clearly visible from its entrance: a real example of light at the end of the tunnel. I always find it reassuring in tunnels when I can see light at both ends: it is much more fruitful than giving the candle the same treatment.

After the tunnel, the last two stopping places are not far and both are near the junction with the Canal Lateral a l'Oise. The first and larger is Noyon. It got under way in the 6th century when St Medar had the first church built; Charlemagne was crowned here in 768 and Calvin was born here - a rich historical mix indeed. There are many ancient monuments and the stunning 12th and 13th century Notre Dame Cathedral. After Noyon, Pont l'Eveque is quite small fry, but in its own way it is still a challenger. The church has the strange votive offerings of the Oise bargemen and virtually all the denizens are friendly.

Before we move on to the Oise, we'll retrace our watery steps to Etrun with its Bassin Rond and the junction for Valenciennes (for Belgium) and the St Quentin Canal to Cambrai.

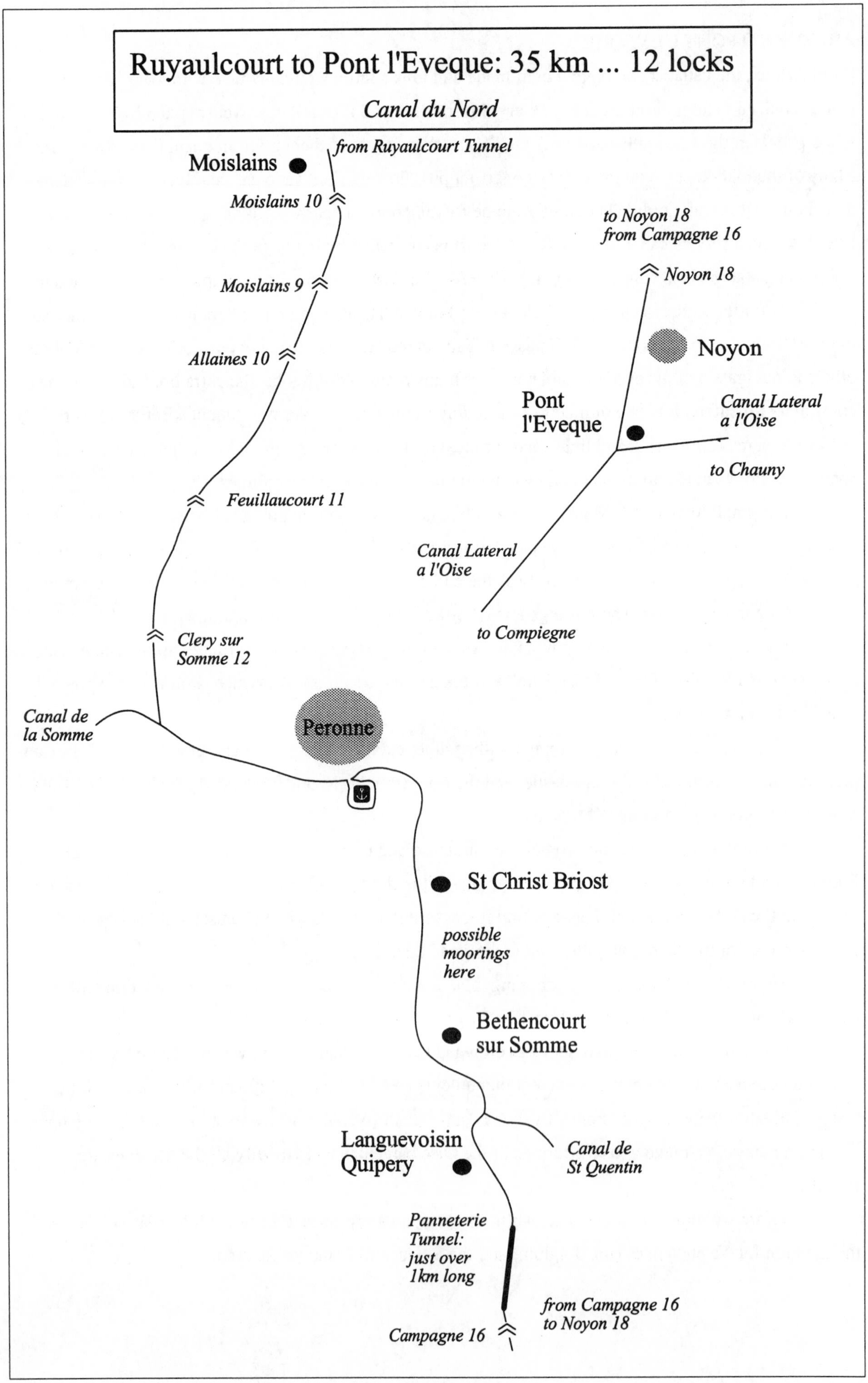

Ruyaulcourt to Pont l'Eveque: 35 km ... 12 locks

Canal du Nord

from Ruyaulcourt Tunnel

Moislains ●

Moislains 10 ≫

to Noyon 18
from Campagne 16

≫ *Noyon 18*

Moislains 9 ≫

Noyon

Allaines 10 ≫

**Pont
l'Eveque**
●

*Canal Lateral
a l'Oise*

≫ *Feuillaucourt 11*

to Chauny

*Canal Lateral
a l'Oise*

*Clery sur
Somme 12* ≫

to Compiegne

*Canal de
la Somme*

Peronne

⚓

● St Christ Briost

*possible
moorings
here*

**Bethencourt
sur Somme**
●

**Languevoisin
Quipery** ●

*Canal de
St Quentin*

*Panneterie
Tunnel:
just over
1km long*

*from Campagne 16
to Noyon 18*

Campagne 16 ≫

CANAL DE ST QUENTIN - ETRUN TO ST QUENTIN

Bassin Rond is well known as an area devoted to the Speedy Gonzales water Jet Set; and 'Last Round The Island Is A Cissy' is a favourite of young and old alike. However, this area soon gives on to a very pleasant scenic stretch with really efficient paired locks that allow an easy passage.

At Etrun there are posts indicating an halte fluvial at Bouchain, 350m away; but I could not find any sign of it. There is a medium-sized pontoon in good order in the back water, immediately next to which, just by the bridge on the corner, is a small boatyard. There are also many private pleasure craft moorings, incuding some for small dinghies. Perhaps more significantly in this isolated area, that while there is no shop in sight, there are at least two telephone kiosks and the boatyard advertises a bar. Valcon went aground at the entrance to the boatyard so clearly it is not a feasible proposition for craft drawing much more than a metre. There is a small sailing school, but in spite of the number of boats and the established Centre Nautique du Bassin Rond, the sloping quaysides and general shallowness make it suitable only for craft of less than 1m draught. The area by Paillencourt is littered with warning signs for various dangers: lack of depth, turning areas, sailing areas ... and on and on. It is in fact a very good holiday area for people with children, but otherwise of little appeal. The restricting depth round Paillencourt is 0.9m, so few boats will be able to complete a circumnavigation of the Bassin Rond. It is a calm and peaceful spot with lots of trees, but it is necessary to carry all you need with you.

Moving into the St Quentin Canal, the first halte is the Cantimpre Port in the centre of Cambrai. Once it was a port de plaisance, but it is now a base nautique - a much fairer description. The town is a pleasant agricultural centre known world-wide for its eponymous fine white linen (Cambric) that used to be bleached in the local fields. It is also well-known for its Betises de Cambrai (mint sweets of universal appeal) and its Andouillettes (tripe sausages of less than universal appeal). Cambrai has been an important bishopric since the Middle Ages and once had as bishop the famous Fenelon, nicknamed the "swan of Cambrai".

Pleasant villages and countryside take over, with Masnieres being perhaps the favourite stopping place. There is an halte fluvial at Honnecourt 15 with a pontoon. It has no services but is situate at a very pleasant and cheerful spot near the village; however, the small pontoon is half filled by a tourist office in the form of a boat with a pretty awning. The halte fluvial called 'les Rue des Vignes' is to be found at Vaucelles 12 and consists of nothing more than a quay and a pretty bit of grass with a picnic area.

Along the St Quentin there are various methods of operating the automatic lock system including the old fashioned quarter-turn hanging-pole suspended mid-canal. There can be hiccoughs: if caught in a bief with the automatic signals not in operation at all (and this can apply between locks 17 and 15) the problem is solved by pulling the red bar to summon the navigation staff. This is quite different from other automatic locks where such an 'alarm' is used exclusively to halt the process of locking when there has been a technical/mechanical problem, and not, as here, just to summon the supervisor to organise the bief.

Next comes the principal feature of the canal: the famous summit reach. This lies between locks Bosquet 17 and Lesdins 18, with two tunnels: the Grand Souterrain (5670m) and the Lesdins (1098m).

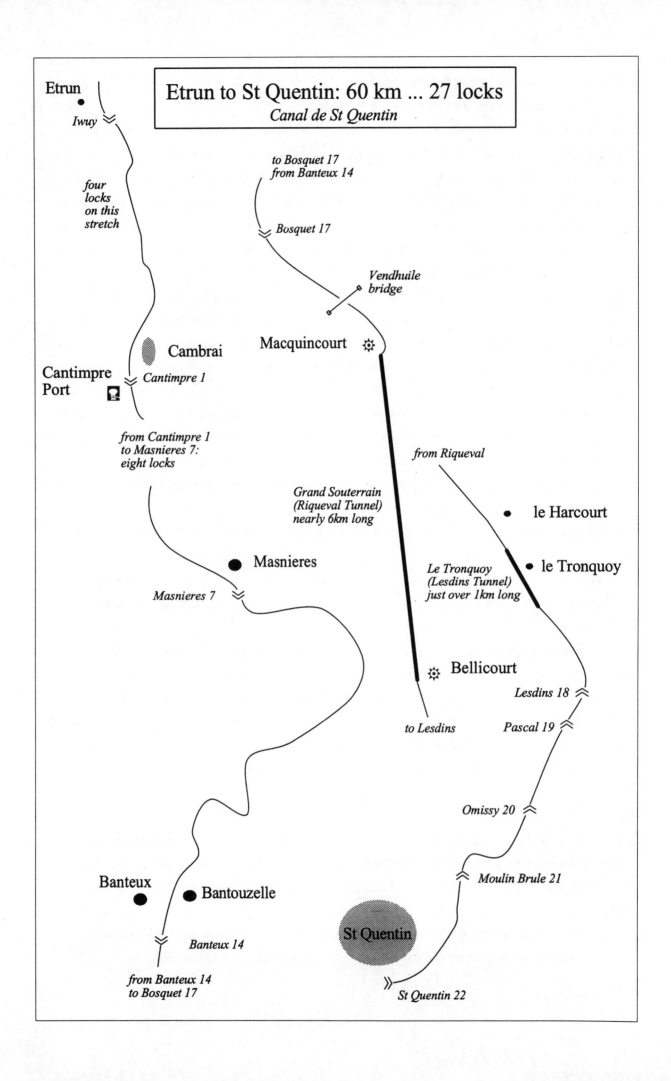

Etrun to St Quentin: 60 km ... 27 locks
Canal de St Quentin

Etrun

Iwuy

four
locks
on this
stretch

to Bosquet 17
from Banteux 14

Bosquet 17

Vendhuile
bridge

Cambrai

Macquincourt

Cantimpre
Port

Cantimpre 1

from Cantimpre 1
to Masnieres 7:
eight locks

from Riqueval

le Harcourt

Grand Souterrain
(Riqueval Tunnel)
nearly 6km long

le Tronquoy

Le Tronquoy
(Lesdins Tunnel)
just over 1km long

Masnieres

Masnieres 7

Bellicourt

Lesdins 18

Pascal 19

to Lesdins

Omissy 20

Moulin Brule 21

Banteux

Bantouzelle

St Quentin

Banteux 14

from Banteux 14
to Bosquet 17

St Quentin 22

Just being towed through the Grand Souterrain makes this route something special. Fees for the Grand Souterrain are levied at the St Quentin lock 22.

Bellicourt is situate close by the southern end of the Grand Souterrain. It is a pretty village worth the climb to see the beginnings of the Escaut and the end of the Mont St Martin abbey - if you have the time that is.

At one time, the whole summit level was crossed under tow; convoys setting off from both ends, crossing between the tunnels and changing over. Now, though the 25km summit bief is still in convoy, only the Grand Souterrain has a tug. Southbound convoys muster on the right bank below the bridge at Vendhuile, generally leaving at 1200 and 1930; while northbound convoys meet on the left bank upstream of the Lesdins tunnel, leaving normally at 0630 and 1500. Neither has an obvious marshalling station and the organisers approach their work in what might be called a cavalier-to-informal manner. You can inspect the remains of earlier versions - and marvel at the scale and scope of it all.

The monster tug can cope with up to 30 commercial barges. Craft tie up to the boat in front using ropes of equal length, preferably crossed to inhibit lurching when under way and regulations require the heaviest craft in front and the lightest at the rear. You will need at least 30m of rope. The tug men are expert at dealing with all and sundry from disenchanted professional bargees to wide-eyed amateur novice crews. Regulations also insist that while the boat is under tow, you must stay at the helm - as if you would want to do otherwise. Fees are levied at St Quentin lock 22, but gas-masks are not included in this charge!

Cambrai and St Quentin are the obligatory watering holes on opposite sides of the main tunnel.

ST QUENTIN TO TERGNIER

St Quentin is very different if approached from upstream rather than downstream. The upstream approach gives onto a very clear open view of modern buildings as opposed to the other more commercial and degraded aspects of the town.

St Quentin has a modest port de plaisance with restricted facilities. Built on a hillside, the town is on the major railway line running to Northern Europe and its industry and commerce have dominated its past. The area is of interest to nature lovers with its Musee d'Entomologie containing over half a million butterflies and other insects, and the Reserve Naturelle des Marais d'Isles, with its hectares of protected waters, beds and banks for the thousands of plants and birds. There is also the museum of Antoine Lecuyer with a splendid collection of pastels by Maurice Quentin Delatour as well as enamels, pottery, paintings and tapestries.

The entrance to the small Souterrain de Lesdins is controlled by lights well ahead of it and there is theoretically a quayside. While not very deep it is no serious problem to boats drawing less than a metre and a half.

The area between locks 24 and 23, including the new halte nautique at Seraucourt le Grand is being very well cared for. This under-proclaimed facility has mains water and electricity with first-rate pontoons. It is in a very quiet spot but close to the village which has all facilities and much appeal.

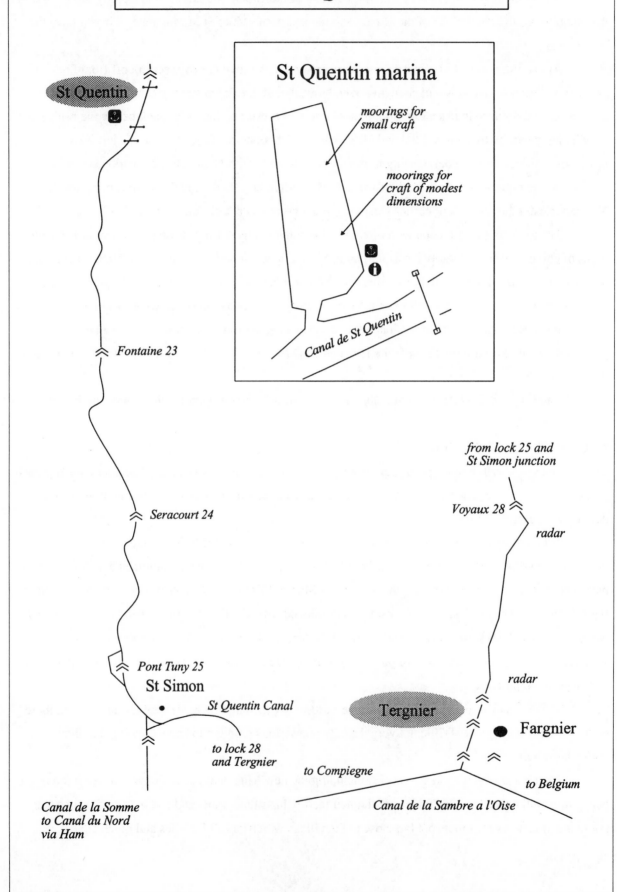

St Quentin to Tergnier: 35 km ... 9 locks
Canal de St Quentin

St Quentin

St Quentin marina

moorings for
small craft

moorings for
craft of modest
dimensions

Canal de St Quentin

Fontaine 23

from lock 25 and
St Simon junction

Voyaux 28

radar

Seracourt 24

radar

Pont Tuny 25
St Simon

Tergnier

Fargnier

St Quentin Canal

to lock 28
and Tergnier

to Compiegne

to Belgium

Canal de la Somme
to Canal du Nord
via Ham

Canal de la Sambre a l'Oise

The maintenance of the paths on each side of the bank is a positive joy to behold since so much has been left to go to seed. Between lock Jussy 26 and the junction at St Simon the canal sides suddenly come in and the waterway narrows into a deep valley. On each side there are woods that dramatically change almost every 100m, offering amazing, naturally sculptured shapes and patterns, hanging climbs and vines. It is a magic place. The small community of St Simon sits at the junction of the St Quentin Canal and the Canal de la Somme, after which it is just over 15km to Tergnier.

Here there are two communities facing each other across the canal: Tergnier and Fargnier, important railway junctions. The Picardy Museum is devoted to local, particularly military operations, in the Somme, the Aisne, and the Oise. There is an intriguing collection of weapons and memorabilia.

After Tergnier, it is necessary to watch out for the remnants of old pontoons reaching towards the middle of the canal. Some are just in a very bad state; others are partly broken down and some are just dangerous posts, lurking. In poor visibility they are difficult to spot as they melt into the background.

CANAL DE LA SOMME
CANAL DU NORD TO CANAL DE ST QUENTIN

Theoretically, there is a choice of routes at the junction of the Canal du Nord and the Canal de St Quentin; one of them being the supposedly agreeable rural detour through the famous old town of Ham. However, the canal and its locks are generally in poor repair and the depth is 'slight' at best (Valcon was touching bottom most of the time). In addition, the overhanging branches over-reach themselves to such an extent that at places they form a complete overhang - creating a real navigational problems. On the whole it it must be looked upon as a negotiation to be avoided; a consummation devoutly to be missed.

For those who must seek it out, Ham, in the centre of the canal, is an ancient fortified town, with the famous sugar refinery nearby at Eppeville. It has items of interest: the crypt of the Abbey is 12th century and well conserved. There is also the residual feudal 13th and 18th century castle. It was, in its prime, the master of the area and can claim fame for holding prisoner one Napoleon III - but not for long since he escaped in the guise of a mason.

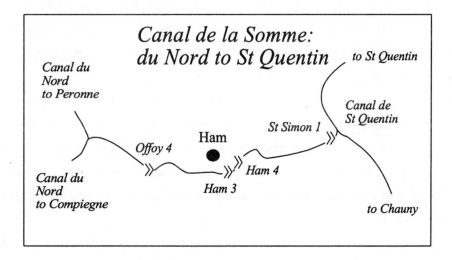

So; with a final warning not to be tempted by this stretch unless your craft is no more than 1m in draught and 9m LOA, let us return to the canal that brings us in from the Channel at St Valery sur Somme.

PART THREE: CANAL DE LA SOMME

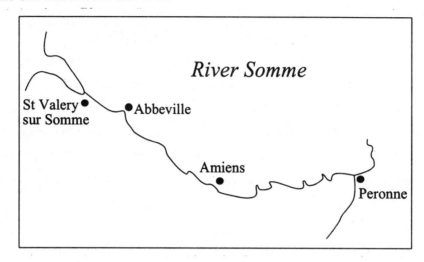

ST VALERY SUR SOMME TO PERONNE

St Valery is not a place to approach at night or in poor weather. The approach to St Valery is straightforward, and even on neaps, craft with up to 1.40m draught should have no problem with shortage of water. However, the buoys are not as effective as they could be and strangers very often find the approach confusing. The most convenient and secure berth will be found at the yacht club pontoons which lie beyond the town quay. Most berths are bow-to pontoons, with a stern-line buoy. Craft with anything less than 2.0m will not ground at Low Water. So; unless you want to sit on the mud for a tide, you must reach the yacht harbour between 2hrs before and 2hrs after HWN. There are good facilities here at the Sport Nautique Valericain where you will find yorself made more than welcome. Another possibility is to tie up alongside the town quay, after checking it is a vacant berth. Here also you will take the ground. However, the sandbanks are there to be explored especially for samphire and sea lilies.

The sea-lock into the canal is beyond the yacht club berths. The keeper generally opens on demand between 90 minutes before and after High Water, but that can be better at Neaps. Mooring is available between lock 25 and the mobile bridge. (It is worth noting that you can get as far as Abbeville along the canal, without taking your mast down.)

Basically founded in 610 as an abbey community, St Valery is a pleasant town with a long history - including the salutary fact that William set sail from the port for England in 1066. It has an intriguing miniature railway that runs a tourist/commuter trip along what used to be the "bains de mer" network. It permits a shoreside visit to Le Crotoy; the intriguing small port across the 'estuary', not easily achieved by yachts. It was a fort of Ponthieu, and the residual castle is a reminder of where Joan of Arc was held before being taken to Rouen.

Leaving St Valery, the scenery on the first stretch of the Canal de la Somme is often hidden by splendid trees. The two villages of Saigneville and Cambron both possess interesting churches with

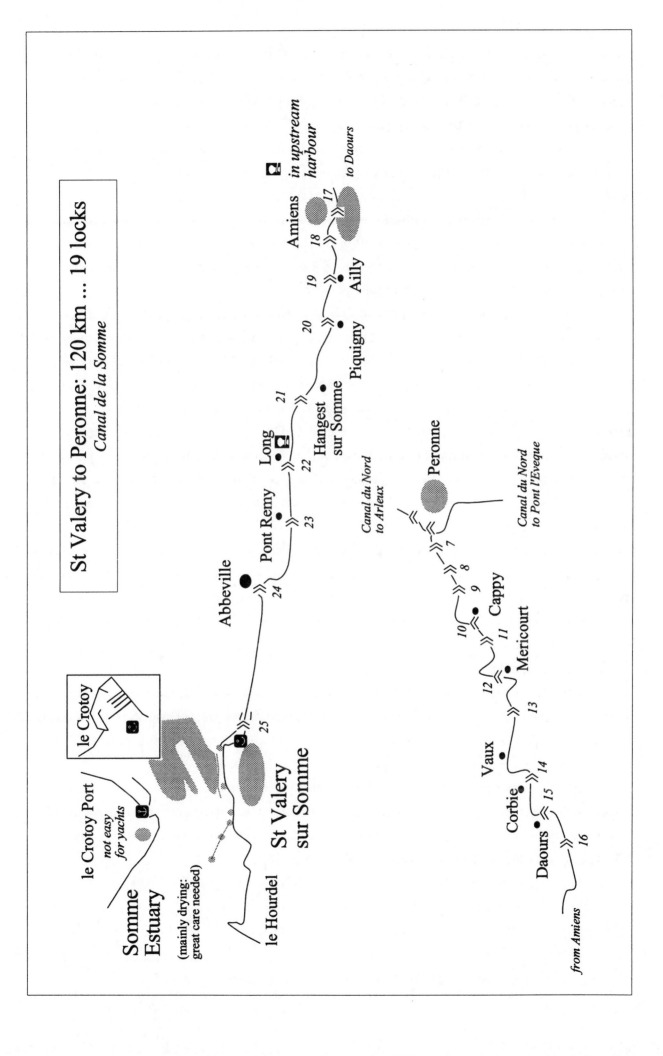

St Valery to Peronne: 120 km … 19 locks
Canal de la Somme

Somme Estuary

(mainly drying: great care needed)

le Crotoy

le Crotoy Port
not easy for yachts

le Hourdel

St Valery sur Somme

25

Abbeville

24

Pont Remy

23

Long

22

21

Hangest sur Somme

20

Piquigny

19

Ailly

18   17

Amiens

in upstream harbour

to Daours

Canal du Nord to Arleux

Peronne

7

8

9

10   11

Cappy

12

13

Mericourt

Vaux

14

15

Corbie

Daours

16

from Amiens

Canal du Nord to Pont l'Eveque

architecture and choirs from the 12th to the 16th centuries. Most significant are the lock and five swing bridges of the dead-straight Canal Maritime d'Abbeville. There is a sound quayside mooring at the northern end of the non-navigable branch of the river. The centre of Abbeville, the regional capital is close by and of its many historical features, perhaps the most stirring is the World War Musee d'Histoire "France 1940" near the Chateau Bagatelle; a 17th century chateau built by a local loom-maker to the cloth and carpet trade. The town's hypermarket is usefully situated with its own riverside quay just outside the town.

There are many villages and attractive banksides along the Abbeville-Peronne stretch with its 17 locks, some of which are 'doubles' with two sets of gates; others have the dreaded sloping side walls, which can be a problem if the keeper is uncooperative. The usual bankside problems for craft with draught of more than a metre apply throughout.

The first small village of note is Epagne Epagnette with its classic stone and brick chateau, restored in the 19th century. Pont Remy, five km along, by lock 23, has a 14th century island fort and the church has some very fine 16th century windows. The pretty village of Long comes next, also by a lock, where there is good mooring. Here there is another grand brick and stone chateau - a good example of Louis XV and there is also a 16th century church with a fine stone spire and inside an excellent organ. The village of Longpre les Corps Saints is a short walk inland but it has a fine 12th and 15th century church with links to the Crusades. Hangest and Piquigny are the other two villages to view before Amiens. The first has (yet another) amazing church and the second the ruins of one of the largest fortified castles in the area, complete with drawbridge posterns, a vaulted kitchen and underground tunnels. There is, of course, a fine church.

Amiens is an industrial centre and has both a commercial quay (Port d'Aval) and a leisure craft facility in the upstream harbour. There is much of interest in this, the capital of Picardie. Of particular note are the Notre Dame Cathedral; the Musees de Picardie ... d'Art Local ... de Costume ... d'Histoire; the Hotoie Zoological Gardens and the Jules Verne Centre, which promotes a walk: "In the Steps of Jules Verne". However, it cannot be said that the moorings are attractive enough to tempt one to taste all that is available in this splendid place.

After Amiens, once again, there are many potential riverside and village halts (all governed of course by draught) but the usual plan is to make reasonable haste for the junction with the Canal du Nord. Small villages apart, the exception has to be Corbie with its collection of remarkable churches and chapels. They need two full days for a complete exploration and appreciation.

Peronne, another industrial centre, sits at this junction, and boasts a first-class port de plaisance. However, this is not quite the case (please see page 41) and one is best advised to move on to Moislains and the Ruyaulcourt Tunnel or south to one of the many villages in the next 50km to Noyon and Pont l'Eveque for the junction of the Canal Lateral a l'Oise.

PART FOUR: CANALS OF THE OISE AND THE AISNE

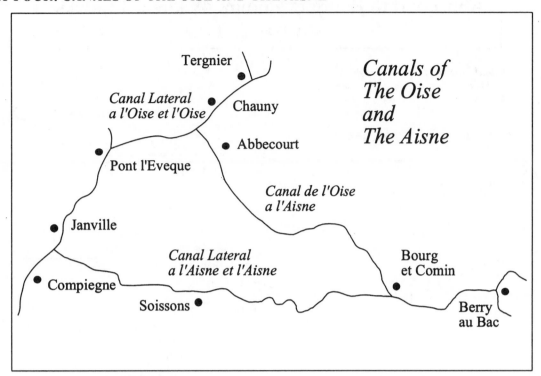

CANAL DE L'OISE A L'AISNE

ABBECOURT TO BOURG ET COMIN

This stretch of canal is best divided into three parts: beginning, middle and end. To begin at the beginning with Abbecourt: a small town at the junction of the Oise with few services and not a lot of appeal, but with an unusually complete absence of pretentiousness. To end at the end with Bourg et Comin, another small community at a junction (with the Aisne) also with few services and short on charm. So, like a jam sponge, any richness has to be found in the middle - and there is some for those with an eye.

After quitting Abbecourt, the first choice is at the twinned community of l'Avaloire and Guny: very rural, very real and very basic. Not far away on the other side of the canal is Coucy le Chateau: a fortified city that from a superb position overlooks the valley. The ruined castle of the Sires de Coucy castle with its underground passages; the War Museum Tower; the 18th century gates and the Granjere gardens are all worth a visit.

Twelve km along the canal is Anizy le Chateau, twinned across the water with Pinon. There are aquaria in the area open to the public together with walks centering on flora and fauna. There is good shopping here, with a decent supermarket. Five km later, on the other side just set back from the canal, is the village of Chavignon. It is a centre devoted to bees and Royal Jelly extraction can be witnessed.

The last middle 'delights' of the canal are two: the first one is a real delight and that is the Monampteuil lake which is now a leisure centre for swimming, sunbathing, fishing, boating and wind-surfing. The other is an actual undelight: quite under lit and given to creating quite long (and apparently unnecessary) waits, it is the small Braye Tunnel. It is just over 2km in length and its one-way system is controlled by traffic lights.

Abbecourt to Bourg et Comin: 48 km ... 13 locks
Canal de l'Oise a l'Aisne

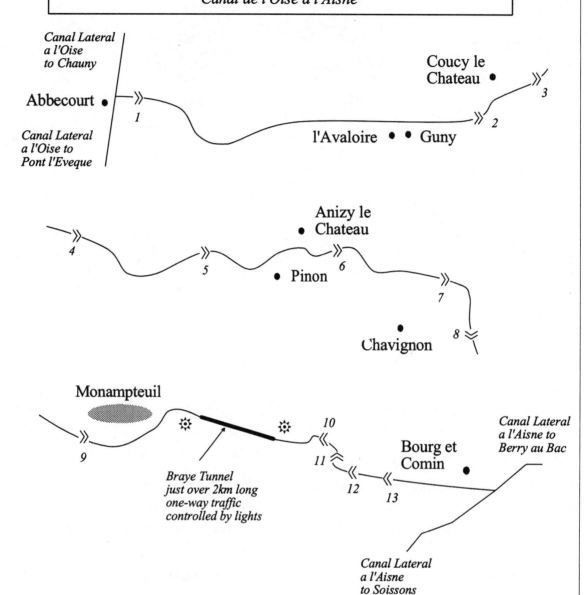

Canal Lateral a l'Oise to Chauny

Abbecourt •

Canal Lateral a l'Oise to Pont l'Eveque

1

Coucy le Chateau •

3

2

l'Avaloire • • Guny

Anizy le • Chateau

4

5

• Pinon

6

7

8

• Chavignon

Monampteuil

9

☼   ☼

Braye Tunnel just over 2km long one-way traffic controlled by lights

10

11

Bourg et Comin •

12   13

Canal Lateral a l'Aisne to Berry au Bac

Canal Lateral a l'Aisne to Soissons

CANAL LATERAL A L'AISNE ET L'AISNE CANALISEE

COMPIEGNE TO BERRY AU BAC

Moving north from Compiegne, the most obvious landmark is the massive Colgate conglomerate at PK99. Just after this point we leave the Oise for the canalised River Aisne. This is a very attractive waterway: picturesque with abundant wild-life, including heron that are nearly at ease and friendly. The slow, quiet boater will be able to observe deer grazing on the banks - happy to stand and stare without fear. The whole stretch combines this kind of peace and quiet with friendly efficiency from the lock-keepers. They all manage to be speedy - but nice with it.

There are many places where it is worth tying up and staying overnight, and they will be chosen to taste. Favourite stopping places are Choisy au Bac; the three communities of Breuil, Attichy and Vic sur Aisne (an area with flight after flight of heron), and Port Fontenoy.

They lead to the crown of the navigation which is undoubtedly Soissons, where you can moor for a week free of charge at the quayside. It has no mains service, but the town is magnificent, capable of entertaining one and all easily for a week. The quayside can become a little boisterous at week-ends in the holiday season, but this is not the rule. The town was almost entirely rebuilt after the 1914/18 War, but its high-reaching towers remain and it is still has many old monuments. The civic museum, the St Jean des Vignes church and the mansion known as the Hotel de Barral are all worth special visits. It is a quite gorgeous place.

As in the stretch before Soissons, there are plenty of smaller places for one night stands in the 50km from Soissons to Berry au Bac, at the confluence of the Aisne and Marne systems. The first favourite is Vailly sur Aisne, a pretty spot actually on the real River Aisne, which is navigable for shoal draught craft up to the town bridge. The next possibility is Bourg et Comin, but it does not compare with Berry au Bac near the end of the navigation. There are plenty of choices of mooring places - all at the banksides, but for once there are some stretches with good depth. Near PK18 however, which is close to a canal hamlet known by the unusual name of La Ferme de Moscou, there is difficulty in closing the bank with more than a metre draught. Further from the hamlet, to the north, and on the other side of the lock at PK19, there is a barge mooring with good depth and usually a place for a small boat to sneak in. The lock-keeper is most co-operative, and there are generally a couple of barges staying overnight for company.

Berry au Bac was once a floating marshalling yard for both commercial traffic and leisure craft. Now there is little evidence of either. Facilities in the immediate vicinity are restricted: the small bar/shop at the junction is a must if only for the experience of life at the minimal edges: its supplies are strictly limited. However, in the village of Berry itself, no more than a short walk away, there are excellent shops and restaurants - of a much larger size and better quality than the size of the place itself would suggest.

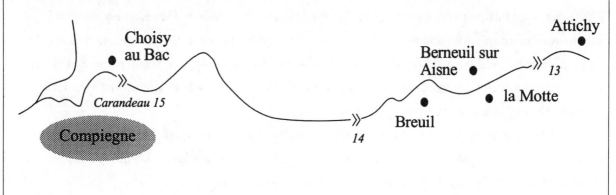

Compiegne to Soissons: 40 km ... 6 locks
Canal Lateral a l'Aisne et l'Aisne Canalisee

*Canal Lateral
a l'Oise
to Pont l'Eveque*

Choisy
au Bac

Attichy

Berneuil sur
Aisne

la Motte

13

Carandeau 15

Breuil

14

Compiegne

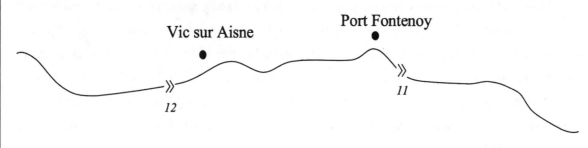

Vic sur Aisne

Port Fontenoy

12

11

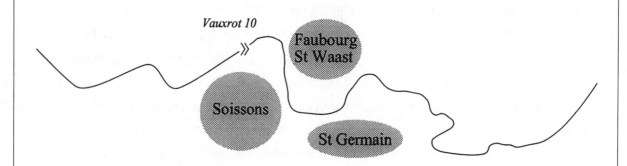

Vauxrot 10

Faubourg
St Waast

Soissons

St Germain

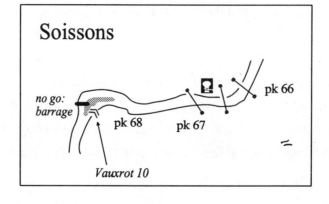

Soissons

*no go:
barrage*

pk 66

pk 68

pk 67

Vauxrot 10

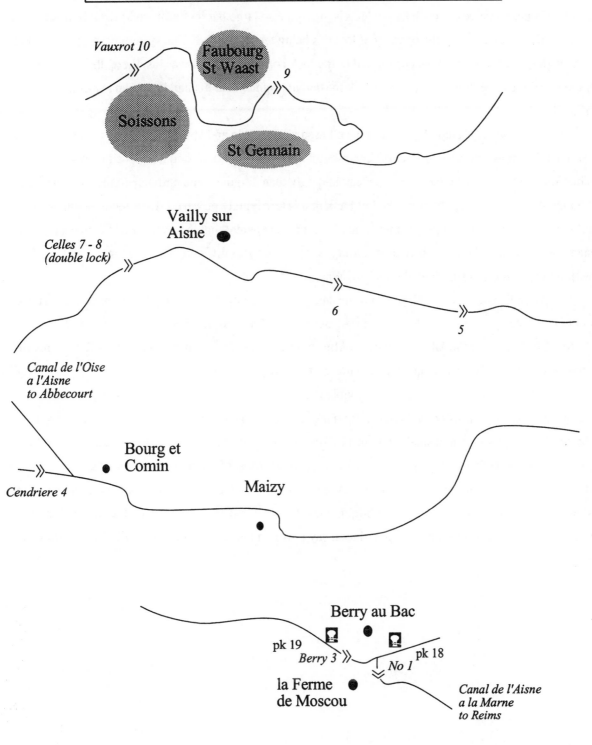

Soissons to Berry au Bac: 44 km ... 6 locks

Canal Lateral a l'Aisne et l'Aisne Canalisee

Vauxrot 10

Faubourg
St Waast

9

Soissons

St Germain

Vailly sur
Aisne

*Celles 7 - 8
(double lock)*

6

5

Canal de l'Oise
a l'Aisne
to Abbecourt

Bourg et
Comin

Maizy

Cendriere 4

Berry au Bac

pk 19

Berry 3

No 1 pk 18

la Ferme
de Moscou

Canal de l'Aisne
a la Marne
to Reims

CANAL LATERAL A L'OISE ET L'OISE
TERGNIER TO COMPIEGNE

Tergnier is heavily industrial with a full range of services in the town. It is not an appealing parking place and it is better to move on to Chauny which is not quite so large but less grim and grisly. In this area, a new method of controlling the opening of locks is being tested by VNF. The system uses a portable battery device that transmits an electric signal to the lock controls. When I was last there, they were still having technical teething troubles. The lock master at Tergnier said his handset wasn't working because of the heat!

The town of Chauny has always been based on its castle and abbey. The quay at Chauny on the left bank is not in a very good state of repair, but it does have pontoons and it is possible to get to the side. Some may find the area little less bleak and ugly than Tergnier. The entrance to the first lock at Chauny has an emptying sluice on the left bank that is terrifyingly powerful. It all looks broad and peaceful until you move into centre channel, when it becomes apparent that the water-thrust comes out with such narrow-channel power that boat-handling is made tricky-to-difficult. The town museum is packed with relics from pre-history and both World Wars.

After Tergnier and Chauny comes the small settlement of Abbecourt (already mentioned above) at the junction with the Canal de l'Oise a l'Aisne. After 15km, another junction: this time with the Canal du Nord at Pont l'Eveque (also see above). After this, the next place of rest is Janville, a few kilometres above Compiegne (dealt with in Chapter Three: The Seine).

Janville is busy with barges, the double locks working almost non-stop, but there is usually a vacant spot on the north side of the locks for a modest yacht to creep in. There is also a vast barge park to the south of the locks, and a small quay just before the one-way system round the island. It is a welcoming community, with a very good basic selection of shops. Most of them are run by a single soul, most of them eccentric, peculiar or idiosyncratic - but in the nicest possible way. There is a very good hardware shop fronting the canal run by a most obliging lady. I have found Janville to be such a welcoming and magnetic place that I find it nigh impossible to say a word against it. There can hardly be a better way to end a chapter!

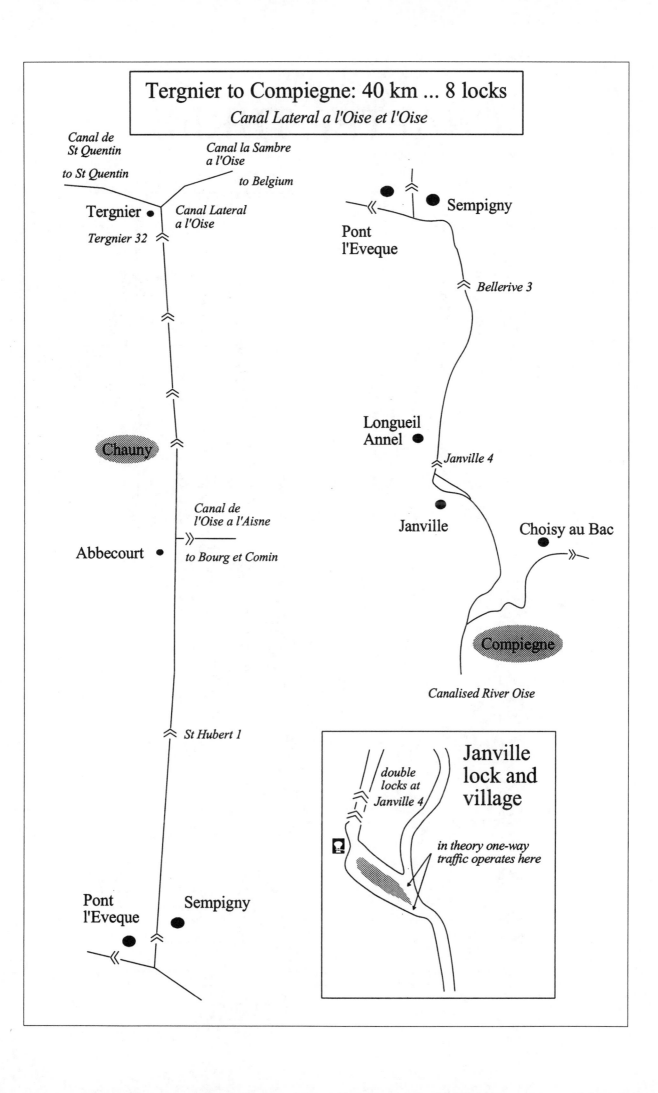

Tergnier to Compiegne: 40 km ... 8 locks
Canal Lateral a l'Oise et l'Oise

*Canal de
St Quentin*

to St Quentin

*Canal la Sambre
a l'Oise*

to Belgium

Tergnier •

*Canal Lateral
a l'Oise*

Tergnier 32

Chauny

*Canal de
l'Oise a l'Aisne*

Abbecourt •

to Bourg et Comin

St Hubert 1

Pont
l'Eveque

Sempigny

Pont
l'Eveque

Sempigny

Bellerive 3

Longueil
Annel •

Janville 4

Janville •

Choisy au Bac

Compiegne

Canalised River Oise

Janville lock and village

*double
locks at
Janville 4*

*in theory one-way
traffic operates here*

CHAPTER THREE

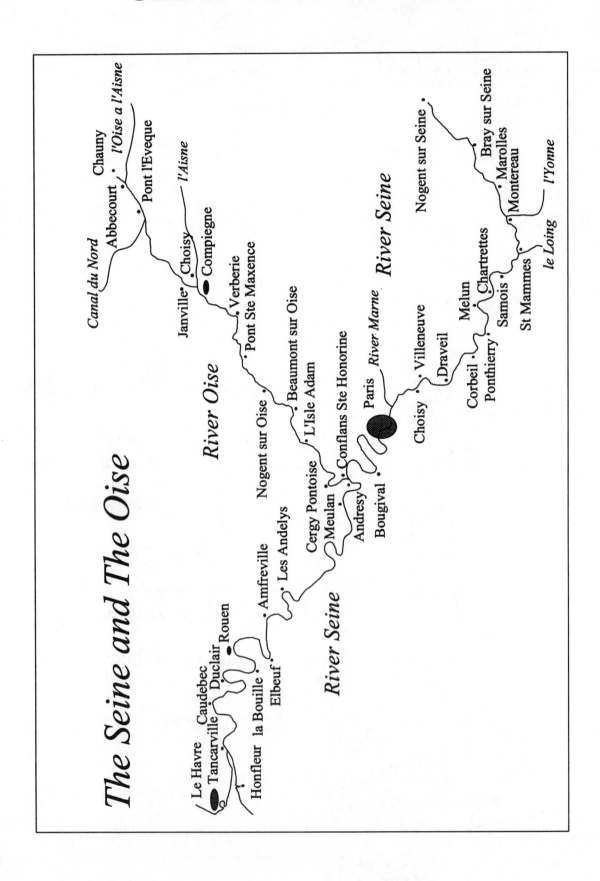

The Seine and The Oise

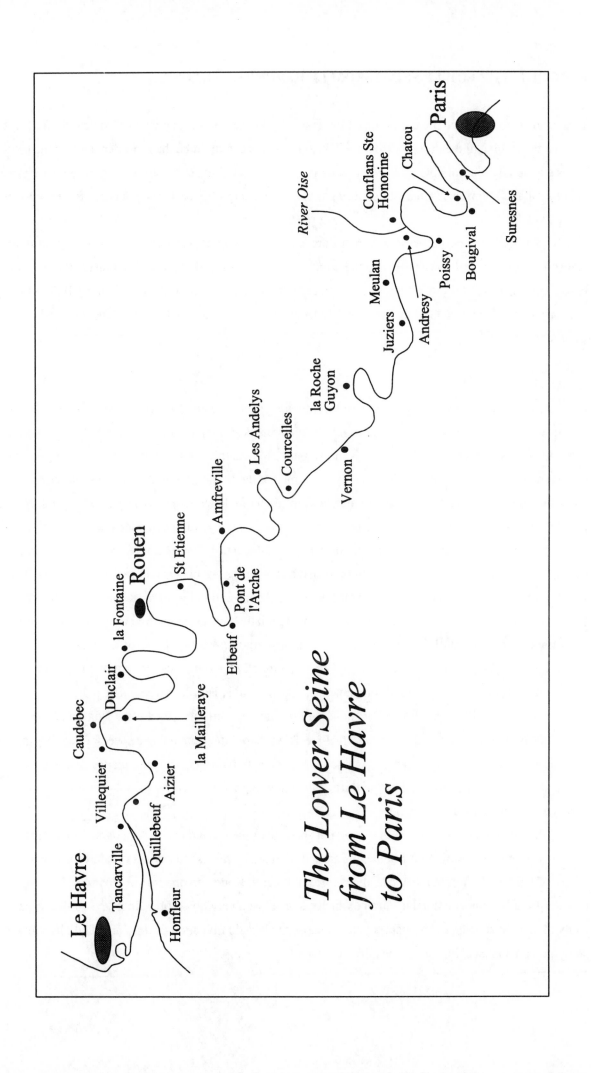

The Lower Seine from Le Havre to Paris

PART ONE: THE LOWER SEINE FROM LE HAVRE TO PARIS

This is not a sea guide, so there is no place for detailed pilotage notes of the channel routes. Sufficient to say that the last leg of the crossing from the UK to Le Havre can often be the most demanding: the estuary is a generally inhospitable spot. When wind is against tide the sea state can be worse than the Thames under similar circumstances: namely suffering those short, sharp little bastards that come from all points of the card.

The harbour approaches and entrance are extremely well buoyed because of the heavy commercial shipping traffic that constantly uses the port. Leisure craft do well to tend close outside the shipping lanes. That is, except for the last stretch, where, to the immediate north of the three buoys LH12, 14 & 16, there is the shoal ground of the Banc de l'Eclat and the Petite Rade, with their attendant wrecks. Caution is required.

LE HAVRE TO ROUEN

Happily for visitors, there is no difficulty in locating the yacht harbour. The port's twin chimneys are conspicuous from afar, and close to, once through the main breakwaters, the marina is immediately to port, protected by its own short breakwater. It is in two parts, and visitors are berthed in the Anse de Joinville. Chaos frequently reigns, but Brits are usually welcomed at the first of the outer pontoons, which are almost straight ahead. They are then despatched as local charm dictates. This typically Gallic enthusiasm or indifference means you are not immediately boarded with money being demanded with menaces.

Le Havre is a large sea port, dating back to the 16th century. It may not be the most charismatic of French ports, but it is efficient, has comprehensive services, is not expensive, and, for British boaters, is not only Porte Oceane (Gateway to the Ocean) as the French call it, but Front Door to Paris and the French Inland Waterways system. Le Havre is a commercially well-used port and town, and while it is not without appeal, most of it is well-distanced from the harbour, and for our purposes it has to be considered merely as a way in. Until recently, Le Havre was virtually the only feasible port of entry to the Seine, but a new lock and general improvements to the system at Honfleur have made a difference - offering skippers a little more flexibility and a most inviting opportunity. (Please see Honfleur below.)

Now, many readers will have craft that are able to cross the Channel at a speedier rate of knots than the six or seven usually achieved by Valcon; but once on the River Seine, no matter what their size or speed, all vessels are governed by the traffic movement regulations. Thirty to 40 knots is of no avail once you are steaming up the river.

Speed through the water is one thing but speed over the ground can be, of course, something entirely different. Cruising up the Seine, progress is affected by the use the skipper makes (or fails to make) of the tide. In summer, you can always steam direct to Rouen on one tide in 20km/hr (11 knot) craft, especially with a favourable current which can achieve a very powerful 5 knots. Nevertheless, a study of sunrise and tide times enables you to choose the best combination of tides and daylight hours to suit your convenience. Please see the tables on page 16 for details.

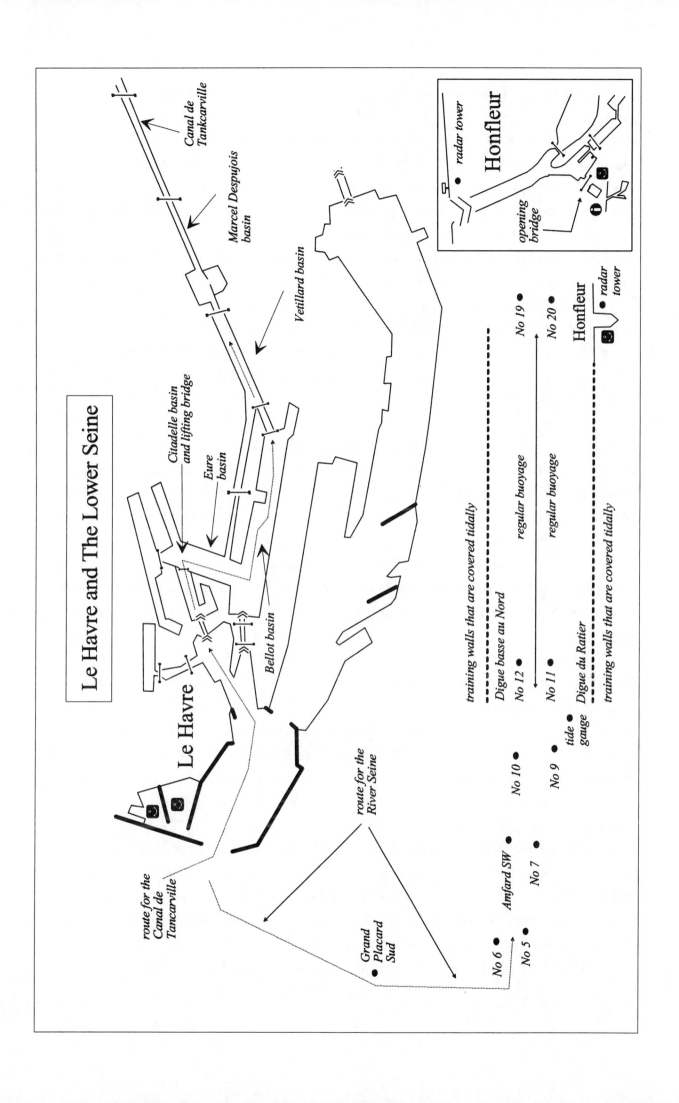

Le Havre and The Lower Seine

Canal de Tankcarville

Marcel Despujois basin

Vetillard basin

Citadelle basin and lifting bridge

Eure basin

Bellot basin

Le Havre

route for the Canal de Tancarville

route for the River Seine

Grand Placard Sud

No 6

No 5

Amfard SW

No 7

No 10

No 9

tide gauge

training walls that are covered tidally

Digue basse au Nord

No 12   regular buoyage   No 19

No 11   regular buoyage   No 20

Digue du Ratier

training walls that are covered tidally

Honfleur

radar tower

Honfleur

radar tower

opening bridge

When leaving Le Havre for the Seine, there are various hazards to be avoided. Perhaps the most seductive is the Tancarville Canal syndrome. This route, which avoids the estuary, is much used by commercial traffic. Merchant ships have their own locks, known locally as 'SAS' - surely enough of a warning in itself! These are Quinette de Rochemont, into the Bellot basin close to the harbour entrance, or Francois 1st, further towards Tancarville. Neither is avaiable to leisure craft which must use the Citadelle basin and the moving bridge into the Eure basin. Next is Bellot basin into the Vetillard lock and basin and finally into the Tancarville Canal. Citadelle operates on demand 24 hours a day when sea levels permit, although its bridge is closed at certain times. Vetillard lock is open from 0600 to 2230, while Tancarville opens on demand from -4 to + 3 HW at Le Havre. Traffic control lights are in operation.

Many first-time visitors are tempted to use the inner canal/basin route, believing it to be calmer (because protected from winds & tides) and overall much less hassle than the Seine estuary. This is not a completely accurate perception since the canal route requires confrontations with all those low slow bridges, wearisome locks and generally unpleasant surroundings. In addition, masts must be lowered in Le Havre before you can pass through the canal. The river is, in my opinion, much the less challenging itinerary and also the more scenically attractive proposition.

The obvious menace, apart from inclement weather, is the commercial traffic. With adverse weather conditions, since nothing can be done to avoid them, it is best to stay and enjoy the shoreside attractions of Le Havre. But the big ships are so obvious and conspicuous that it is no problem to see and to steer well clear of them. The fact of the matter is that more sinister, inconspicuous dangers lurk in the shoal banks at the entry to the river. Inconspicuous, that is, except for the excellence of the buoyage. The cautious route is westerly to YBY LH11, standing off southerly to YBY Duncan Clinch, and only then rounding the Red No.4 to access the main channel on an easterly course. After that, you keep just to the north of the channel (as in the Traffic Regulations) and wait for the open bleakness to change to pleasantly wooded cliffs.

The first place of note is Honfleur: which is fascinating enough to be visited in its own time and its own right for its own delight. Until recently it was not possible to combine a visit with a passage up river, but the whole harbour is now locked and consequently more accessible than before. Leisure craft use the inner basin, entry into which is governed by the opening of the bridge across what used to be a locked basin. To gain the best tide and time to go upstream for Rouen means steaming past Honfleur at or shortly after Low Water. Honfleur's bridge opens three or four times a day; on the hour after the first opening. (If you have it in mind to use Honfleur, the best plan is to contact the Cercle Nautiqe de Honfleur for current tidal and bridge information. Write or phone them at CNH, Club House, 8, rue Saint Antoine B.P. 118 14600 Honfleur. Tel: 00.33.31.98.87.13. They also publish a most helpful brochure.)

Generally speaking, mooring below Rouen is a laborious and perilous affair. The two main dangers when mooring are first being effortlessly and unknowingly crushed by a big ship; and second drying out on foul mud ground. In addition, the general condition of the river bed, the heavy commercial traffic and the aggressive tides combine to make anchoring unsafe.

Mooring for short periods is tolerated and indeed cannot be avoided when cruising from Rouen

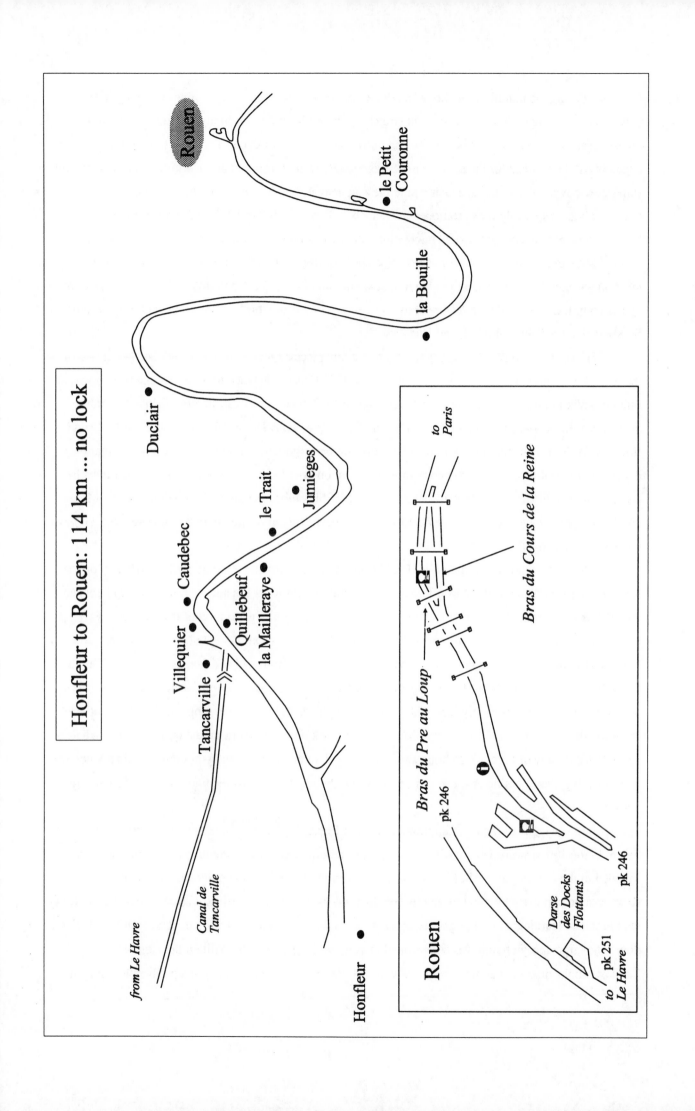

Honfleur to Rouen: 114 km … no lock

Rouen

from Le Havre

Canal de
Tancarville

Tancarville •

Villequier •

Quillebeuf •
la Mailleraye •

Caudebec •

le Trait •

Jumieges •

Duclair •

la Bouille

le Petit
Couronne

Honfleur •

Rouen

to
Paris

Bras du Cours de la Reine

Bras du Pre au Loup →

pk 246

Darse
des Docks
Flottants

pk 246

to   pk 251
Le Havre

to the sea during the months with shorter daylight hours, because of the ban on night travel by leisure craft. It is important to avoid open straight stretches where big ships pass at high speeds; to avoid mooring too near the bank, since a heavy wash can push you against it or even lift you on to it and to avoid the apparent safety of inlets for the same reason. It is prudent to find a spot near a working ferry since the big ships slow down when passing, causing much less upheaval. The ferrymen and pilots are usually willing to offer advice, especially those stationed at Caudebec. It is essential to let the navigation authorities know if you have to stop and correct navigation lights are compulsory throughout the night.

Most quays are reserved for cargo ships and mooring by pleasure boats is prohibited. In any case, most quays have no ladders, are too high to disembark and do not have bollards suitable for small craft. Quays completely forbidden to leisure craft are: Quay de Seine at Honfleur, the Radicatel, Port Jerome, St Wandrille, Le Trait, Yainville, and Duclair.

However, coming alongside is tolerated at a few places: Quillebeuf and Caudebec being two of the few. Quillebeuf sur Seine, a commercial quay, at PK331 is no distance up river. At one time it was an infamous Viking hideout. Caudebec is not far away at PK310 and is now little more than a commercial quay-place. It was once the main town in Pays de Caux, and Henri IV called its church of Notre Dame 'the most beautiful chapel in the kingdom'. It must not be forgotten that there is always the danger of drying out on foul ground and someone should remain on board at all times not only to adjust lines for the tide but also to attempt to fend off when the wash of big ships assaults with maximum force. Many are the skippers I have met who have decided or have been 'forced' to tie up on the tidal stretch: all have unpleasant tales to tell.

The river stations at Tancarville (PK337 on the right bank) and Passage du Trait (PK299 on the left bank opposite) can sometimes offer sound mooring possibilities. Leisure craft must tie up between the piles or to the inner (bank) side of commercial craft. Correct navigation lights are compulsory.

In between these two, Villequier (PK313.5) may have a vacant buoy, but leisure craft are allowed to use them only under sufferance and competent crew must be on board and prepared to cast off at all times. The village is in a beautiful setting and houses the Victor Hugo Museum. Strictly speaking, the Villequier buoys are exclusively reserved for merchant ships, and are in non-stop use. There are other buoys on the river that can be used, but there is always risk and leisure craft must quit them immediately upon demand - day or night. A 24 hour watch by competent crew is necessary not only for this: when the tide turns, big ships passing at speed can cause craft to be heaved against the buoy or even thrown right onto the bank.

Jumieges, one of the most impressive ruins in France, occupies a splendid site on the Lower Seine. In the 10th century Duke William Longsword rebuilt Jumieges on the ruins of the former abbey founded in the 7th century by St Philibert and destroyed by the Vikings and the new Benedictine abbey soon became popularly known through its benefactions as the Jumieges Almshouse. Charity did not however preclude learning and Jumieges also became widely recognised as a centre of scholarship and wisdom. The large abbey church was consecrated in 1067 in the presence of William the Conqueror. The last monks dispersed at the Revolution and in 1793 the abbey was bought at a public auction by a timber merchant from Canteleu who intended to turn Jumieges into a stone quarry and used explosives to bring down the lantern in the church. A new proprietor in 1852 set about saving the ruins which now belong to the nation.

It is true that these possible-to-chancy mooring opportunities are nearer to the sea than to Rouen and may seem tempting. I cannot do other than urge skippers to plan to make the trip to Rouen at one go. After a possibly sluggish start getting to Honfleur about Low Water, the flood tide can be exploited all the way.

If you need to take down masts and haven't done so in Le Havre, you must do so at Rouen, where the place to moor is the yacht pontoon in the St. Gervais basin on the south quay of the Darse Babin.

Skippers gain permission and can also arrange for boat work or maintenance to be done by visiting the harbour office. To do this, moor at the Rouen Port Authority pontoon on the de Lesseps quai, upstream from the Darse Babin. Craft are allowed to stay for a maximum of 48 hours in the St Gervais basin, but most skippers and crew will probably want to leave after 48 minutes. There are few domestic facilities nearby and a late night trip to find a good but inexpensive restaurant or take-away can be a bit of tedious affair - for those on foray as well as those left aboard for the very necessary guard duty.

Skippers with craft that can get under the bridges can proceed straightway to the the Rouen pleasure boat harbour. This is just upstream of the Pont Corneille, and the pontoons are on the left bank of the right arm: the Bras du Pre au Loup branch. The pontoons have been improved over the past few years. There is mains power and water, but they still leave much to be desired in stability and roping points. In general the authorities also leave you much alone. They are usually conspicuous by their absence when help is needed to tie up; but then, they do not unnecessarily pester for money. Of course, they have been stating for nearly ten years now that vast improvements and refurbishments are 'in hand'; and I must add that the mooring facility is by no means the worst or the worst value for money in France. It is important to know that traffic is permitted to move in the Bras du Pre au Loup only against the flow; that is: traffic proceeding upstream may do so only during (against) the ebb tide and traffic going downstream may do so only during (against) the flood.

All general services and stores are available in the immediate vicinity; while all other things French that bring the visitor to the Seine are to be found in Rouen itself; undoubtedly one of the most beautiful and interesting cities in France. I have no fault to find with this city.

ROUEN TO MANTES LA JOLIE

Finding places to stop is no longer a serious problem after Rouen. The next marina-type facility is at Elbeuf on the right bank at PK218, no more than 24km from Rouen. Things have improved dramatically here: the restricting draught, now at a good 2.5m, is a full metre better than it used to be and access is no longer limited to 2h +/-HW. It is not set in the most salubrious of surroundings, nor is it surrounded by many domestic or social facilities but it is a very sheltered and secure haven with some boating services and access to mains power and water.

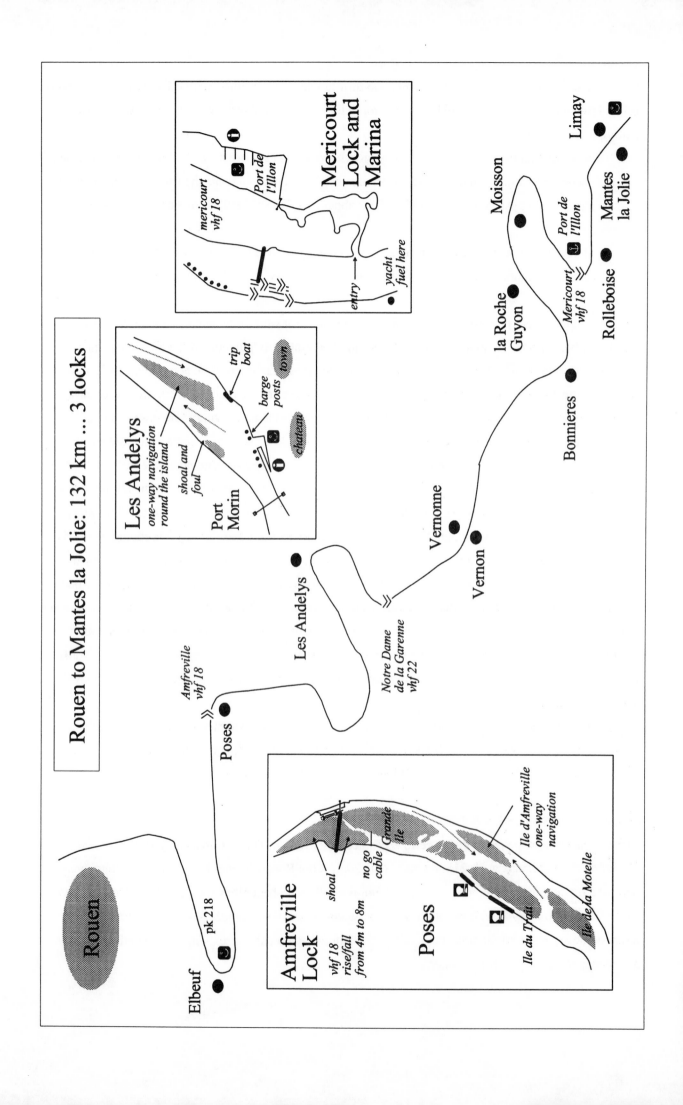

Rouen to Mantes la Jolie: 132 km ... 3 locks

Rouen

Elbeuf

pk 218

Amfreville Lock

vhf 18
rise/fall
from 4m to 8m

Poses

shoal

no go
cable

Grande
Ile

Ile du Trait

Ile d'Amfreville
one-way
navigation

Ile de la Motelle

Poses

Amfreville
vhf 18

Les Andelys

Notre Dame
de la Garenne
vhf 22

Les Andelys
one-way navigation
round the island

shoal and
foul

Port
Morin

trip
boat

barge
posts

town

château

Mericourt Lock and Marina

mericourt
vhf 18

Port de
l'Illon

entry

yacht
fuel here

Vernonne

Vernon

Bonnieres

la Roche
Guyon

Moisson

Port de
l'Illon

Mericourt
vhf 18

Rolleboise

Limay

Mantes
la Jolie

The Seine from here on gets more dramatically scenic with magnificent cliffs with every passing PK; not that every marker post is present, but it can be quite intriguing to catalogue them. The very first lock is d'Amfreville just 16km after Elbeuf. D'Amfreville has operators who are generally friendly, but their operation can be a long-winded (90 minutes for example) assignment; but neither the lock nor its keeper was threatening and the experience turned out to be an advancement on many English locks.

The lock and the upstream islands together with the small community of Poses make for an intriguing and restful stop after the potentially demanding trip up the tidal Seine. I met not one unfriendly soul.

The next staging post is the port de plaisance at Les Andelys, another 45km on. It is preceded by the small yacht club Paris-Normandie on the right bank with a depth of 1.5m where there is seldom room or welcome for a visitor. Andelys has a dog-leg entrance encumbered with small buoys, with little room to manoeuvre. It has now been dredged, has mains power and water and is a most pleasant haven with an attractive village with good shopping. The marina is overlooked by the splendour of the Chateau Gaillard atop its precipitous small mountain.

Thirteen kilometres after Les Andelys is the second lock: Notre Dame de la Garenne. Three kilometres after it, on the right bank there is a deviation round the three large islands that take up the next 5km. If you take the deviation, you will see very shortly on the starboard hand a collection of small pontoons. It could be useful in an emergency - but so could the lock itself. Otherwise there is no attraction.

The twinned towns of Vernon (left bank) and Vernonne (right bank) have a yacht club tucked away behind the small islands just before the town bridge. There is little depth at the pontoons and there are (obvious) shoal areas at the 'headlands' of the islands. Just after the bridge, there is another small pontoon facility. The same kind of yacht club small boatyard pontoons exist at Bonnieres, past the main part of the town. Once again, they are on the right bank and nearly hidden by islands. Indeed, it is easier to see them after you have passed them than to find them in the first place. They are followed by equally small pontoons at la Roche Guyon (right bank) and Moisson (left bank).

The best place to aim for is the really neat and nice marina known as Port de l'Illon, just past the lock at Mericourt. At nearly 50km from Les Andelys it comes after a pleasantly easy leg and has a lot to offer. It is situate literally in the backwoods and is an up-to-date facility with a very good boatyard and repair setup. All standard marina services are provided ashore and on the pontoons (except for the phone which has always been erratic). Shopping does not exist, so you either take it with you, or use the dinghy to cross the river to the village of Rolleboise, which also has riverisde fuel for yachts. Port de l'Illon is a quiet reserved place; inexpensive and ideal for a few days away from almost everything but nature.

Just over 10km upstream are the twinned towns of Mantes la Jolie and Limay at PK110. There is an halte de plaisance just below the bridge (Pont de Mantes) in the minor channel to port. It is far superior to the broken-down pontoons at the boatyards you see first after you have passed under the bridge connecting the two islands. It affords easy access to all the services of the large town across the river and the smaller community closer by.

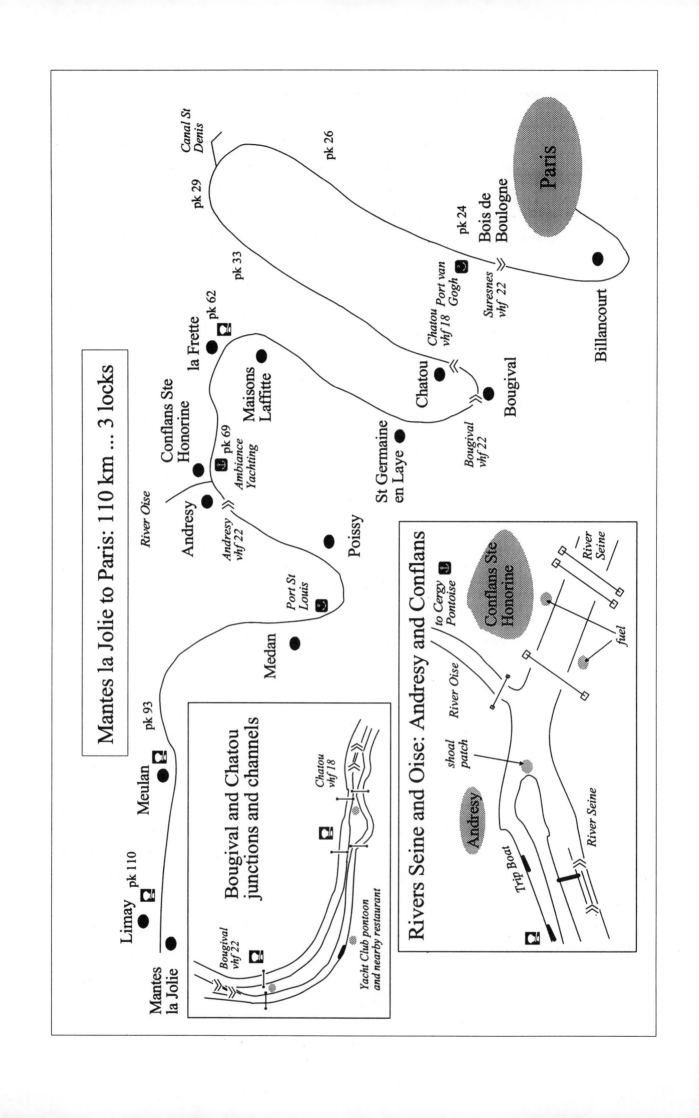

Mantes la Jolie to Paris: 110 km … 3 locks

Canal St Denis

pk 29

pk 26

pk 33

pk 62

la Frette

Conflans Ste Honorine

River Oise

Andresy

Andresy vhf 22

pk 69

Ambiance Yachting

Maisons Laffitte

Poissy

Port St Louis

Medan

pk 93

Meulan

Limay   pk 110

Mantes la Jolie

St Germaine en Laye

Chatou

Chatou vhf 18

Port van Gogh

pk 24

Bois de Boulogne

Suresnes vhf 22

Paris

Billancourt

Bougival

Bougival vhf 22

Bougival and Chatou junctions and channels

Bougival vhf 22

Chatou vhf 18

Yacht Club pontoon and nearby restaurant

Rivers Seine and Oise: Andresy and Conflans

River Seine

fuel

Conflans Ste Honorine

to Cergy Pontoise

River Oise

shoal patch

Andresy

Trip Boat

River Seine

MANTES LA JOLIE TO PARIS

The community of Meulan is another 17km upstream at PK93. It has a similarly well placed halte. It is a charming place with an excellent shopping centre and a very good open air market.

There are various boatyards and pontoons along the 20km to the next lock, Andresy, but they are of little use or appeal. In particular, the pretentiously named Port de Plaisance de Port St Louis is a broken down affair with neither facilities nor welcome and should you be unhappy enough to be caught out and put in a berth, extortionate fees may well be demanded. Far better to steam non-stop up to the lock and on to the junction with the River Oise. There are then five choices: the halte de plaisance at Andresy in its quiet backwater; the new Mediterranean-style marina at Cergy Pontoise (10km up the River Oise); the packed and busy-to-bursting right bank quaysides and barges at Conflans Ste Honorine; the small boatyard of Ambiance Yachting just past Conflans at PK69 or the small Halte de Plaisance de la Frette on the right bank at PK62.

To get to Andresy you round the headland at a good 20m off and head back up the backwater. You pass the barge park and the trip boat jetty and the halte with its five mooring buoys is to starboard. Andresy is small community with a splendid Saturday market. The pontoon (with mains usually working) is behind the police sub station, near a public telephone and a splendid Moroccan restaurant. Nearby Conflans has everything including confusion and noise. Cergy Pontoise is quiet and sophisticated in a swish and rural manner, while Ambiance has an ambience of quietly disorganised industry in the middle of the countryside. La Frette sits quietly under the trees with a nearby telephone and excellent cave. Its mains services have been known to work. They are all first rate in their own way. You pays your money (or not as the case may be) and you takes your choice: Andresy and la Frette are completely free; Conflans usually is; Ambiance is inexpensive if they actually take your money and Cergy takes full whack for its finesse.

After Conflans, the lock at Bougival is just over 20km away. There is a choice of routes: the River Neuve arm or the Marly arm. The lock-keepers at Bougival have always advised me to use the Marly stretch, which is reached through the Bougival lock itself. The Neuve leads to the Chatou lock but has no stopping place or amenities of interest to cruising folk, whereas on the Marly line there are two haltes and a splendid new yacht club pontoon. Hugh McKnight said Bougival was a haunt of Impressionist painters, and that intrigued me. It has a splendid photographic museum and a terrifying road traffic bridge. Chatou has big town facilities and lots of noise. Ironically, it is not sited on the Chatou lock arm. The yacht club pontoon is an under-used dream.

THE RIVER ROUTE TO THE BASTILLE

Paris is no more than a few hours hours away and most British boaters will now cruise up the Seine to bow low or brusquely nod the head at Notre Dame and then make immediate smoke for the well-known Port de Plaisance Paris Arsenal, commonly known as the Bastille. Few there are who venture into the inner sanctuary of the canals that meet in the heart of the city: the l'Ourcq, the St Denis and the St Martin. A decision to use this route must be taken well in advance of the last lock before the city centre,

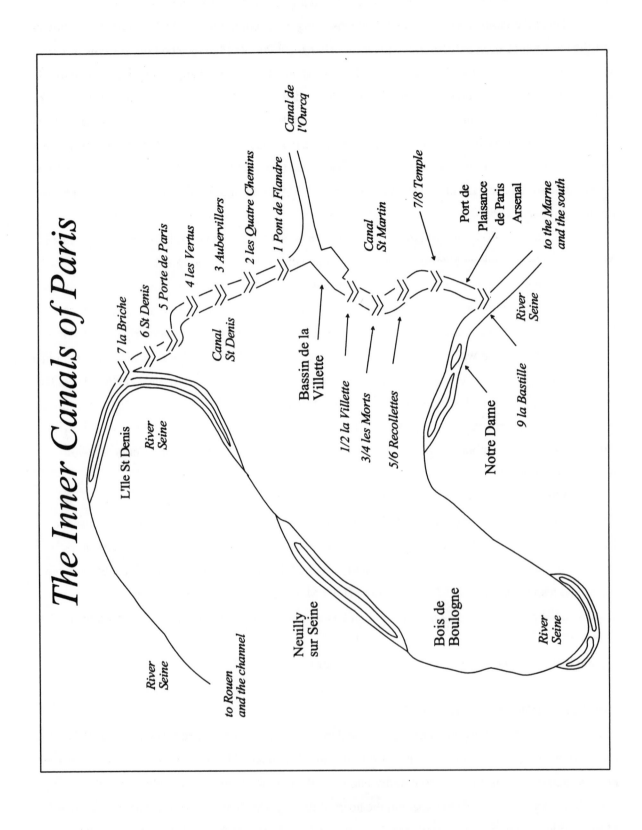

The Inner Canals of Paris

Suresnes, since it is necessary to take the port arm of the river and leave the Ile de St Denis to starboard at PK33. We will return to this circuitous canal system later.

The entrance to the St Denis Canal is not until PK29, but if you don't intend to use it, you may wish to avail yourself of one of the many free moorings that can be found on the route on the other side of the Ile St Denis. The two arms do not join up again until just after PK26. Two kilometres after they do, there is a new facility at PK24, Port Van Gogh, where there are many obvious berths for very large craft - while those for smaller boats (10 -12m) are quite hidden away ... as are frequently all members of staff.

After this comes the last of the locks before Paris, Suresnes. From here on, there are many mooring places for small boats on the banks of the Seine, including the well-known but not so well-appointed Port de Champs Elysee and the Touring Club de France. Although they have reputations for being welcoming to visitors, seldom do they seem to have a vacant berth. It must be said that they are suitable only for those souls who are not troubled by the nearly-night-long noise and wash of the river traffic: from the biggest of barges to the smallest of bateaux mouches as they ply their noisy trade: son(g) et lumiere at its worst. This applies also to the many possible (free) wall moorings that can be found all along the banks of the Seine as it makes its way through Paris. These stretches abound with visual glories: many of the capital's bridges are in scrubbed stone and freshly painted gold and green and there are some excellent examples of post Corbusier/Bauhaus architecture. There is the remarkable perspective of the Eiffel Tower when viewed from the river, and dramatically contrasting glass mountain of TF1, HQ of French TV.

After the greater glory of Notre Dame, round which there is a one-way system, it comes as something of a disillusionment when you come face to face with the entrance to the Port de Paris Arsenal. But renovation and refurbishment are the order of the day, being tied in with the massive expansion of the underground Metro just nearby/above/underneath. Although the most expensive berthing facility in Paris, the Port de Plaisance de Paris Arsenal, with its relative peace and quiet, and superb location by the Place de la Bastille, has to be the prime candidate for anyone proposing to stay for more than a quick stopover. You can call up on VHF or wait until you arrive and then announce yourself from the listening post on the river pontoon. No matter how good your French, you will probably be welcomed in English. We shall return to the subject of the 'Bastille' Port de Plaisance after the round tour of the inner canals.

From Rouen the journey to Paris is 241km (130 miles) with 6 locks that rise 26m (86ft). For those who want to get there fast, it can be done, under favourable conditions, in two days. Legend has it there are those who have, without breaking the speed limits, cracked it in a day. I have yet to meet such a person in person.

THE CANAL ROUTE TO THE BASTILLE
The inner city canals, the St Denis, the St Martin and the l'Ourcq are hardly ever frequented by visitors. True, the last kilometre or so of the St Martin Canal is well and truly known, since it is the Paris Arsenal marina itself, leading, via lock No. 9 La Bastille straight into the river and thus known as 'the gateway to the Seine'.

These three canals offer more than just a change from the regular route up the Seine from PK33 to Paris Arsenal just past PK0. There is some fuel economy: the total canal distance being no more than 12km but this must be offset by the time spent negotiating the 16 locks; not only filling in forms, but also talking to lock-keepers and passers-by all of whom want to know from whence you came. Then there is the time taken exploring the soft under-belly of the city; perhaps musing on Maigret, Toulouse Lautrec and Genet, as archetypal voyeurs, painters and poets of the city's back-street life.

In general, the navigation is open to leisure craft free of charge, as are the locks and the lifting bridges on l'Ourcq. There is a small charge for locking through the canals of St Denis and St Martin. Mooring is free for the first day within Paris, and some of these moorings have water and electricity.

CANAL ST DENIS

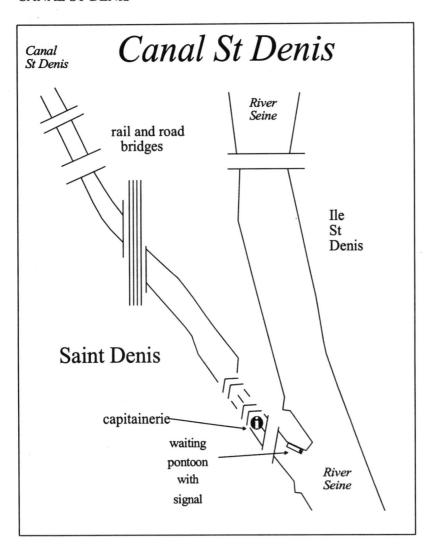

After the junction with the Ile St Denis, you continue for 4km until the dark arches of the double lock appear on a bend on the port hand. There is a new waiting pontoon to starboard from which to signal the lock-keeper. The Canal St Denis runs from the Seine to the Canal de l'Ourcq and the Bassin de la Villette. It is the busiest workhorse waterway in Paris, passing through predominantly industrial suburbs, with numerous private quays used by commercial barges.

It takes about half an hour to sort out the fees and admin with the helpful staff at the first lock. The next two are remotely controlled and the rest are manned. It is an easy passage all the way to the last lock, Pont de Flandre. After more admin, next comes the Canal de l'Ourcq to port with the Bassin de la Villette to starboard.

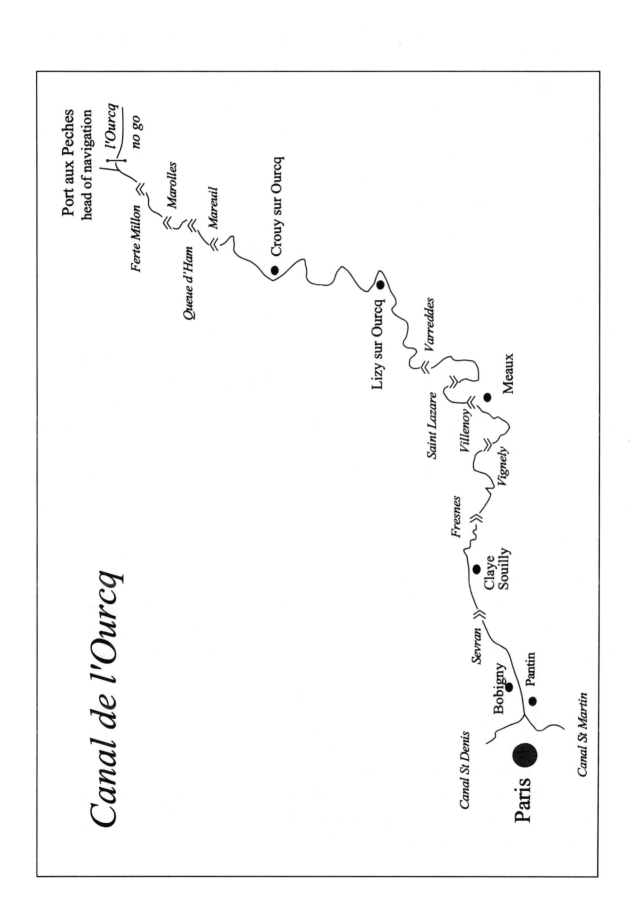

Canal de l'Ourcq

Paris

Canal St Denis

Canal St Martin

Bobigny

Pantin

Sevran

Claye Souilly

Fresnes

Vignely

Villenoy

Meaux

Saint Lazare

Varreddes

Lizy sur Ourcq

Crouy sur Ourcq

Mareuil

Queue d'Ham

Marolles

Ferte Millon

Port aux Peches
head of navigation

l'Ourcq

no go

CANAL DE L'OURCQ AND THE BASSIN DE LA VILLETTE

The lifting bridge on the l'Ourcq side of la Villette is automatic and always in operation and there are well-placed mooring bollards. Mooring is free for the first seven days on the canal and canalised River l'Ourcq outside Paris. This canal is different from the St Denis and St Martin as it is more a deviation into Paris's outlying rural regions. Sevran, its first lock, is manned and permits passage between 0900 and 1700. After this, all the l'Ourcq locks are self-service for which a Key 'A' is necessary. Congis bridge is the same way, but for craft of more than 2.0m air draught it is necessary to contact the authorities. A key may be obtained from the lock-keeper at Sevran and the Capitainerie at Paris Arsenal. The permitted draught in the first, 'Grande' section of the canal is 2.6m. After Sevran the 'Petite' section is technically limited to 0.8m, but craft up to 1.1m draught are permitted at owners' risk.

The Canal de l'Ourcq very quickly becomes a non-Parisian experience; soon enjoying the rural companionship of the River Marne. It is for those who care not for la dolce vita, speed and prying eyes - but for those with life/time to stand and stare. Back in the city section, the Bassin de la Villette is very busy: a fully dynamic tourist attraction. Its main attractions are its centrality and inexpensive moorings.

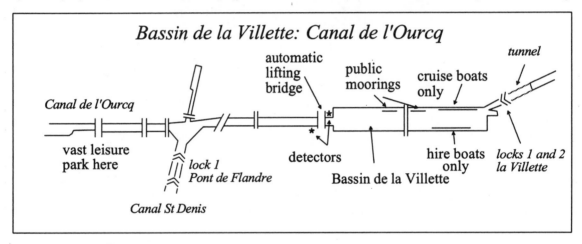

CANAL ST MARTIN

The Canal St Martin runs from the Bassin de la Villette to the Seine. It is 4.5km long with 9 locks and consists of alternating open biefs and tunnels that run under many boulevards and even the actual Place de la Bastille. Its one-way system is controlled by lights. The canal has long been a tourist attraction with a regular trip-boat service. Situate in the heart of the city with inexpensive quayside moorings - some with water and electricity, it is a boater's delight. It finally gives onto the Paris Arsenal marina which is a delight for the trip-boat sightseers who enjoy observing life aboard.

In the Bassin de la Villette, all and sundry delight in telling visitors where to go - and not to go - as well as how long they will have to wait. Take note: they do not exagerrate; it can take hours for your 'leisure craft' turn to come after all the trip boats. In spite of any wait, the entry into Paris Arsenal marina must always afford at least a small thrill: one can moor within metres of the Place de la Bastille, its splendid Opera Centre, and, of course, some of the finest eating places in the world. Locking out into the Seine we then move upstream for the major routes to the Med.

Port de Plaisance de Paris Arsenal

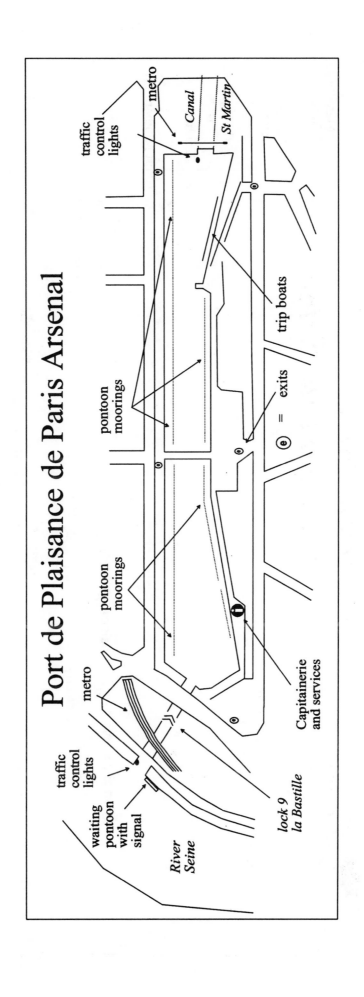

metro

traffic
control
lights

Canal

St Martin

pontoon
moorings

pontoon
moorings

trip boats

ℯ = exits

Capitainerie
and services

metro

traffic
control
lights

waiting
pontoon
with
signal

River
Seine

lock 9
la Bastille

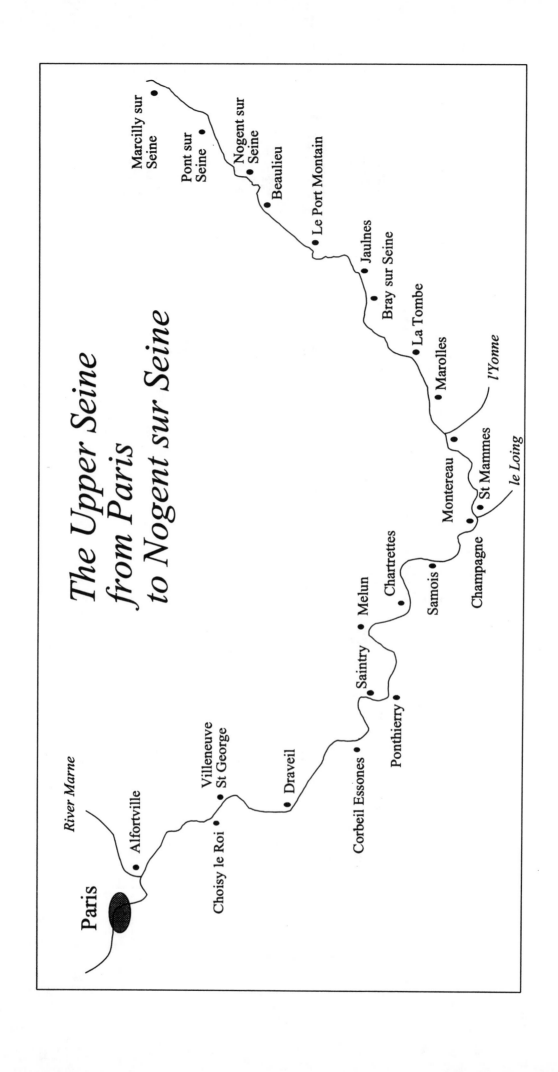

*The Upper Seine
from Paris
to Nogent sur Seine*

Paris

River Marne

Alfortville

Choisy le Roi

Villeneuve
St George

Draveil

Corbeil Essones

Ponthierry

Saintry

Melun

Chartrettes

Samois

Champagne

Montereau

St Mammes

le Loing

l'Yonne

Marolles

La Tombe

Bray sur Seine

Jaulnes

Le Port Montain

Beaulieu

Nogent sur
Seine

Pont sur
Seine

Marcilly sur
Seine

PART TWO: THE UPPER SEINE, PARIS-ARSENAL TO MONTEREAU

PARIS TO PONTHIERRY

The Haute Seine starts virtually from the Arsenal marina. Immediately across the river are the police, who sometimes check fuel tanks for 'red' diesel (illegal in leisure craft). It is less than 5km to the junction with the Marne, which goes more or less straight ahead with the Seine tending to starboard. The first of its 19 locks is the appropriately named Port a l'Anglais at PK161. It is large and smoothly operated, and the only hindrance to progress may be the lock-keeper's insistence on inspecting all the ships' papers, often referred to as 'papiers' or 'cartes' - but most frequently signalled by the lock-keeper drawing a rectangle in the air with one or both hands: this will include the VNF licence, officially known as a 'vignette',

The first boatyard at Choisy le Roi (PK158) has a strong mooring buoy in the river: while its setting is not salubrious it is a useful emergency service. The next possible stop is the so-called port de plaisance just before Villeneuve St George (PK154). It is mainly a yacht club devoted to those in the fast lane, and they have neither the time, space nor propensity to welcome visitors. The public marina facility is of suspect depth, with rusted posts and nasty overhead wires permitting access only to craft with less than 2.5m air draught. There are few facilities directly to hand and although free public moorings may be an attraction, on balance it is better to move on.

The first choice comes with the very new and up to date Port Premier at PK148. It is 2km past Ablon lock, on the right bank tucked away immediately after the railway bridge. It is a private marina, becoming a residential development, but visitors are welcome. While not inexpensive it has a lot to offer - but shops are a goodly walk away.

Only 2km after Port Premier is the Port Aux Cerises marina at PK146 near Draveil. The pontoons are sound, depth is good and the all-night security is first rate; but there are few water taps, no mains electricity and the toilets are basic. It is important to arrive, pay up and get a key - otherwise, while you may get a free mooring, you will be berth-bound for the night, unless you unship the dinghy and brave the security guard. About 5km after Cerises there is a public quay next the Vert Logis restaurant just upstream of the Pont de Ris Orangis. The Champrosay Club Nautique is next door but the area is generally calm and restrained.

There are moorings for small craft at Evry Petit Bourg and Corbeil Essones. In the main they are occupied by modest sailing boats, dinghies and canoes and much used by ski enthusiasts. The same applies to the well-advertised Port Saintry, which turns out not to be of much substance, both metaphorically and literally. Craft of more than 8m LOA must strain its pontoons when attacked by the big wakes of big barges. Actually, the next best halt is at Coudray. It is a large lock, and while the sluices are well-controlled, it can still require constant attention to rope work. Nearby however, there is a spacious wall with wooded verges.

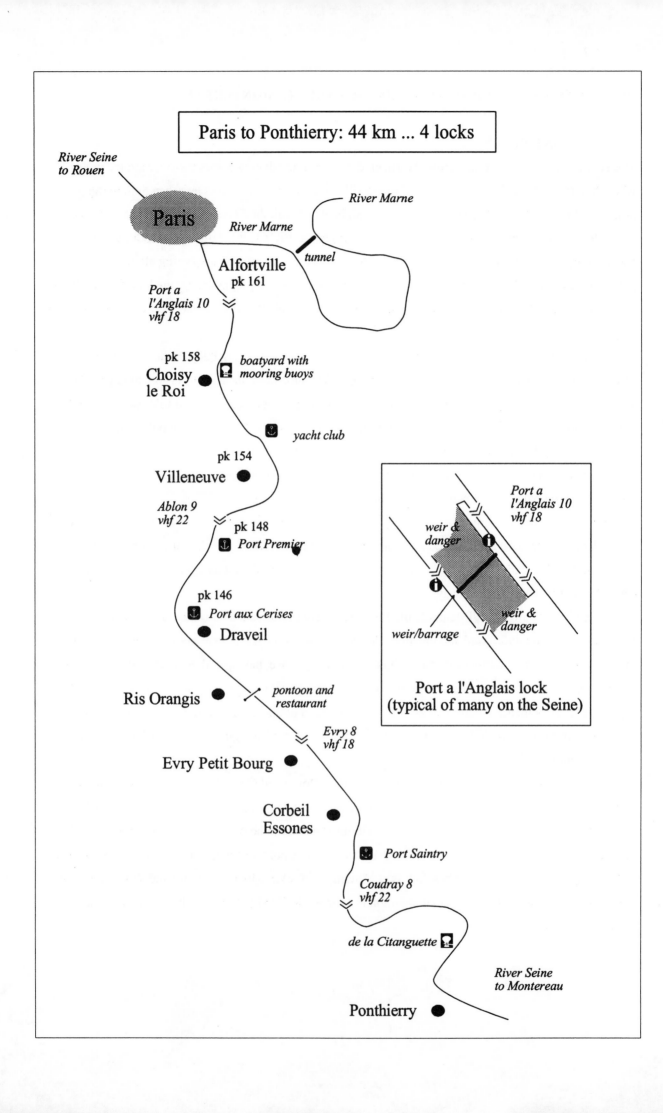

Paris to Ponthierry: 44 km ... 4 locks

River Seine to Rouen

Paris

River Marne

River Marne

Alfortville
pk 161

tunnel

Port a l'Anglais 10 vhf 18

pk 158

Choisy le Roi

boatyard with mooring buoys

yacht club

pk 154

Villeneuve

Ablon 9 vhf 22

pk 148

Port Premier

pk 146

Port aux Cerises

Draveil

Ris Orangis

pontoon and restaurant

Evry 8 vhf 18

Evry Petit Bourg

Corbeil Essones

Port Saintry

Coudray 8 vhf 22

de la Citanguette

River Seine to Montereau

Ponthierry

Port a l'Anglais 10 vhf 18

weir & danger

weir & danger

weir/barrage

Port a l'Anglais lock
(typical of many on the Seine)

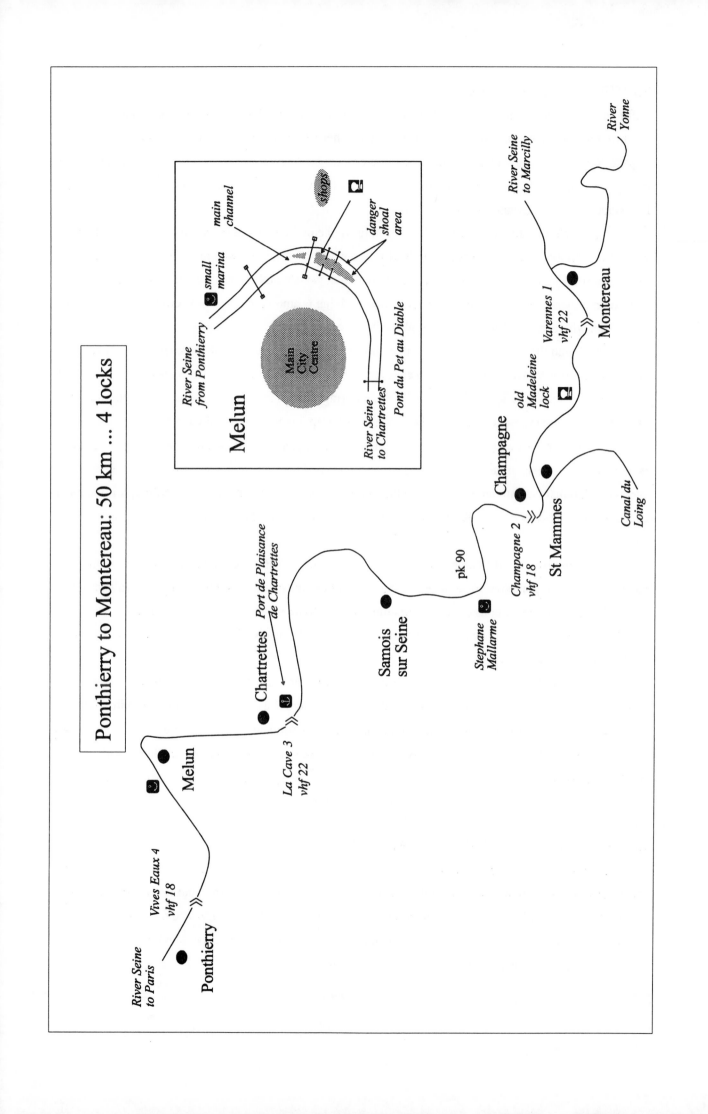

Ponthierry to Montereau: 50 km ... 4 locks

River Seine to Paris

Ponthierry

Vives Eaux 4
vhf 18

Melun

Chartrettes

Port de Plaisance
de Chartrettes

La Cave 3
vhf 22

Samois
sur Seine

pk 90

Stephane
Mallarme

Champagne

Champagne 2
vhf 18

St Mammes

old
Madeleine
lock

Varennes 1
vhf 22

Montereau

River Seine
to Marcilly

River
Yonne

Canal du
Loing

Melun

River Seine
from Ponthierry

small
marina

main
channel

danger
shoal
area

shops

Main
City
Centre

River Seine
to Chartrettes

Pont du Pet au Diable

PONTHIERRY TO MONTEREAU

Before the next main feature, Melun, there are many modest sailing clubs with very small pontoons. Two are different: first is by the old lock de la Citanguette where there is small quay for the hotel and perhaps a space between the many barges. The second comes after lock Vives Eaux 4 (lively like Coudray) where there is a small marina just before Melun. It does house some large boats in spite of its narrow entrance. Its riverside stone quay has a very good depth.

To reach the halte nautique at Melun, you leave the main navigation and proceed to port after which the pontoon is on the starboard hand, with five white mooring buoys to port. None of it is in best repair, but it affords convenient access to the town, which is a gem of a place. This is a must of a stop-over for enthusiasts of French cheeses, since Brie de Melun is among the best and certainly the most singular Brie, with a strong salt bite and a mighty after taste.

Although the halte branch rejoins the main line later, the through route is unnavigable. Back on the main arm, it is less than 10km to another splendid stopping place: the Port de Plaisance de Chartrettes, to port just after La Cave 3 lock. The moorings are best taken bows-to, since depth runs out and weed takes over close to the bank. The place is run from the barge at the downstream end of the moorings: mains power and water and the first night's mooring are free. It is a quiet spot, with a restaurant close by and a supermarket twenty minutes' walk away. For an even quieter spot, there is an anchorage a few kilometres upstream not far from the village of Samois sur Seine. It is a small loop off the main channel, much used by barge folk taking recuperation. Red buoys designate it as a definite Slow Boat strait.

A stop-over quite different from Chartrettes and Samois is Port de Stephen Mallarme on the left bank at PK90. The pontoons are all new and some facilities are so new that they are not yet up and running. The last pontoon is set aside for visitors: moor downstream and as near to the bank as you can, as the flow can hinder mooring and the wash from peniches can be heavy. There is a bar at the nearby cross-roads, but shops are distant.

Just over 10km ahead comes the parting of the ways for most Brits, for to starboard is the Central Canal route for the Mediterranean via the Canal du Loing. There is a big fuelling station to port after the junction. It is much used by barges and you may have to wait, but being a barge centre, services are available. St Mammes lies on one side of the river and Champagne sur Seine on the other. On the starboard bank of the Seine, there are good moorings with easy access to the town. If it is full, you just move on 1km upstream to the base nautique and Sailing Club of St Mammes.

LA PETITE SEINE: MONTEREAU A MARCILLY

The next major halt, Montereau, is also at a junction: with the River l'Yonne, also for the Bourgogne and Nivernais canals. There is spot at the old Madeleine lock where mooring is free, but it is often taken over by motley craft and the immediate surroundings cannot be described as salutary. The pleasant green sward just to starboard after the bridge and Yonne junction at Montereau must be a favourite: there is usually a vacant place and there are plenty of shops nearby.

We are now off the main track to the Med, and any further cruising up the Seine means a return trip since Marcilly, head of the navigation, is a dead end. However, for those with the time, here are some brief notes.

The Seine changes its character subsiding into a generally serene milieu, with lock-keepers more given to passing the time of day than passing you speedily through their lock. The first lock, Marolles, is a first-rate place to rest with deep mooring to a grassy bank. Bray has a double pontoon in good order, pleasantly sited by a park and shaded by trees. It is a delightful spot (no mains) in a delightful village. Village shops and bars are to the right; food and DIY supermarkets to the left.

Jaulnes lock should be approached with caution, for the current can exert quite a pull, and to starboard where the weir has its run, there are dangerous broken piles. Fortunately, there are well-placed traffic control lights. Vezoult lock is entirely different: everything is new and all is sweetness and light - the infamous sloping sided locks having been eliminated. There is a quiet mooring just before the lock, with nothing but nature to serve you. Supplies are in fact 17km distant at Nogent sur Seine, with three locks in-between. After Vezoult, there is a 10km straight canal stretch, with the unnavigable river to starboard. When the two reunite after Beaulieu, it becomes a secluded river (with just a short speedboat basin). Nogent itself appears after 4km of really winding waterway. The town quay is to starboard, with a sign to indicate the depth of water available. Industry and commerce are obvious, but the town itself is an attractive example of a traditional French community rooted in the past but missing out on nothing that is up-to-date: offering indeed, the best of both worlds.

And what a pleasant note on which to leave the Seine, for although there are nearly 20km of canal and river to Marcilly theoretically navigable for craft up to 1.4m, I am advised that such a depth is optimistic, and Nogent is best viewed as the head of the waterway. And so back many kilometres to an equally attractive river, the one we left at Conflans and Andresy: the Oise.

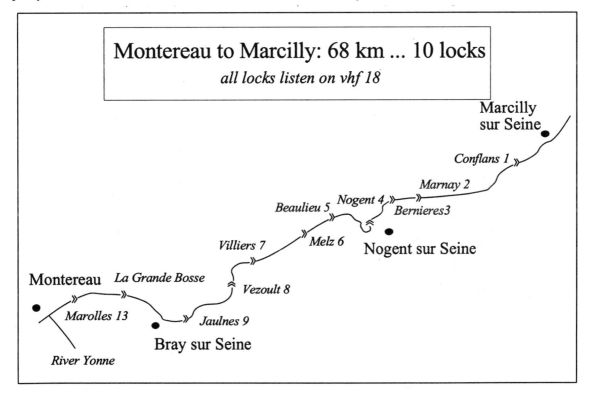

Montereau to Marcilly: 68 km ... 10 locks

all locks listen on vhf 18

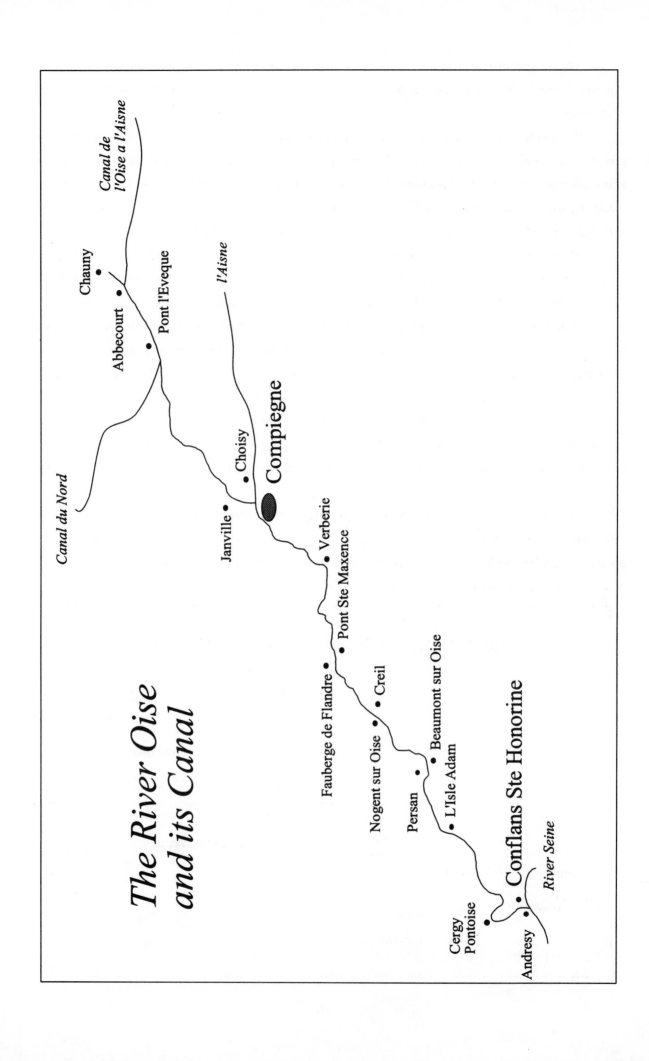

The River Oise
and its Canal

Canal de
l'Oise a l'Aisne

Canal du Nord

l'Aisne

Chauny •

Abbecourt •

Pont l'Eveque

Janville •

Choisy •

Compiegne

Verberie •

Pont Ste Maxence •

Fauberge de Flandre •

Creil •

Nogent sur Oise •

Beaumont sur Oise •

Persan •

L'Isle Adam •

Conflans Ste Honorine

Cergy Pontoise •

Andresy •

River Seine

PART THREE:THE RIVER OISE AND ITS CANAL

CONFLANS STE HONORIN TO COMPIEGNE

After the large-spread breadths of the Seine, the River Oise offers a more modest feeling - once, that is, the heavy commercial section dominated by Conflans has been left behind. In fact, it is no more than a couple of kilometres before the country joys of Jouy le Moutier hove into view; soon followed by the prettily laid-out and well-kept mooring at Vaureal (prohibited to yachts); and at PK9, the Port de Plaisance of Cergy Pontoise. This new marina in the clay-brick-glaze, stone and glass Mediterranean style is an overnight alternative to Conflans and Andresy; while for those who left there early in the morning, its bread-shop and restaurant must be a temptation.

The marina, on the right bank, has clean and new pontoons each provided with full facilities. Even electric heating is provided without extra charge while the boat is in use. Half of the development is private while the other half, 110 berths, is open to the public. All modern sanitary, social and leisure facilities are immediately to hand; while a few minutes walk away the old village offers all the charm, goods and chattels that one expects of a rural, riverside community.

Just over 1km before the first lock on the river, Pontoise 7, is the Base Nautique de Jaux on the left bank. It has first-rate pontoons with good depth and basic services. Their welcome is warm and friendly, and the halt leaves nothing to be desired. Just after the lock, the twinned towns of Pontoise and St Ouen l'Aumone offer a sound pontoon and good shopping facilities - but also a goodly measure of town and auto-route traffic. So for sylvan peace one moves on another 5km to a quiet wooded backwater at PK20, near the village of la Bonneville. There is little but tamed wild life and very appealing it is. Shortly after, also quietly found, are the modest pontoons at Auvers and Butry; both extremely pleasant spots.

Next comes the lock and very singular community of L'Isle Adam. There are a few pontoons on the banks well before it but they are all very small. L'Isle Adam is a veritable shrine to good food, wine, and hedonism writ large. The district has been laid out with some flair to entice the epicurean good, the self-indulgent bad and the sybaritic rich from near and far to spend, spend, spend. There are pontoon places and buoys for no more than six boats. The banks also afford secure mooring for craft of no more than 1m draught. The mooring (with restaurants) is to starboard just before the bridge and the lock.

If a more economical stop is preferred, there is a well-laid out halte on the Persan side of the river opposite Beaumont sur Oise. There is a very large Leclerc superstore nearby and only metres away, the small bar/cafe 'Chez Nicole'. Both offer a good choice but Nicole, the lady with the bar and a person of curious character gives extraordinary value.

From Beaumont to Nogent is 24km with 2 locks, but there are plenty of modest places to moor en route. At PK49, on the left bank, the Toutevois hotel has its own pontoon. Navigationally, this is the only tricky stretch: on the bend there are some of the very few buoys to be found on the river. These red buoys mark a shoal area that extends well out towards the left bank. They are not particularly obvious - especially from downstream.

Andresy to Precy: 50 km ... 3 locks

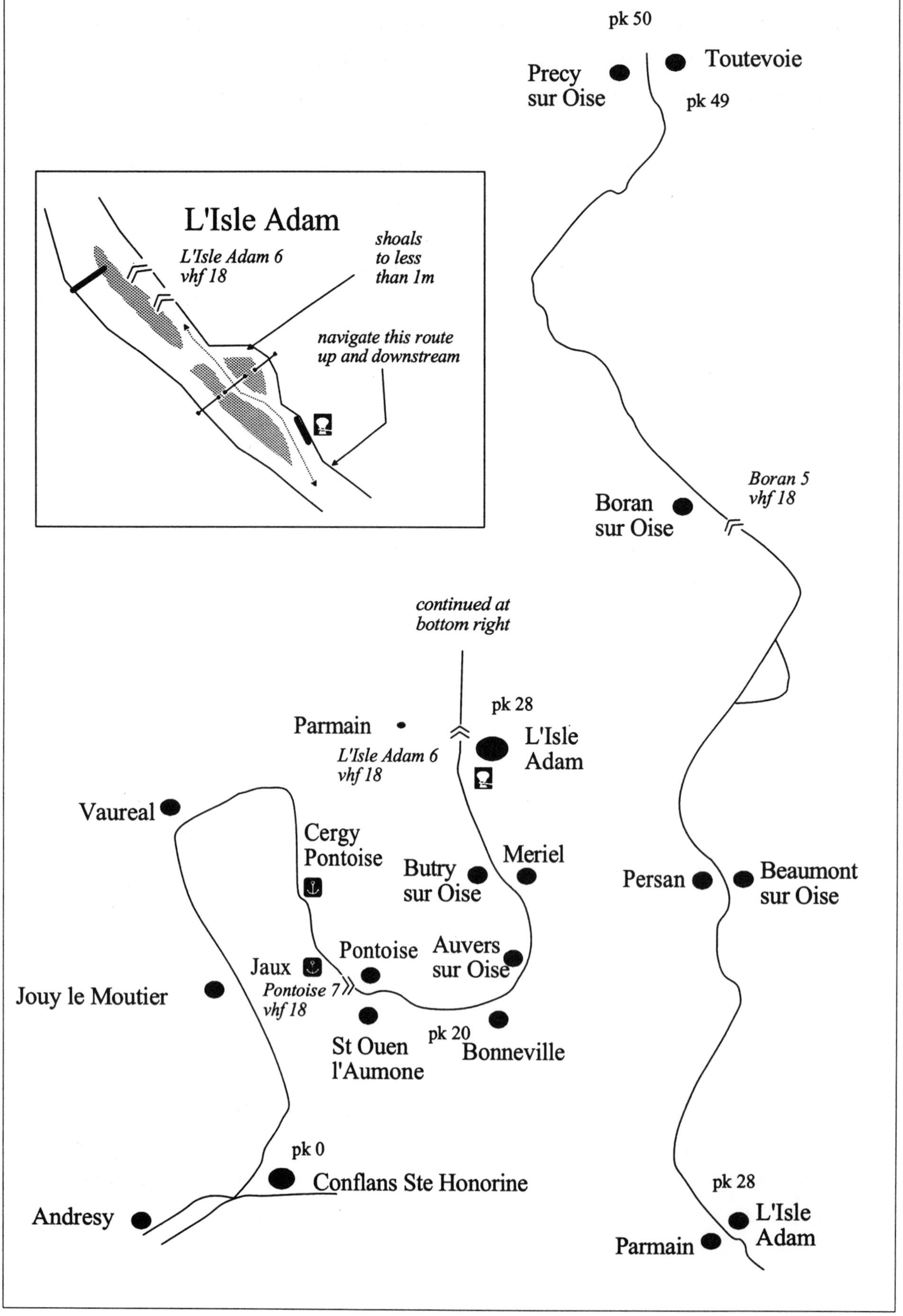

L'Isle Adam

L'Isle Adam 6
vhf 18

shoals to less than 1m

navigate this route up and downstream

pk 50

Precy sur Oise

Toutevoie

pk 49

Boran sur Oise

Boran 5 vhf 18

continued at bottom right

pk 28

Parmain

L'Isle Adam 6 vhf 18

L'Isle Adam

Vaureal

Cergy Pontoise

Butry sur Oise

Meriel

Persan

Beaumont sur Oise

Pontoise

Auvers sur Oise

Jaux

Pontoise 7 vhf 18

Jouy le Moutier

St Ouen l'Aumone

pk 20

Bonneville

pk 0

Conflans Ste Honorine

Andresy

pk 28

L'Isle Adam

Parmain

Nogent sur Oise is on the port-hand opposite the larger town of Creil. For once there is a good choice of quay moorings and the two commerce-based towns have plenty of facilities. Just before the next lock at Sarron (10km on) are the two small communities of Faubourg de Flandre and Pont Ste Maxence. It is possible to moor after the bridge to starboard where the depth is good. A certain dexterity will probably be required to rope up, and an equally certain agility required to scale the steeply sloping banks. There are some steps that reach all the way to the street. It is not absolutely easy to get the boat next them and without them the ascent can be tricky and sloppy. But please do not be put off: Maxence is a joy and well worth a stop-over.

It is now about 25km and 3 locks to Compiegne. There is a stream running at between half and a full knot against you - but the speedy efficiency of the double lock-keepers on this stretch makes up for any small delay the stream may cause. The next lock is Verberie, a pretty and well-cared for place, where the nearby village of Port Salut is unfortunately not the home of the famous cheese. There is a small pontoon and mooring wall in attractive setting.

Compiegne is a must - and worth the long wait you may have at the last lock, Venette 1, because of the continuing preference given to commercial craft, no matter how illogical or how long the delay. The Yacht Club marina base is welcoming with all services; and hardly demanding when it comes to moorings fees. It is unexpected but reassuring to discover that its president is the head of the local police force. There are good shops and eating places nearby. In particular, an inexpensive Routier restaurant to the left outside the gates and a splendid Moroccan indoor market towards the town on the left; and on the river near lock No.1 there is a first rate chandlery - one of the best I have found in France.

Just upstream of Compiegne is the junction with the Canal Lateral a l'Aisne et l'Aisne Canalisee taking you to Berry au Bac. This section is described in Chapter Two.

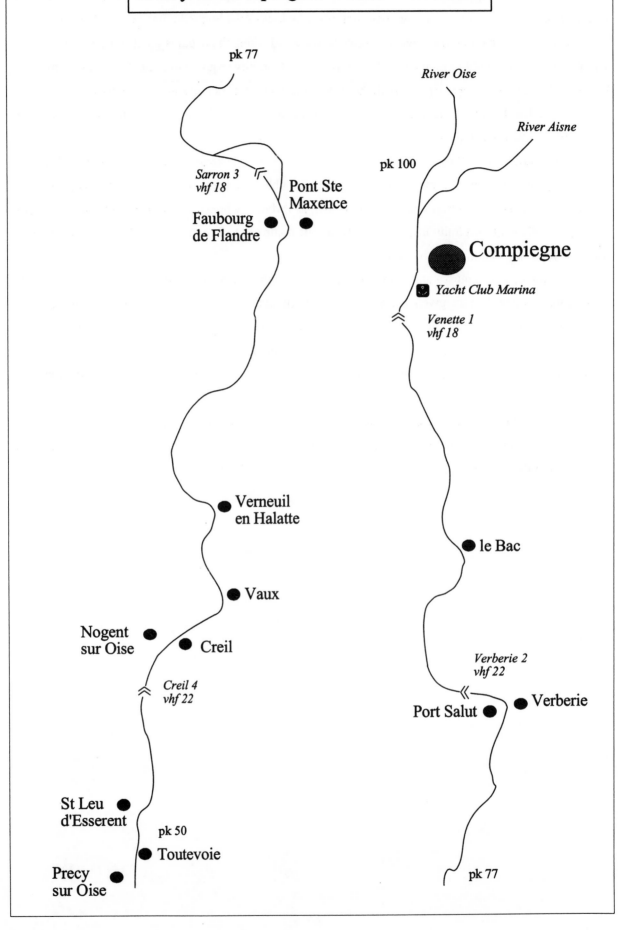

Precy to Compiegne: 50 km ... 4 locks

pk 77

River Oise

River Aisne

pk 100

Sarron 3
vhf 18

Pont Ste
Maxence

Faubourg
de Flandre

Compiegne

Yacht Club Marina

Venette 1
vhf 18

Verneuil
en Halatte

le Bac

Vaux

Nogent
sur Oise

Creil

Creil 4
vhf 22

Verberie 2
vhf 22

Port Salut

Verberie

St Leu
d'Esserent

pk 50

Toutevoie

Precy
sur Oise

pk 77

CHAPTER FOUR

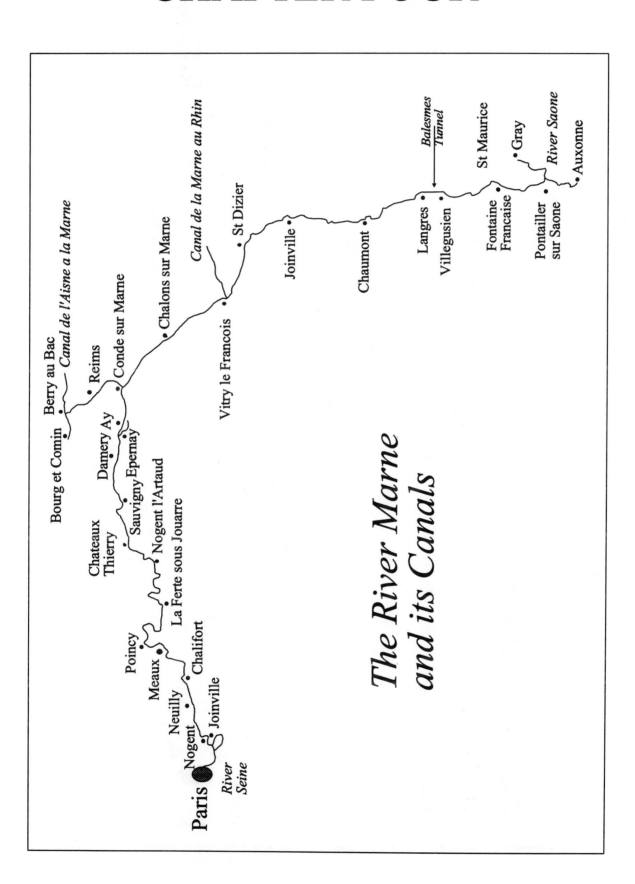

The River Marne and its Canals

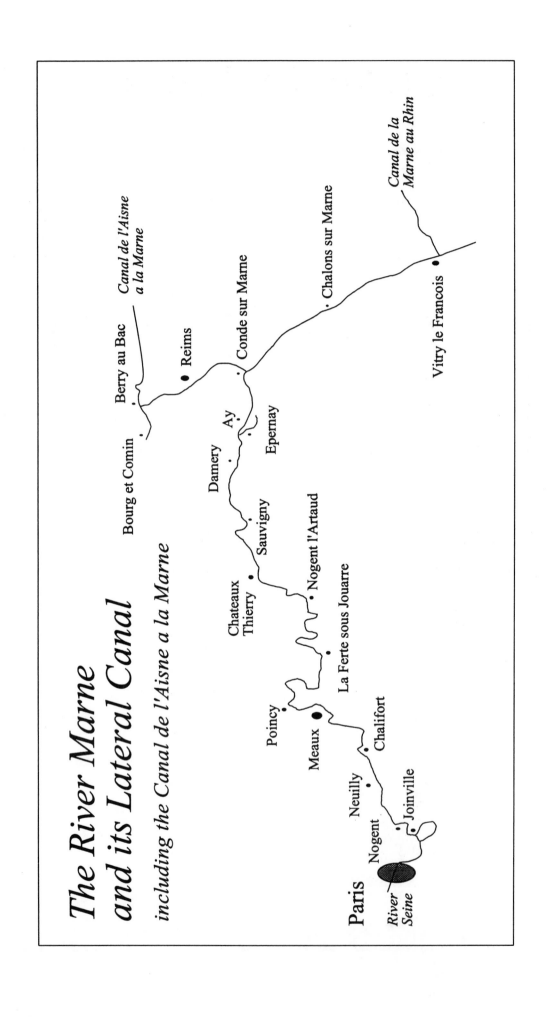

The River Marne and its Lateral Canal

including the Canal de l'Aisne a la Marne

THE RIVER MARNE

The confluence of the Rivers Seine and Marne represents not only Points of Departure but also Point of No Return, since this is decision time for the trip to the south. All roads lead to the Saone and on to the Rhone, but there are choices to be made here: the Marne river-and-canal route straight through; or the Seine and the consequent choices of the Bourgogne or Central canal routes. At no more than 10km upstream from mighty Notre Dame, the confluence can nevertheless still contend with its own spectacle: possibly the Biggest Chinese Restaurant in the world. The Marne could hardly have a more manifest marker. You pass it where the Seine peels off to starboard and the Marne goes more or less straight ahead.

JOINVILLE TO MEAUX

Passing under four bridges and the easy first lock, No 18, you are passing through the basically industrial complex of Alfortville, Maisons Alfort, Saint Maur des Fosses and Joinville. After more bridges, this uninspiring area gives on to the St Maur Tunnel and lock which are controlled by lights and present themselves as more threatening and less prepossessing than they really are. The lock is to port on the right bank while the river goes straight ahead into the classic Ox-bow of a hairpin bend to return to the canalised navigation at the other end of the tunnel. In fact, the river is fully navigable to the commercial Port de Bonneuil, a place of little interest to yachtsmen. The remaining stretch is appalling: it abounds with detritus and water-logged trunks and suffers a general lack of water. It is best left to those with oars and fishing rods.

Before the tunnel, there are good waiting pontoons after which it soon becomes apparent that the St Maur negotiation offers no serious challenge. Once through its brief dark shadows, the light at the end of the tunnel shows the area to be vastly improved. The first mooring opportunity comes immediately after the exit with the modest facilities of the Port de Joinville. Although in the centre of commerce and industry, it possesses a tranquil and beflowered charm. The halt is pleasant enough but there is little point in lingering here, and if all domestic needs were not acquired in Paris, and a shoresides visit is necessary, then it will be best to postpone it until the nearby next possibility which is the modest but smart Port de Nogent marina. Here another scene altogether draws attention to itself. All bright and white, as are most of the boats that live there, it is situate at the very heart of affluent suburbia, and everything about its fixtures and fittings tends to reflect this. It is an extremely convenient resting place as well as a good base for the comprehensive facilities all round. It is a floating headquarters of the leisured life that is the essence of the "Bank of the Marne", a domain that has been the spiritual home of painters, writers and other artists for over a century. The banks are well-kept; the trees pruned; the houses, villas and mansions all immaculately cared for, while all the celebrated local taverns ("guingettes") are dressed en fete to suit the lavish dispensation of white wines for which they are renowned. This stretch of the Marne is extremely popular with Parisians. There can hardly be another stretch of waterway mustering as many riverside restaurants, auberges, bars and cafes as the few kilometres between Joinville and Neuilly. They look enticingly good, and most are full to capacity in season. Their high prices do not seem to deter the world

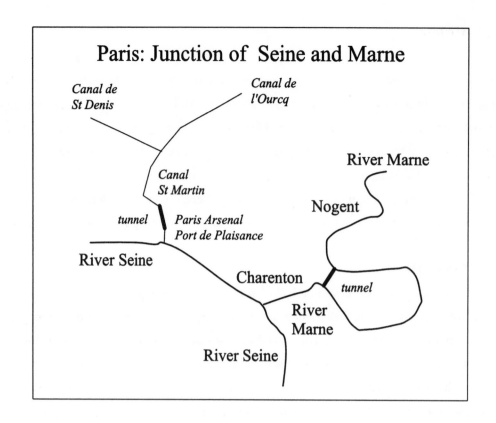

Paris: Junction of Seine and Marne

Canal de St Denis

Canal de l'Ourcq

Canal St Martin

River Marne

Nogent

tunnel

Paris Arsenal Port de Plaisance

River Seine

Charenton

tunnel

River Marne

River Seine

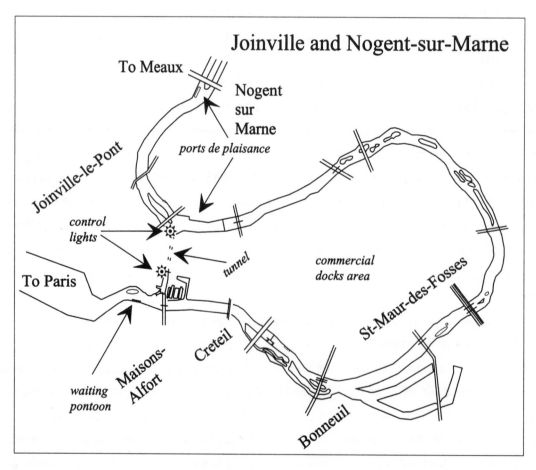

Joinville and Nogent-sur-Marne

To Meaux

Nogent sur Marne

ports de plaisance

Joinville-le-Pont

control lights

tunnel

commercial docks area

To Paris

St-Maur-des-Fosses

Creteil

waiting pontoon

Maisons-Alfort

Bonneuil

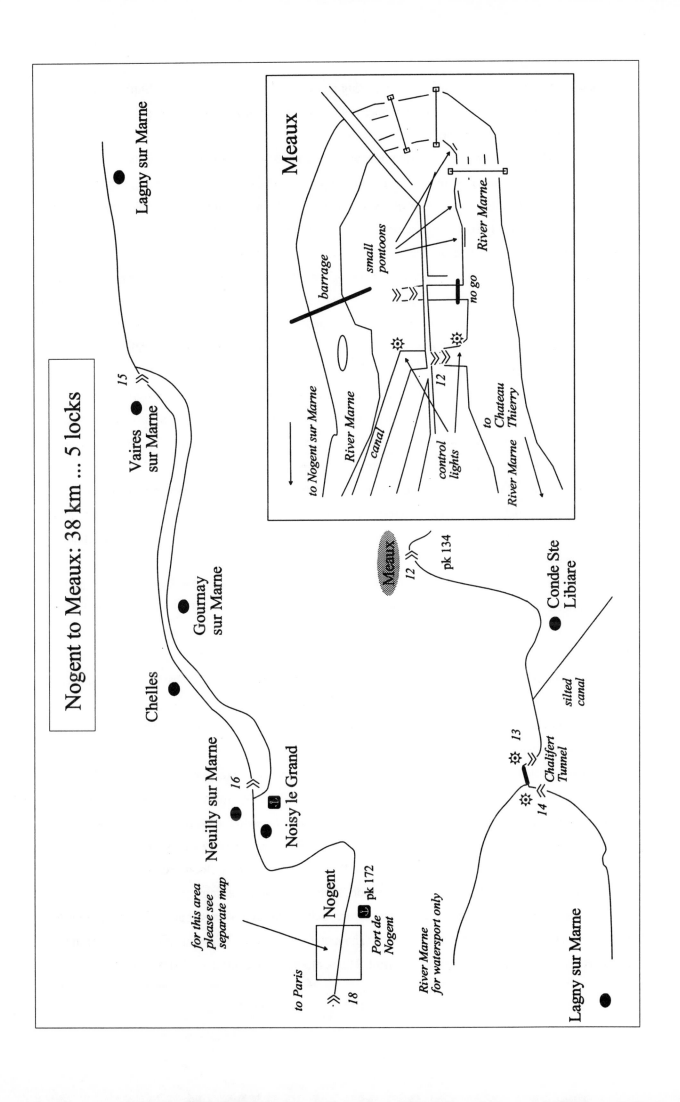

Nogent to Meaux: 38 km … 5 locks

Lagny sur Marne

Vaires sur Marne

15

Chelles

Gournay sur Marne

Neuilly sur Marne

16

Noisy le Grand

for this area please see separate map

Nogent

to Paris

18

Port de Nogent   pk 172

River Marne for watersport only

Meaux

12   pk 134

Conde Ste Libiare

silted canal

13

Chalifert Tunnel

14

Lagny sur Marne

Meaux

barrage

small pontoons

River Marne

no go

to Nogent sur Marne

River Marne

canal

control lights

12

to Chateau Thierry

River Marne

and his wife from eating and drinking out, rejoicing and generally making whoopee. Entirely in keeping with the genus loci are the two islands that appear shortly after: Ile d'Amour and Ile aux Loups. The islands are governed by a one-way channel system.

It is only 5km to the next watering hole at Neuilly sur Marne. (And indeed for those with a passion for staying at marinas, having easy access to comprehensive facilities and shopping, as well as generally appreciating la dolce vita, it is worth using these early marinas as much as possible since later on they disappear completely from the system - and even small villages will be difficult to discover.) The marina at Neuilly comes just before lock 16. The lock is on the canalised section, while the marina is to starboard and on the right bank of the island. Coming the other way, the turn into the marina is upon you almost before you know it with a very sharp bend. Once near the marina, the flow can be quite strong, so care is needed when negotiating the pontoons. The range of craft is intriguing: from huge residential barges, through a variety of cruising boats, to dinghies and canoes. Speedy trip boats, dogs, children and swans also take to the surrounding water in large numbers. The marina office is not always attended; both service and fees being honoured in the breach more then the observance. Nearby is a leisure park and fish restaurant. To stay here is to experience a marina that is different. At night it is quiet; as if in a secluded preservation area. At no stage along these stretches does bankside mooring present a problem for craft drawing less than a metre. Others are better served by the marinas.

The canal still moves through heavily built up conurbations: Chelles, Gournay , Vaires and Lagny - all 'sur Marne'. The HQ of the famous Touring Club de France is to be found at Lagny. In general the moorings are suitable only for modest craft - and the locals cannot be described as the most hospitable of boating folk.

The next stretch of the canal is known as Chalifert and is just over 20km long with a terrain that is half wooded and half industrial. At the end there is a short tunnel (300m) with locks before and after (14 and 13) where it is possible to moor. Traffic is controlled by lights. Facilities are restricted in the area. The river branch-line to port is navigable for a couple of kilometres only up to Noisiel. It passes old locks, underwater obstructions and backwaters, finally leading to dangerous old barrages. Its main attraction is to be found in its quaint and quiet charm - but it should be approached only by those who have it in mind to explore every last kilometre and have a shoal craft that can safely live with it. It is much used by the water-sporting fraternity.

In the following 12km there is little to tempt anyone to linger except perhaps for the small community of Conde Ste Libiare - especially since Meaux itself is so close and of such appeal. The entry into the dark arches of the narrow Canal de Meaux comes as a bit of a shock. Meaux's working lock is only part of what was once a massive construction, used in the days when the city was a thriving commercial centre. Movements are controlled by traffic lights. When the waters are in flood, extreme caution is required when entering or leaving the river section, as the flow can be strong.

It is possible to moor on the canal just before locking through Meaux, but I prefer the pontoons on the river stretch which comes after the lock. The moorings are to port, just past the entrance to the canal, and the town centre is very close to hand. The pontoons have everything but reliable mains power.

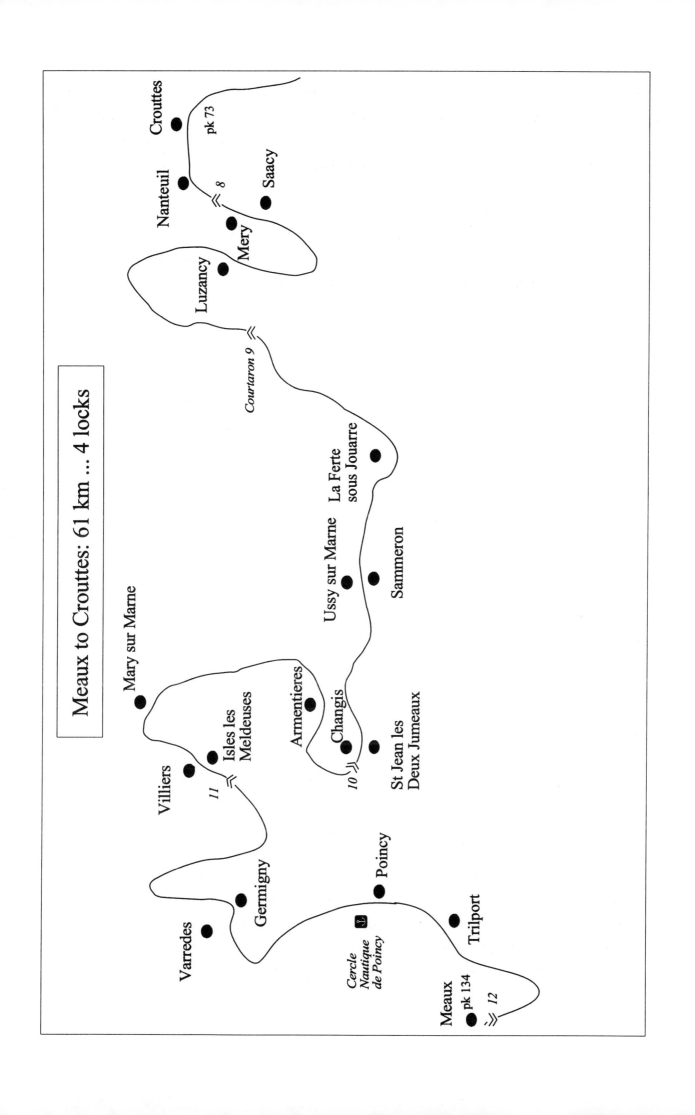

Meaux to Crouttes: 61 km ... 4 locks

Navigation is permitted only up to the bridge just past the pontoons, and there is a barrage further along round the continuing wide bend. Gourmet enthusiasts will recognise the town's name as the handle for one of the most celebrated of French cheeses, the famous Brie de Meaux. The splendid cathedral dominates the town and the surrounding countryside, no doubt proud of its eminence in the heart of Brie territory. The Cathedral Gardens and the Bossuet ('Eagle of Meaux') Museum are worth a visit. The old town is packed with interest and services. In particular, its food shops are excellent ... and its fresh cheeses do taste that soupcon better. All in all a splendid place.

Just outside Meaux, on the road to Soissons, is the monument that commemorates the September 5th, 1914 halt of the advance of the German army and the beginning of the French counter-attack.

MEAUX TO CROUTTES

The first mooring after Meaux is in the town of Trilport, almost immediately after which comes the miniature Cercle Nautiqe de Poincy. Although sometimes proclaimed as a fully fledged and public marina the incumbents have decided to sport a Port Prive notice that really declares Keep Out - and that means you! In any case, there is little room to manoeuvre and there is no great depth once inside the self-proclaimed Port.

Next comes a positive cavalcade of small villages: Germigny l'Eveque, Isles les Meldeuses (lock 11), Mary sur Marne, Changis sur Marne and St Jean les deux Jumeaux (PK100 and lock 10), Ussy sur Marne and La Ferte sous Jouarre. Changis has a welcoming yacht club. La Ferte is a happy-go-lucky small town with shops for all and a pleasing riverside. For those wanting spiritual nourishment, the well-ordered Benedictine Abbey that dates back to the 7th century is only 3km away at Jouarre. It has been massively rebuilt many times, lastly in the 17th century, and has famous features that include the tombs in the Merovingian and Carolingian crypts and its outstanding tower. While the villages all have endearing names, not all possess that little extra that tempts the traveller to stay, and mooring is not easy at any of the villages. La Ferte is undoubtedly the best bet. However, the river itself continues to oblige with broad turns and narrow twists through very attractive surroundings.

Just after La Ferte, craft with less than 0.2m draught can gain access to the small pontoon in the backwater just behind the island near Courtaron lock 9. It is possible to moor happily for both the twinned villages of Mery and Saacy, while Nanteuil, although not the proper halte it is supposed to be, has a very good wall but is without mooring rings. It is worth the extra effort since it is a charming village.

CROUTTES TO DORMANS

After more wide curves of the river, complete with U-turns and potential Ox-bow lakes, comes Charly where there is good mooring, but with the village a smart walk away. Just past Charly is the small community of Nogent l'Artaud. This is another village with an advertised halte which it does not possess. But, once again, there is a wall in good repair with plenty of depth and useful moorings rings, but with hardly room for more than one boat at a time. The village is pleasantly quiet with a good range of shops

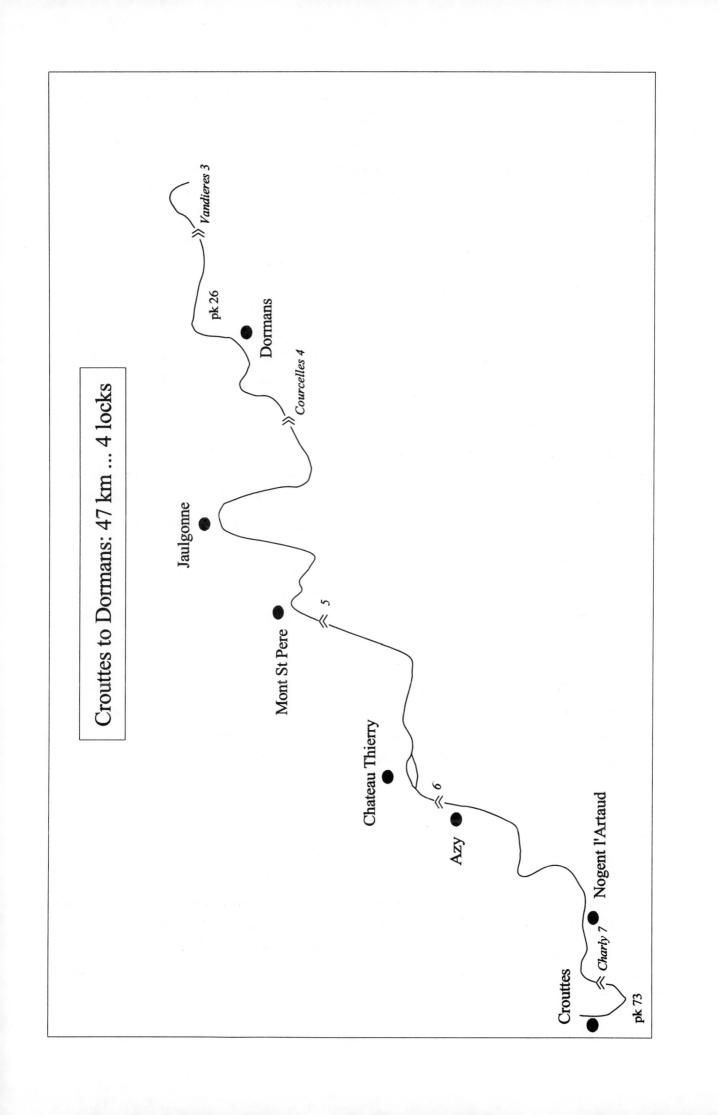

Crouttes to Dormans: 47 km ... 4 locks

Vandieres 3

pk 26

Dormans

Courcelles 4

Jaulgonne

Mont St Pere

5

Chateau Thierry

6

Azy

Charly 7

Crouttes

Nogent l'Artaud

pk 73

and a fascinating 12th century church. Larger boats should find places on the quay just under the bridge on the left bank. The river continues to wend its way through heavy woodland with nothing to divert the attention but the scenery to Chateau Thierry, where there is a sound but small pontoon just by the main bridge to starboard. There is no mains supply, but there are plenty of town facilities on both sides of the bridge. The road traffic can be really horrendous, but don't let that prevent you from arranging a break here. You are now in the vine-growing area, and the promise of champagne by the gallon must be in most crews' minds. All the nearby cellarmen will tempt you with tasters. Be warned: guard your head, liver and your wallet.

After Chateau Thierry, the two small communities of Mont St Pere and Jaulgonne do not offer good moorings. The halte at Jaulgonne was recently in a state of complete disrepair - but, of course, repair and refurbishment are promised. It is the next place that is the temptation: the leisure centre with ski club, beach and swimming pool at Dormans. This one is overlooked by a Louis XIII château and the famous Chapelle de la Reconnaissance which commemorates the First World War battles of the Marne.

DORMANS TO VITRY LE FRANCOIS

Undoubtedly, the next place of major interest is the champagne centre of Epernay, situate down its own branch line. However, before that (no doubt necessary) deviation there are one or two experiences to be enjoyed or avoided. The latter comes first at lock Vandieres 3 and both Damery 2 and Cumieres 1 have the (in)famous sloping walls. Locks 1 and 2 have keepers that permit craft to 'sit' in the centre and let the waters move around them but Vandieres 3 has new piles and the keeper can insist that they are used. When combined with the force of crudely released water, the sloping walls and vertical steel piling can be a really serious threat. Not only are boats thrown and tossed about in a thoughtless fashion, which is worrying enough in its own right; but there is the very real possibility of physical damage to the craft. It is best to be well prepared with lots of big fenders, much stout rope and as many hands as possible to hand.

Port a Binson, no more than two kilometres after Vandieres is the next recognised stop, where there are the small pontoons of the yacht club. The region is pleasantly surrounded with vineyards and there are all the facilities of the next-door camping site at the disposal of visitors. After, the small communities of Reuil, Damery and Cumieres all offer modest moorings, but the target has to be Epernay.

EPERNAY

The Epernay branch leaves the main line just before lock Dizy 15. The main canal goes straight ahead while you take the wider route to starboard for the navigation to Epernay which is generally wide and deep. True, some small stretches are broken down and ugly, but on the whole it is pretty and pleasing. Soon the huge stone tower dedicated to champagne will be seen, as it completely dominates the area - but then this is the country of champagne, and Epernay does claim to be the Capital de Champagne. The Port de Plaisance d'Epernay is on the starboard hand just under 5km from the junction. The marina, which is run by the Societe Nautique d'Epernay, has a popularity in and out of season that testifies not only to the

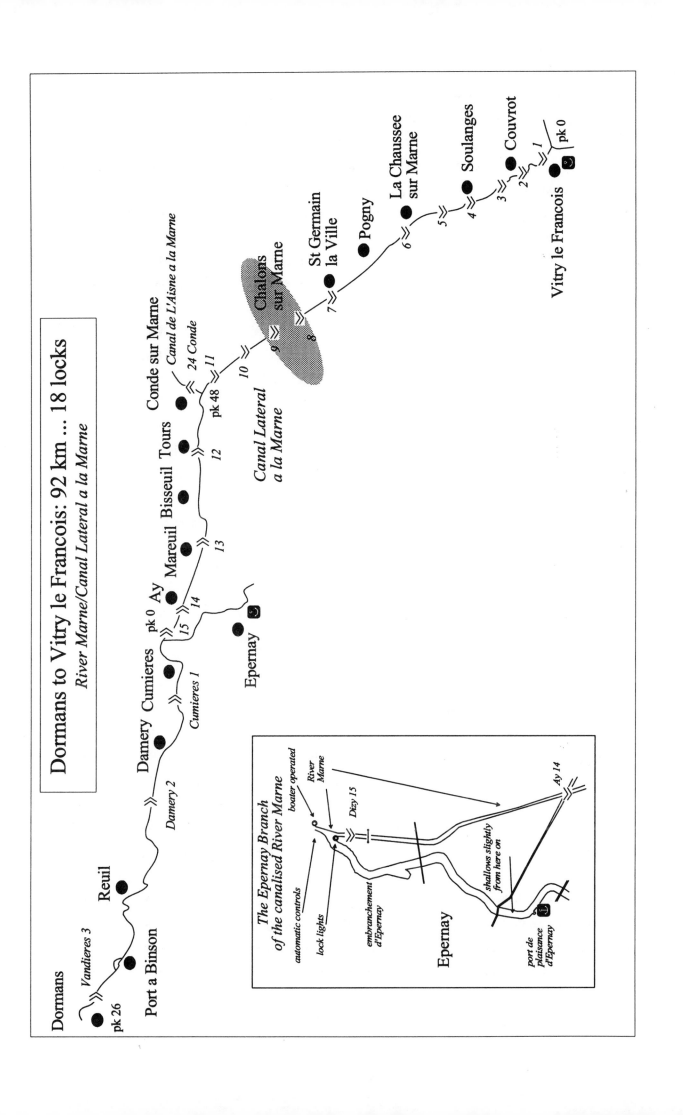

Dormans to Vitry le Francois: 92 km ... 18 locks
River Marne/Canal Lateral a la Marne

Dormans

Vandieres 3

pk 26

Reuil

Port a Binson

Damery Cumieres

Conde sur Marne

Damery 2

Cumieres 1

pk 0 Ay

Mareuil Bisseuil Tours

Epernay

Canal de L'Aisne a la Marne

24 Conde

11

pk 48

10

9

8

7

6

5

4

3

2

1

*Canal Lateral
a la Marne*

Chalons
sur Marne

St Germain
la Ville

Pogny

La Chaussee
sur Marne

Soulanges

Couvrot

pk 0

Vitry le Francois

15

14

13

12

*The Epernay Branch
of the canalised River Marne*

automatic controls

lock lights

boater operated

*River
Marne*

Dizy 15

*embranchement
d'Epernay*

*shallows slightly
from here on*

Epernay

*port de
plaisance
d'Epernay*

Ay 14

attractions of the town and its drink, but also to the excellent facilities and friendly reception that awaits all visitors. Not only does it appeal from initial sighting, but it manages to sustain that first impression till you bid farewell. It is a detour that can cost time and money: there is much to attract and delay in the area; and while the mooring charges at the port are reasonable, the prices in the town are as high as the tower. For example, the least expensive glass of champagne I was able to find in 1992 was £3.00, and in 1994 £5.00. There is more: all food and snacks are uncommonly (though predictably) thirst-making and are similarly highly priced. The town is a splendid shopping centre and there is a very good supermarket well placed for the marina, which has all mod cons (including sports facilities, especially tennis) and is very prettily located with deep-water moorings. It is extremely well kept and served by staff who are among the kindest and most efficient I have met in France.

Epernay is in the heart of France's classic Champagne territory, being the headquarters of Moet et Chandon, Mercier and de Castellane. It houses the Champagne Museum in the Chateau Perrier: a pastiche of Louis XIII built in the middle of the 19th Century by one of the foremost negociants of the times.

Back on the main lime at Dizy, 'milestones' suddenly change. You find yourself at PK66, PK5 or PK0 to choice: depending upon on which part of the bank you happen to stand. PK66 relates to the Canal Lateral; PK0 to the river; and PK5 to the Epernay branch. The reason for this is that we now move on from the Marne to the Canal Lateral a la Marne. However, the short trip to Conde seems part of what is behind rather than what is to come. Moving on from Dizy to the junction with the Canal de l'Aisne a la Marne at Conde, there are many pleasant stopping places. Those with the most and closest facilities (and of course the most popular) are Ay, Mareuil sur Ay, Bisseuil and Tours sur Marne. They are all charming and welcoming and will tempt you to stay too long, for the banksides are pretty, accessible and free but before we tackle the 'main' leg of the Canal Lateral however, let us retrace our steps.

PART TWO: CANAL DE L'AISNE A LA MARNE

You may have reached Berry au Bac from the Oise or the Pas de Calais; that is via the Canal de l'Oise a l'Aisne or the Canal Lateral a l'Aisne. From Berry to the junction with the Canal Lateral a la Marne at Conde sur Marne there are not many particularly good stopping places, but there are places where it is just possible to gain decent access to the side. One of these is really worthy of note: it is the chandlery and fuel station 7km after lock Courcy 9. While their prices are not low, they are one of the few stations where it is possible to obtain fuel and gear in any quantity without difficulty.

The canal has two main and special features: the city of Reims with its soaring cathedral; and the underground passage known as the Souterrain de Mont de Billy. Just as the l'Aisne waterway was commanded by Soissons, this one is dominated by Reims: City of Coronations and of Champagne, or alternatively 'ville de champagne avec passion' as its publicists have it. From the cruising skipper's point of view, Reims is a delight. First, it has a fully equipped and well-run quayside marina facility and on arrival you will be issued with 'Rules for the nautical stop-over at the Reims old port'. Second, the harbour-master has contacts in champagne and delivers personally. Finally, there are so many opportunities for shopping, socialising and sightseeing in the city that even the most motley of crews would be seduced suffi-

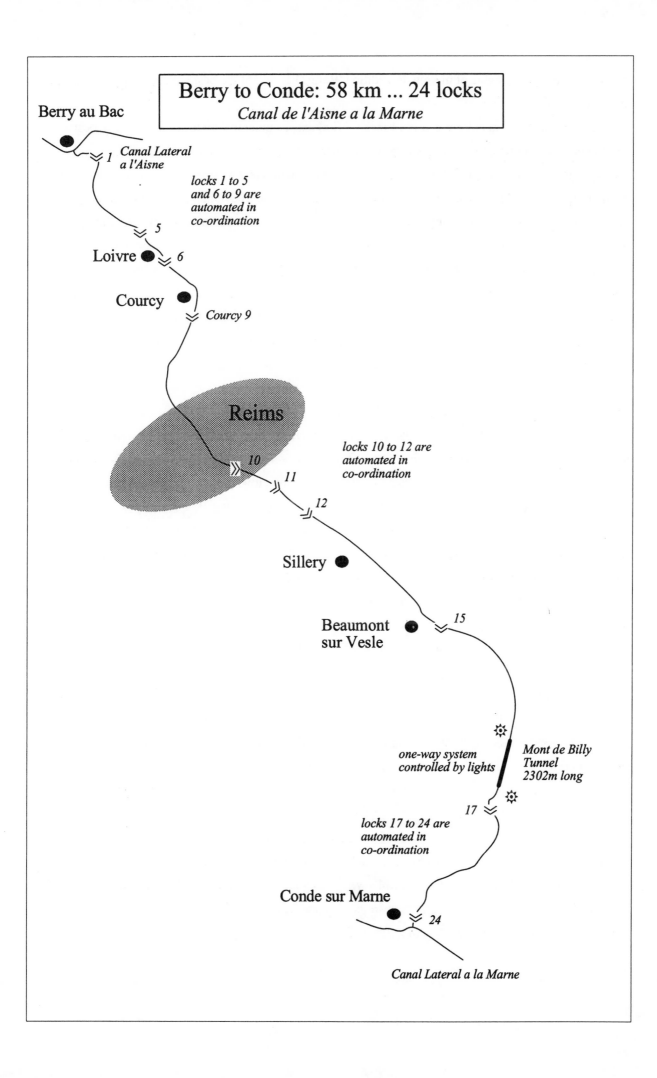

Berry to Conde: 58 km ... 24 locks
Canal de l'Aisne a la Marne

Berry au Bac

1

*Canal Lateral
a l'Aisne*

*locks 1 to 5
and 6 to 9 are
automated in
co-ordination*

5

Loivre *6*

Courcy

Courcy 9

Reims

10

11

*locks 10 to 12 are
automated in
co-ordination*

12

Sillery

Beaumont
sur Vesle *15*

*one-way system
controlled by lights*

*Mont de Billy
Tunnel
2302m long*

17

*locks 17 to 24 are
automated in
co-ordination*

Conde sur Marne

24

Canal Lateral a la Marne

ciently to preclude thoughts of mutiny. In addition, Reims has one of the best bakers in France: M. Zunic of Le Four a Bois.

After the marina at Reims, it is 14 locks, 35km and 1 tunnel to Conde sur Marne. The best overnight halt is found at Beaumont sur Vesle, just before lock 15. The Mont de Billy tunnel is a one-way passage just over 2km long controlled by lights. Although there are warnings that craft may have to wait hours for permission, I have never had to wait more than minutes. The tunnel is straight and well-lit and quite without problems. Once through the tunnel, it is one set of eight automated locks and 8km to the junction at Conde. It is specially important to pass out of these locks slowly, as they are not very sensitive to small leisure craft. However, it must not be done too slowly. If you are in a convoy of, say, three or four, the last out may well hear the harsh and dreaded tones of the alarm bell unless he has been stem to stern with the boat in front. Once this occurs, there are only seconds before the gates begin to close.

Conde has well kept banks and provides a good resting place before the short haul to Vitry le Francois and the long haul from Vitry to Heuilly.

PART THREE: CANAL LATERAL A LA MARNE

This canal actually started at Dizy, by the deviation to Epernay, but it is not until one is past the junction at Conde that it seems one is on a different tack. There is no way that this stretch can be described as a massive experience, consisting as it does of 11 locks, 50km, two towns and three villages. However, what there is, is well worth exploring. You will also have plenty of time to view the passing scene and scenery since some of the biefs are regulated at speed limits of between 2km and 5km/hr. Such speeds are, particularly in a sea-going craft, almost impossible absolutely to observe, but the physical conditions of the canal make it impossible for any craft to navigate except at dead-slow-ahead.

The first port of call, Chalons sur Marne is probably the most appealing and is certainly the most important. The trip from Conde is marked by a straight leg of 15km and 3 locks before it is possible to tie up to the deep-water bankside near the town centre. In fact, everything is close to hand: the real River Marne, the large and lively railway station, shops and restaurants galore. One of the most attractive tree-sheltered mooring spots is opposite the small island, which is known locally as Rat Island because of its infestation. However, this does not seem to deter local youth from besporting itself in and out of the water and on and off the banks. The commercial and shopping centre of Chalons is standard stuff, but the back streets are something else and well worth at leat a day's exploration.

After Chalons, the canal continues its almost dead-straight progress for nearly 20km, passing the villages of St Germain la Ville, Pogny and La Chaussee sur Marne. It is not particularly easy to tie up at any of them and the next two candidates for mooring are those at the public quay by the small village of Soulanges and the marina at the edge of the much larger town of Vitry le Francois. Soulanges offers a pleasingly modest and quiet experience, while Vitry has many more, and much livelier facilities. While Vitry lock 1 is part of this waterway, the town itself is not the end of the Canal Lateral a la Marne, it is in fact the beginning of the Canal de la Marne a la Saone.

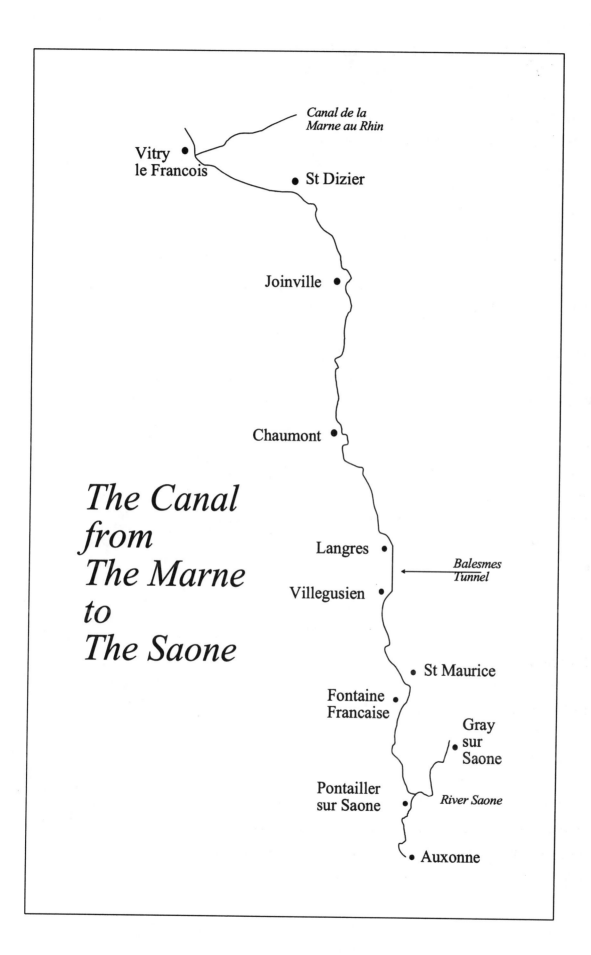

Canal de la Marne au Rhin

Vitry le Francois

St Dizier

Joinville

Chaumont

The Canal from The Marne to The Saone

Langres

Balesmes Tunnel

Villegusien

St Maurice

Fontaine Francaise

Gray sur Saone

Pontailler sur Saone

River Saone

Auxonne

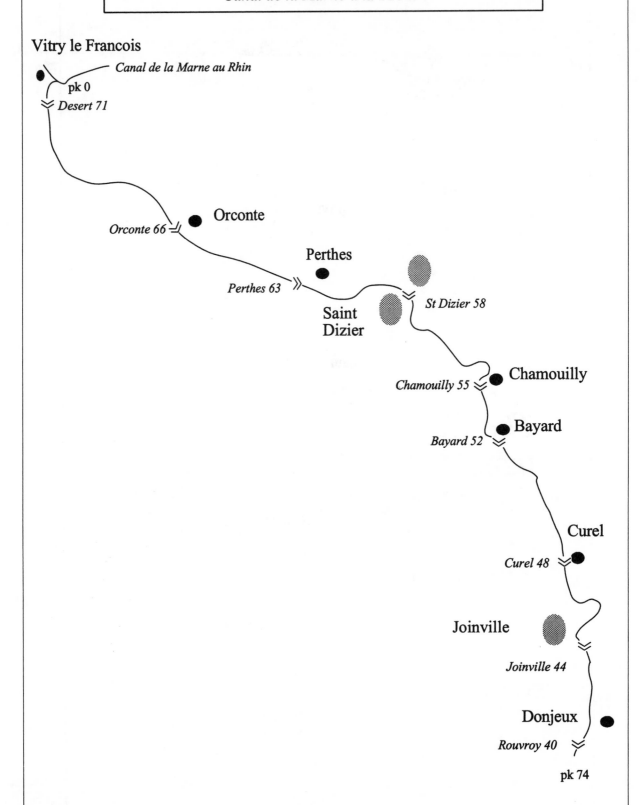

Vitry le Francois to Donjeux: 74 km ... 30 locks
Canal de la Marne a la Saone

Vitry le Francois

Canal de la Marne au Rhin

pk 0

Desert 71

Orconte 66 — Orconte

Perthes

Perthes 63

Saint
Dizier

St Dizier 58

Chamouilly 55 — Chamouilly

Bayard

Bayard 52

Curel

Curel 48

Joinville

Joinville 44

Donjeux

Rouvroy 40

pk 74

PART FOUR: CANAL DE LA MARNE A LA SAONE

The marina is sited on the Canal de la Marne a la Saone, just past its junction with the Canal de la Marne au Rhin. It is an attractively laid-out, well-run public facility with a tourist office on site. There is not a lot of depth in some parts of the actual marina and it is frequently full. It is possible to moor on the outside wall and still reach the mains power and water supplies - if you have good lengths of cable and pipe. The town is a centre of commerce and industry and has all the engineering facilities associated with a big barge marshalling centre. This is a good place to victual and fuel up, for there is no really attractive stopping/shopping place before St Dizier 30km on.

The straight stretch to St Dizier has little to offer in facilities or scenery, and contradicts Stevenson's Virginibus Puerisque 'El Dorado' passage: 'To travel hopefully is a better thing than to arrive.' The marina here is run in an efficient but informal manner, and while it is not the biggest in the world, there is nothing at all to be said against it. Whatever its friendly proprietor cannot provide in person in the way of his very reasonable range of goods and services, he can point you to not far away. General shopping, domestics and restaurants are a goodly walk away in the town centre. It is neither an appealing walk nor an attractive destination. It is however, something of a necessary expedition, since the aforementioned long haul to the junction with the River Saone at Heuilly, which starts in earnest here, is desperately short of accessible facilities, services, shops, bars - and, for many of its biefs, a decent depth of water in the canal. It is also possible to moor at the quays in the town, but they do not afford such an attractive proposition. So; make the most of Vitry le Francois and St Dizier that is no more 30km distant. These two places must be noted in the same way as are London buses: none for ages, and then two at once. It is not a case of tarrying at Jericho until your beards be grown, but the rather younger Boy Scout ethos 'Be Prepared', for, after these two, there is a severe shortage of reliable or comprehensive goods and services for the next 200km and 100 locks.

From Vitry le Francois, through St Dizier and right on to Joinville, the canal cannot be said to be a delight to the eye; nor are the villages appealing in themselves or well- endowed with mooring facilities. There are one or two chances for mooring, but these vary almost from month to month as some parts of the waterway fall into further disrepair and some are actually repaired. Some relief comes with Joinville, an attractive little town, possessing, in a modest manner, all amenities.

It is then nearly 50 km and 20 locks to Chaumont, the last large town before the River Saone. Between Joinville and Chaumont, Donjeux, Froncles and Bologne offer inferior moorings and mediocre facilities; but they are possible stop-over points for occasions when exhaustion takes over. This is a stretch that frequently has problems with its water supply, and it is possible to have to wait hours for one, slightly too heavily laden barge to force its slow way through: ponderously manoeuvering so that it neither strands on the bottom nor jams under the bridge. Those barges working within the legal limits of the waterway cause little problem; but the French seem prepared to tolerate those who go over the top just to keep in work and are ready and willing to accept 'la difference'.

Chaumont's position neither excites nor attracts in a scenic way, but there are good mooring quays by locks 24 and 25 and there have been promises of a well-equipped marina. The town's services

103

Donjeux to Heuilly: 153 km ... 83 locks
Canal de la Marne a la Saone

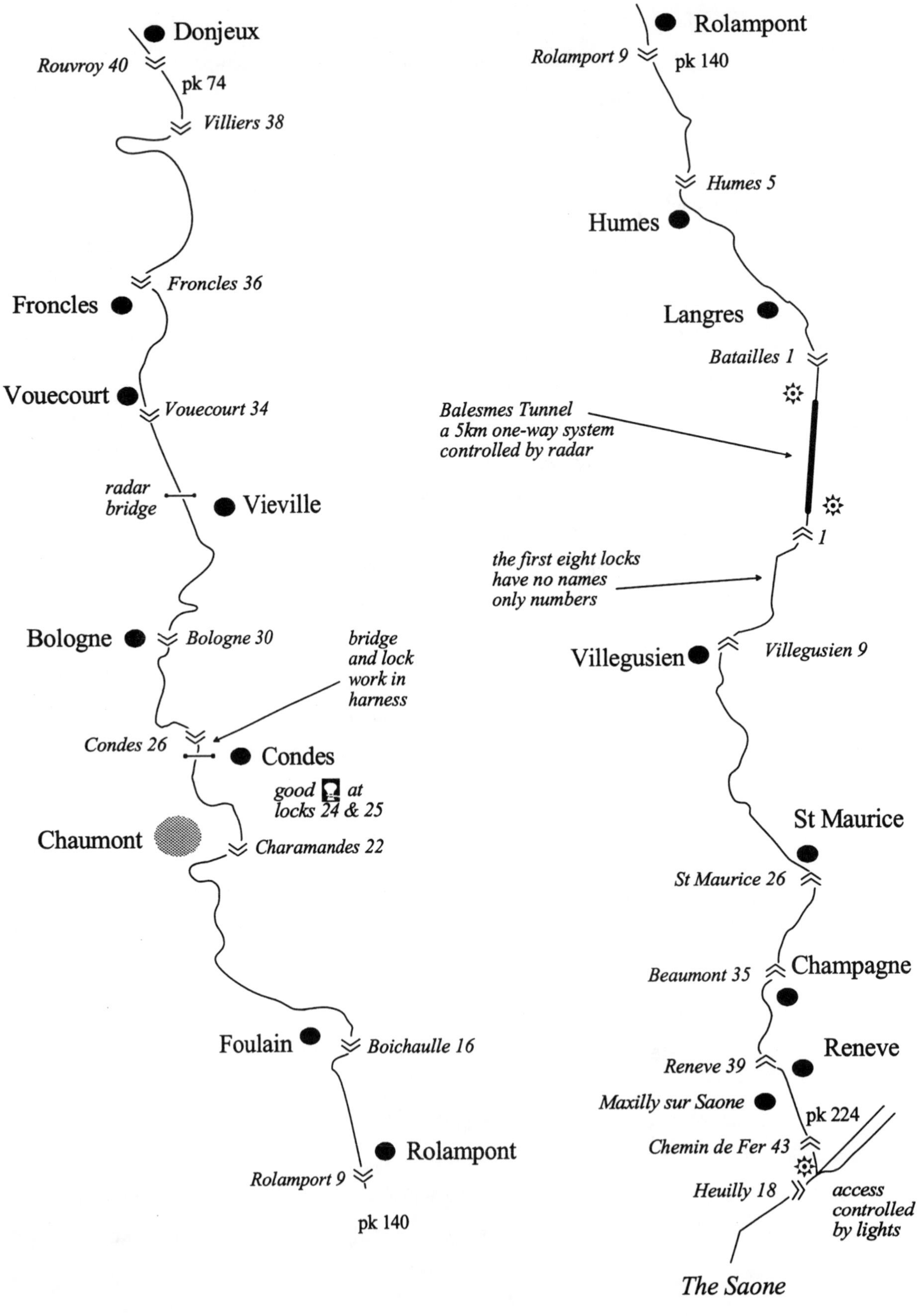

● Donjeux

Rouvroy 40

pk 74

Villiers 38

Froncles ● *Froncles 36*

Vouecourt ● *Vouecourt 34*

radar bridge ● Vieville

Bologne ● *Bologne 30*

bridge and lock work in harness

Condes 26 ● Condes

good 🍽 *at locks 24 & 25*

Chaumont ● *Charamandes 22*

Foulain ● *Boichaulle 16*

● Rolampont

Rolamport 9

pk 140

● Rolampont

Rolamport 9 pk 140

Humes 5

Humes ●

Langres ●

Batailles 1 ☼

Balesmes Tunnel
a 5km one-way system
controlled by radar

☼

1

the first eight locks
have no names
only numbers

Villegusien ● *Villegusien 9*

St Maurice ●

St Maurice 26

Beaumont 35 Champagne ●

Reneve ●
Reneve 39

Maxilly sur Saone ●

pk 224

Chemin de Fer 43

☼

Heuilly 18 *access controlled by lights*

The Saone

are superb, including an excellent supermarket within easy walking distance. So, once again, make the most of it, for after this there are only the very small communities of Foulain, Rolampont, Humes and Langres Marnes. (This latter is not to be confused with the small town of Langres which is some way from the canal.) Apart from Langres, these four communities are essentially hamlets, where the indigens are delighted to welcome strangers but have few services to offer - and all on an irregular basis. For example, I once had to cycle the two kilometres into the nearest village three times; so eccentric were the position, appearance and opening hours of the 'open all hours corner shop'. In the event it turned out to be the back room of a tiny cottage with hardly room to turn. This was merely due to the miniature size of the room and not jam-packed provisioning, for it turned out that customers had to place their orders the day before, after which the "grocer's" wife would drive their ancient Renault van into the next (hardly bigger) village and buy them in.

Next on the agenda is an almost equally inadequate set-up: the 5km Balesmes Tunnel which is a thoroughly depressing experience. It is very poorly lit, so a searchlight is essential. On the other hand, more light would only serve to show up more clearly the generally decrepit state of the construction and the abundance of floating and semi-submerged detritus. The keepers of the locks at both ends delight in over-instruction and over-description. None of it ever dispelled my forebodings before and during the excursion, nor reduced my relief after a safe passage and release. Although the word dungeon springs to mind, I have never experienced, witnessed or even heard of an accident or really bad encounter. Nevertheless, caution should be exercised.

There are now just over 60km and 40 locks to the Saone. There are two choices for a resting place after the tunnel: the small village of Villegusien, just before the lock; or the even smaller one of Piepape, three locks after. The former has a larger choice of shops, but the latter has more character - including a close-by bakery. Batches of fresh bread are ready just after 0500 and the aroma can reach the boat, calling you, John Peel-like, from your bunk in the morning. Of the following villages, there is only one with a reliable mooring for other than shoal craft and that is at Reneve, only 4 locks and 10km from the junction with the Saone, where access is controlled by lights.

Once arrived at the small village of Maxilly sur Saone and lock 43 Chemin de Fer, you can choose from three mooring possibilities. You can stay in the canal, using the recently improved facilties by the lock. You can move into the Saone, passing through the Heuilly lock, and drop downstream a couple of kilometres to Pontailler, where there is a modest marina on the right bank just before the main road bridge. To get in, you have to be able to pass under a bridge with 3m headroom. The alternative is to tie up on the same side of the river just after the road bridge, where there is a sound enough mooring.

CHAPTER FIVE

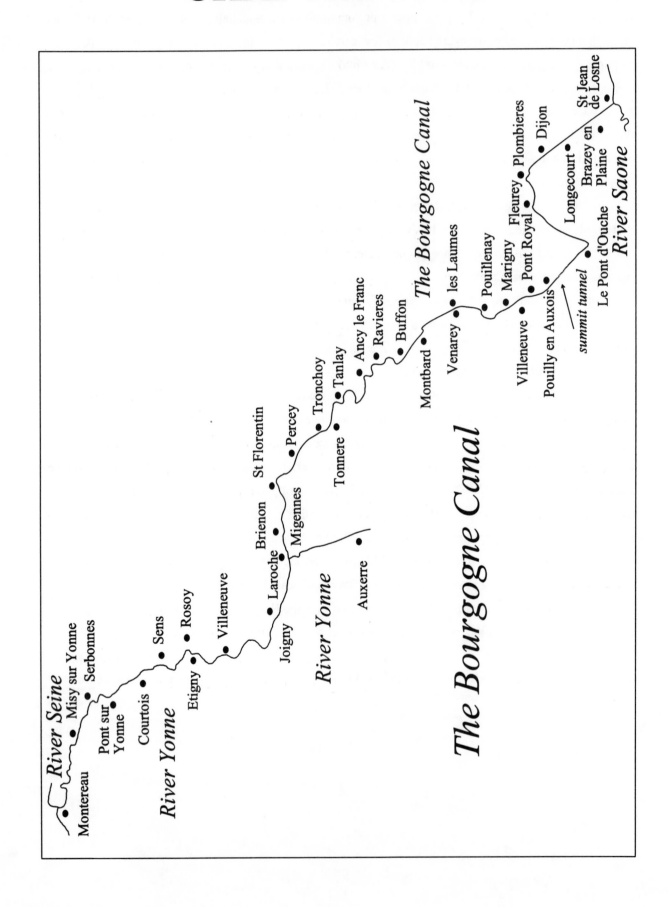

PART ONE: THE RIVER YONNE

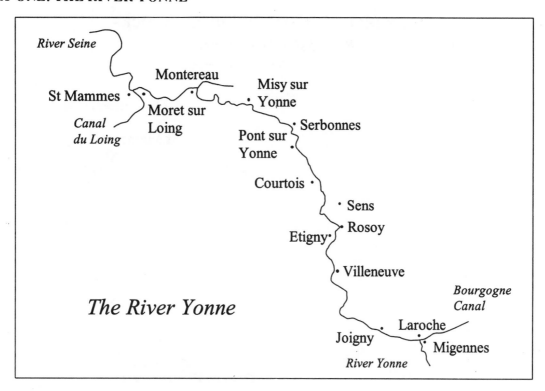

The River Yonne

Map showing: River Seine, Montereau, Misy sur Yonne, St Mammes, Moret sur Loing, Canal du Loing, Serbonnes, Pont sur Yonne, Courtois, Sens, Rosoy, Etigny, Villeneuve, Bourgogne Canal, Joigny, Laroche, Migennes, River Yonne.

THE SEINE TO ST MAMMES AND MONTEREAU

As you approach the Yonne, cruising upstream on the Seine, it comes as something of a surprise to discover that the larger of the two rivers is not the Senior Seine, but the Younger Yonne. Later, it can also be a surprise to discover that the much smaller river can frequently be faster and stronger - especially in autumn and spring. Both rivers are spanned by large bridges at the confluence at Montereau (the full designation of which is Montereau Faut Yonne), and both are dominated by its massive and mighty church: the Collegiale Notre Dame et St Loup.

There is no marina at Montereau. In 1994, the nearest was Port Stephane Mallarme at PK90. There is a possible stop-over at the old Madeleine lock at PK77, where mooring is free. However, there are disadvantages: the huge power station, Centrale Thermique of Electricite de France de Montereau, is very close; the lock is often fully occupied by motley craft in various states of disrepair and the collection of detritus in the immediate surroundings prevents it from achieving any salutary status. However, the city fathers of St Mammes, have planned a marina on the site of the hire-boat pontoons run by the English operator, John Faulkner, whose advice, hospitality and riverside shop are equally known to passing Brits. It is intended that this should be up and running for the 1995 season.

MONTEREAU TO SENS

However, these are no more than last resorts on the final reach just before the Yonne. So; to Montereau, where, in spite of its prime position on the Yonne, the best moorings are to be found on the Seine: namely, the pleasant green sward to starboard at PK68, just round the bend after the bridge. It is a pleasantly

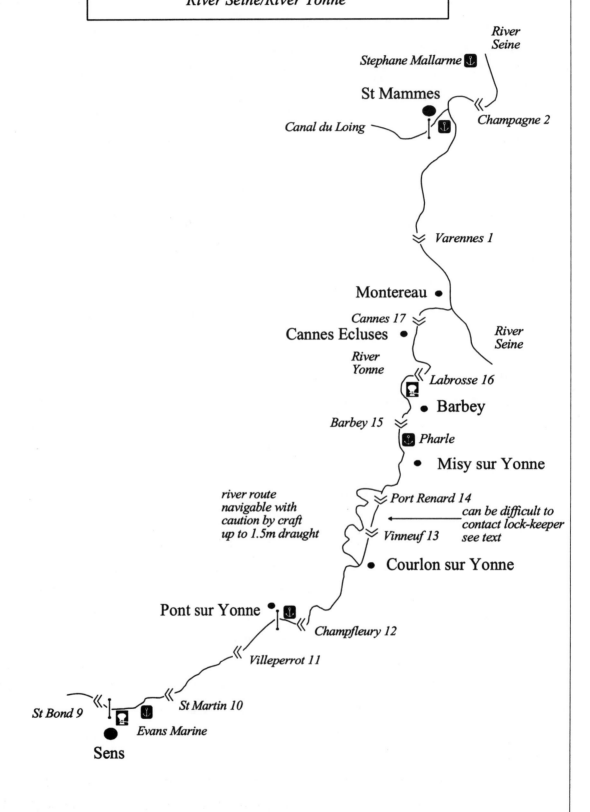

Montereau to Sens: 40 kms ... 8 locks
River Seine/River Yonne

River Seine

Stephane Mallarme ⚓

St Mammes

Champagne 2

Canal du Loing ⚓

Varennes 1

Montereau

Cannes 17

Cannes Ecluses

River Seine

River Yonne

Labrosse 16

Barbey

Barbey 15

⚓ *Pharle*

Misy sur Yonne

river route navigable with caution by craft up to 1.5m draught

Port Renard 14

can be difficult to contact lock-keeper see text

Vinneuf 13

Courlon sur Yonne

Pont sur Yonne ⚓

Champfleury 12

Villeperrot 11

St Bond 9

St Martin 10

Evans Marine

Sens

sheltered spot, backed by a row of cottages with denizens who seem favourably inclined towards the great boating public. All the shops are easily accessible, and there is usually a vacant place; which unfortunately cannot be said for the Yonne stretch of the town. Montereau is an industrial town where most of the possible berthing facilities are fully taken by large barges. The Church of Notre Dame et St Loup (14th - 16th century); the Priory of St Martin (11th century); the nearby prehistoric site at Pincevent; the ruins of "Chateau de Surville" and the Faience Museum in the former Post Office are all of note.

So, for a first stop on the Yonne proper, we must turn to the quiet bank-side moorings just after the first lock on the river, Cannes 17. After the large, well-managed and highly mechanised locks of the Seine, where there is no difficulty in manoeuvring, the locks on the Yonne offer, at first glance, not only a major contrast but also something of a challenge. While the whole operation and the character of the lock-keepers is essentially different, the main change is in the configuration of the walls of the lock itself, which are sloping. (Quite a few sloping walls still exist elsewhere, but apart from three on the Marne, they are all the remaindered halves of what were originally double locks, now given over to single working. Happily, they are of course, experienced 'en passant' as most lock-keepers are prepared to let skippers 'sit' in the middle of the lock.) Some locks have no traffic lights; some have lights that work and others have lights that do not work. It is difficult to know which are which and what is what; so one can only resort to general alertness; good binoculars; common sense and an all-pervading sense of optimism.

Nothing less like the famous Mediterranean coastal resort can be imagined than the small community of Cannes Ecluses, found on the left bank just after the lock. At heart, it is a quiet village, with all basic shopping facilities and a pleasant small bar, the Restaurant Maroc. For very light sleepers, the night trains might prove tedious, but I found it a pleasingly gentle place and a happy introduction to the delights in store along the Yonne. Just after the next lock, Labrosse 16, there is a new mooring quay in good order; most appealing for those who wish to experience a day in the middle of nowhere.

After the lock at Barbey 15, there is the Port de Plaisance du Pharle, just before the village of Misy sur Yonne which is suitable only for small craft. Misy itself appears as a tiny village on the right bank. It is even more scattered than Cannes, with the best possibilities for mooring and access to the few shops being downstream of the road-bridge. About a kilometre after Misy, there comes a parting of the ways: the river itself takes a course to starboard to wind and wind again into isolated woods and fields. This stretch is deemed to be *cautiously* navigable for craft of no more than 1.5m; and if you are in search of quiet woods and pastures, you will not cruise in vain. The canal route is a 5km stretch known as the 'derivation de Courlon' leading through two locks and a set of guard gates to the next village. It is long and narrow with vertical stone walls that command the navigation. Its two locks, Port Renard 14 and Vinneuf 13 are both operated by one agent. The method is to call him in advance on VHF Channel 08 whether navigating up or downstream. Sod's Law being what it is, he is usually to be found working the other locks.

Courlon sur Yonne is quite a big village on the right bank. Its main thoroughfare and shops are about 1km from the river, along a decent road. Good meals and wine are available. It has a small quay just outside the Auberge, where mooring is possible although not easy for larger craft. Shortly after, comes Serbonnes, another very small village on the right bank, with shops about 1km from the banks. Getting close-to is not difficult here, for there is a small quay with good depth as well as electricity. However, craft near maximum draught may prefer to wait until the small town just after the next lock, Champfleury 12. This lock is a newer one, with vertical sides and good breadth. It is also much faster than the others. The small hazard to be avoided on the right bank just before the lock is the hidden ledge just below the waterline.

Pont sur Yonne, no more than a kilometre from the lock on the left bank is quite an appealing smallish town. The original bridge was almost demolished, and a new one built to ease both road and river traffic. The old medieval bridge is a standing invitation to painters and photographers alike, and from its extremities, there are interesting views of the river. There are good moorings just downstream of the new bridge on the left bank at pontoons set at 90° to the river bank. They are of a size to serve smaller craft (up to 8.0m LOA), but careful rope work can ensure a secure berth. It is also possible to moor directly above the pontoons, to the grass banks as well as below them - but this latter is frequently used by the floating hotel trade. The immediate surroundings are shaded and attractive, and the close-by shopping is very good. Toilet facilities leave a lot to be desired and are far less appealing than the 12th/15th century church. Lock Villeperrot 11 requires care on the upstream right bank where it is supposed to be possible to moor but the banks are broken down and encumbered.

The next major city-centre attraction is Sens, on the right bank just over 10km after Pont sur Yonne. Before it, however, comes an important cruising facility: the marina and boatyard known as Evans Marine, a family business run by one Simon Evans. It is well known to many Brits for its English-speaking welcome and its winterising facilities ashore and afloat. Amongst their five or six agencies, they number Volvo and Penta. In addition, they have an emergency repair service, with a 160hp tug and a 1 ton crane. The yard is upstream of St Denis roughly halfway between the St Martin lock and Sens. Hardly more than a kilometre from the centre of Sens, it boasts all the joys of first-rate loos and showers and a good range of boating gear. (Evans Marine Chantier Naval, Chemin du Port de Givet, St Denis les Sens, 89100 Sens. Tel. 86 65 34 66.) After the boatyard, there is a clearly buoyed rocky patch in midstream towards the left bank. The bridge is navigated through a central arch with two-way traffic.

The Cathedral city of Sens is just round the bend after the new road bridge, with its bankside moorings. You keep to the east of the island and moor well before the bridge, to port on the right bank. It has a very pleasant river frontage, and mooring facilities are being improved all the time, with the quay being specially refurbished. It's splendidly convenient for the town centre, which is well worth a thorough (two-day) investigation, dating back as it does to the Romans, when it was the provincial capital.

Sens Cathedral is impressive in many ways. Not only is it the oldest but it is also the largest gothic Cathedral in France. Both inside and out it is magnificent, and its stained glass windows are quite lovely. The Cathedral has two connections with Canterbury Cathedral. The construction of Sens Cathedral was started c 1130 and built mainly between 1140 and 1168. Its first architect, Guillaume de Sens, also undertook the restoration of the choir at Canterbury Cathedral from 1175 to 1192. Thomas a Becket, Archbishop of Canterbury, who had earlier studied nearby, took refuge here in Sens from 1166 to 1170.

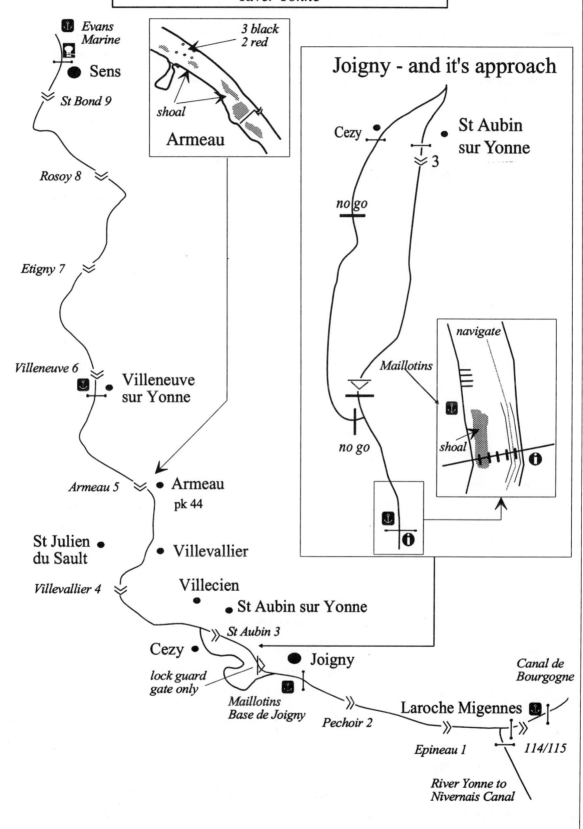

Sens to Migennes: 44 km ... 9 locks
River Yonne

Evans
Marine

Sens

St Bond 9

Rosoy 8

Etigny 7

Villeneuve 6

Villeneuve
sur Yonne

Armeau 5

Armeau
pk 44

St Julien
du Sault

Villevallier

Villevallier 4

Villecien

St Aubin sur Yonne

St Aubin 3

Cezy

*lock guard
gate only*

Maillotins
Base de Joigny

Joigny

Pechoir 2

Laroche Migennes

Canal de
Bourgogne

Epineau 1

114/115

River Yonne to
Nivernais Canal

Armeau inset
3 black
2 red

shoal

Armeau

Joigny - and it's approach
Cezy

St Aubin
sur Yonne

3

no go

Maillotins

no go

navigate

shoal

Walking round the town is a pleasure. While the ramparts remain only as ruins, they are pleasingly lined by trees and there are gorgeous old houses in the rue Jean Cousin. The Mausoleum of the Dauphin Louis de Bourbon and the Treasury are richly endowed, the latter with sumptuous textiles, ivories and ornaments. The mid-19th century covered market is a splendid array of iron and brickwork; while the Municipal Museum proudly boasts Napoleon's Waterloo hat. Above all, the shopping areas are splendid: their wares are nothing if not enticing and it is a veritable gourmet's delight.

SENS TO MIGENNES

The next 17km wind through gentle countryside, becoming more and more rustic as you pass each of the four locks: St Bond 9; Rosoy 8; Etigny 7 and Villeneuve 6. In 1993, Nos 7 and 8 were still manual. There are four small villages that are not too distant from the river, but mooring is very tricky and the best plan must be to continue to the last lock. Here, it is important to tend to the right bank before and after the lock because of shoaling in the centre and near the left bank.

Villeneuve sur Yonne is a small town that was 'new' when created by Louis VIII in 1163 as a fortified royal residence. There are existing remains, as well as the 13th century Great Gates: Porte de Sens (also Champagne) and Porte de Joigny (also Bourgogne). The associated round tower of Louis le Gros, an amazing cylinder of a keep, was actually built by one Philippe Auguste at the beginning of the 13th century as a combined fortress and royal apartment. The first stone of the church of Notre Dame was laid in 1163, but it was not until the 16th century that it was finished.

It is easy to tie up just downstream of the old stone bridge, where there is a newly constructed quayside. Across the river, on the other side of the island, there is the town marina, which calls itself both port and halte de plaisance. It is a secure berth, and water and electricity can be obtained, but only with difficulty since the points are quite distant. At any time other than high season, it is also difficult to find an official who wants to take your money - even though the regulation dues are official. This small town makes a pleasant break between the two main centres on this stretch of the Yonne: Sens and Joigny, which is nearly 20km distant. The river is still fairly wide in this area, and there are three locks before Joigny; Armeau 5; Villevalier 4 and St Aubin 3.

The stretch has only one minor navigational hazard, and that is 4km after Villeneuve sur Yonne and 1km before the first lock at Armeau. There are shoals and rocks at a place where there is considerable barge traffic; and some of these have difficulty in turning into the quarry on the left. There is no real threat, but it is only sensible to be vigilant and cautious when approaching the last kilometre before the lock (see inset). Armeau lies on the right bank, at PK44, just after the lock. It is a very pretty little place, perhaps the prettiest on the stretch, with all basic village amenities. It has an interesting claim to fame, in that the Chateau le Grand Plateau was once owned by the Man in the Iron Mask. It is just over 2 km to the east of the village and is open to the public.

A couple of kilometres from Armeau, along the Bassin de Vitesse, come these two opposing villages: Villevallier on the right bank, close to the river; and St Julien, set a little further back on a hill. Both have village basics, but St Julien has just that little extra: a 16th century timber house and the

Vanguillain chapel from which there are splendid views of the Yonne valley. Shortly after the Villevallier lock come more settlements. Villecien and St Aubin, both on the right bank, are little more than hamlets; the first without a shop and the second with just that little more including a 13th century church atop the modest hill. However, Cezy, on the other side, is a much a larger place with a good range of shops and a restaurant. It can be approached by road across the two bridges; a walk of no more than a kilometre or so if you moor close by the St Aubin lock. Mooring is just possible on the right bank along the last kilometre before the lock, but not entirely problem free anywhere in this area. Just before the lock the waters divide: the river goes to starboard and the canal to port. It is possible, with great care and modest draught (1.2m being the maximum for safety in mid channel, and 1.0m being better) to navigate up the river arm. If you are lucky, you may find a vacant spot to moor at the no better than modest quay. It is chancy navigation - but, of course, the scenery does improve as one might expect when leaving the man-made navigation. Back in the canal, it is just two locks and 4km to Joigny, the last port of call before the parting of the ways with the junction of the Canal de Bourgogne.

The delightful old part of this town sits atop a steep slope rising from the river bank to its narrow streets around the St Thibault and St Jean churches. There are many quaint houses, with carvings and pottery built into their fabric; but the 17th century Porte du Bois is perhaps the most famous and intriguing. The quality of the general shops is excellent and food shops and eating are first rate. The official 'name' for the inhabitants is Joviniens, but they have been nicknamed Maillotins ('Hammerers') since the 15th century when coopers slaughtered the local aristo, the Count of Tremoille, with their wine barrel mallets. Predictably, Joigny is known for its local wines St Jacques; and it is possible to moor at the private quay of the famous Cote St Jacques restaurant, on the right bank downstream Tel : 84. 62. 09. 70.

The modern part of the town is on the left bank, with access from across the 18th century stone bridge. However, there is nothing 18th century about the type, quantity, quality or speed of the traffic that uses it: even simple road crossing is hazardous. There are good, free moorings, with rings and bollards, downstream of the bridge on the right bank immediately next the main road. They are, though, fairly noisy at night because of the heavy commercial road traffic. For craft of shallow draught, it is usually possible to find a bankside space on the left bank, but the place is without amenity. The best place, for security, quiet and access to immediate shops must be about 100m downstream of the bridge on the left bank, at the Port des Maillotins - Base de Joigny, where Locaboat Plaisance run a small, but extremely efficient marina. Their services include fuel, water, loos, showers - a staff who are friendly, informed and efficient. The pontoons are soundly constructed and easy to use. (Locaboat Base: Tel: 86.62.06.14.)

Between Joigny and the junction with the Canal de Bourgogne there are only 8km and 2 locks: Pechoir 2 and Epineau 1. Both locks are speedy with powerful water-flows. In no way can this leg be described as an odyssey, but arrival at the lock at Migennes will transport the boater from one world to another.

You turn left for the Canal de Bourgogne, and right for the continuation of the River Yonne. The Yonne, however, leads to the Nivernais Canal and that route is not covered by this guide since the navigation can pose severe problems for craft of more than 1.0m draught.

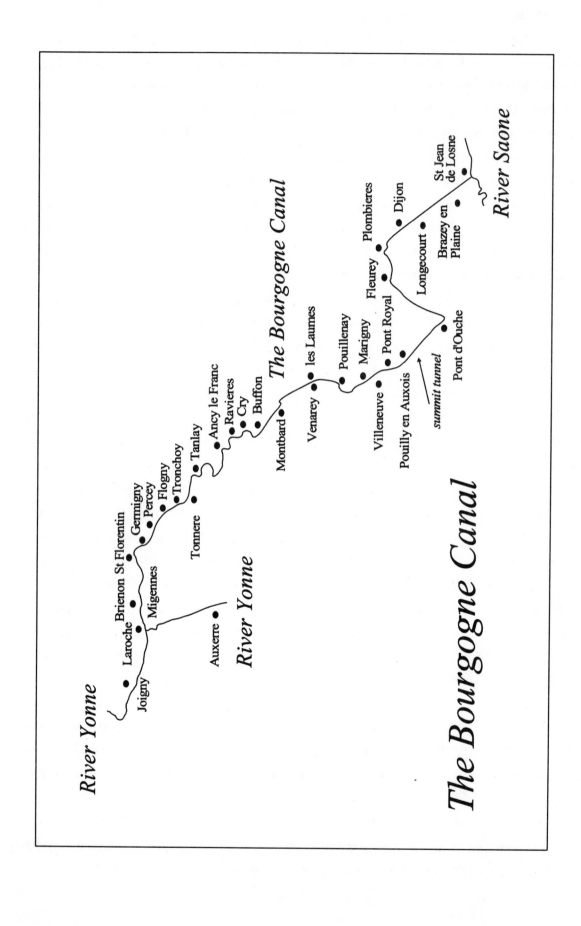

PART TWO: THE CANAL DE BOURGOGNE

The Canal de Bourgogne is magnificent from whichever end you tackle it. True, its close approaches may not be scenically impressive, but essentially the waterway is a spectacularly picturesque experience, especially when navigating from Migennes towards St Jean de Losne in the autumn. Even from the barest facts and figures, it is impressive: 242 kilometres long, with a grand total of 189 locks; 113 of which are on the Yonne side and 76 on the Saone. The crowning glory of the Canal de Bourgogne is the summit tunnel reach at Pouilly en Auxois: at nearly 400m above sea level, it is the highest in France. Its length is often given as 3349m. long, but I prefer the more magical alternative of 3333m. In theory, the canal permits passage to vessels of Freycinet gauge with 3.1m air draught and theoretically a permitted draught of 1.8m; but in 1993 it was restricted to craft with draught of less than 1.4m, and in April 1994 some stretches were restricted to 1.2m. Today, commercial traffic has virtually gone and the canal is left for leisure and pleasure.

Designed to link the Seine and Rhone basins, it was on 28th December 1832 that the first boat crossed the watershed reach opening up a waterway originally conceived 300 years before. The idea of linking the Atlantic and the Mediterranean through Burgundy goes back possibly to Louis XII. However, it was Henry IV, in 1606, who set things in motion, canalising a stretch between Dijon and Saint Jean de Losne. In 1696, Vauban drew up a report recommending joining the Yonne to the Saone with a summit at Sombernon or Pouilly. Lack of finance prevented progress until 1775 when limited work began between Laroche and Tonnerre. In 1781 Burgundy decided to open the canal between Dijon and the Saone and on 14th December 1808 boats actually entered the Port of Dijon. In 1822, a loan of 25 million FF enabled the completion of the navigation, but another 11 years were to pass before five feeding reservoirs were built. The last stage, enlarging the canal to Freycinet, was completed in 1882, after massive works to raise banks, heighten bridges and lengthen locks.

In more recent times, trouble has raised its head again. The canal was first threatened with complete declassification, then 'partial declassification' - this particular notion involved the construction of a mighty motorway right down its centre. Then it was closed to traffic on Sundays, just as the pleasure boat industry was developing. The fact that we can now navigate the canal today must surely be due to divine intervention on behalf of those masterpieces built by our ancestors, because, with two or three exceptions, the folk on the planet have done little to help.

LAROCHE MIGENNES TO TONNERE

The entrance to the lock is through a large outer basin directly off the Yonne, but mooring in it is virtually impossible, and jilling around is the order of the day. The lock enjoys a double-barrelled number, 114-115, but this belies the actuality. It is neither large nor double, and while not Stygian, it is certainly Cimmerian; and when it comes to literary references, the lock-keeping couple, veritable ancients, could have sprung fully-fledged from Shakespeare or Victor Hugo; Macbeth or Les Miserables according to taste. They will issue you with a leaflet containing dire warnings about the lack of water in the canal. In

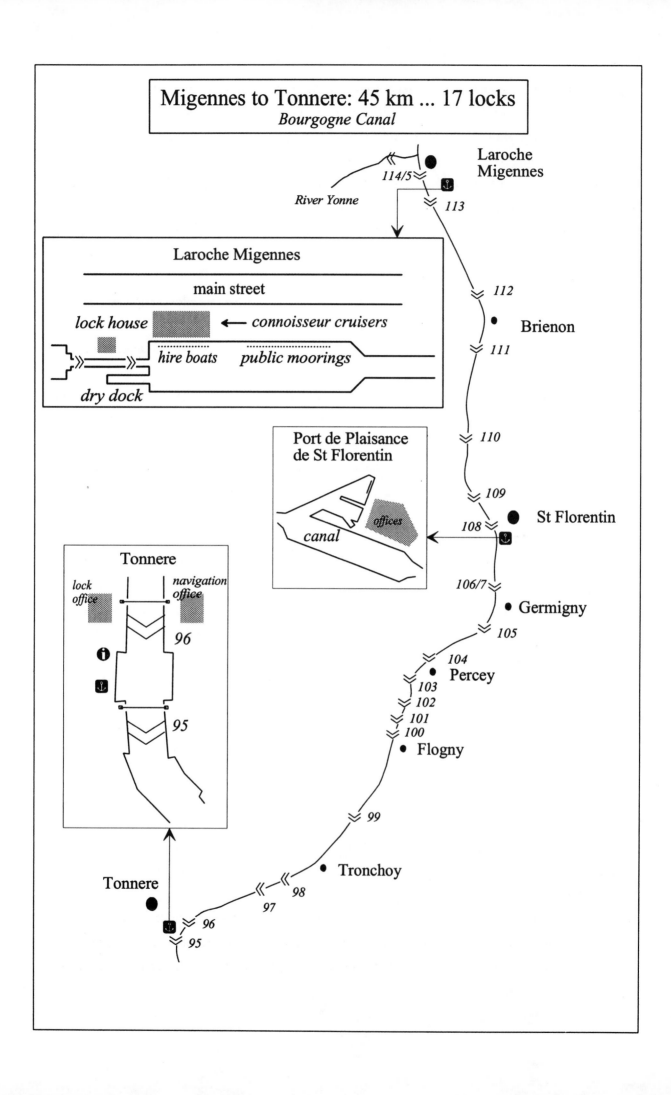

Migennes to Tonnere: 45 km ... 17 locks
Bourgogne Canal

Laroche
Migennes

114/5

River Yonne

113

Laroche Migennes

main street

lock house   ← *connoisseur cruisers*

hire boats   *public moorings*

dry dock

112

● Brienon

111

Port de Plaisance
de St Florentin

110

109

offices

108   ● St Florentin

canal

106/7

● Germigny

Tonnere

*lock
office*   *navigation
office*

96

95

105

104
● Percey

103
102
101
100
● Flogny

99

Tronchoy

Tonnere

●

96

95

97   98

fact, for craft of much more than 1.0m draught, mooring can pose problems when away from the main stopping places. The most critical stretch for lack of water is in the area of locks 100-95: if you can negotiate those there is little likelihood of further trouble - provided you travel slowly and always in the centre.

The keepers will also issue the standard leaflet regarding the illegality of using tyres for fenders. They will also give you a small card (referred to as a 'fiche', 'carte' or 'papier') that will be stamped from time to time to mark your progress through the system run by the Direction Departmentale de l'Equipement de la Cote d'Or. If you are going the whole hog, it will stay with you until you reach the Saone at St Jean de Losne.

Once through the somewhat daunting lock, you enter a large basin, with good depth and plenty of good mooring places with electricity, water and fuel. Quayside visitors are well served by the hire-boat Connoisseur Cruisers' team of Dominique and Isobelle Fourre; hirers and non-hirers alike get the benefit of their friendly help and advice.

That advice will certainly draw attention to the following possible pitfalls: not all the advertised ports de plaisance, haltes fluviales & nautiques deserve the name, so all should be approached with a contingency plan if your draught exceeds 1.0m and you have have a strict schedule. Not all the radar detectors work well and it is a good idea to have an axe, large hammer or a saucepan to wave near them to ensure they trigger the lock routines as they should. In terms of over-all planning, about three weeks should be allowed to get from Migennes to St Jean de Losne without breaking any speed limits. It will not be possible to stop everywhere, but you will be neither rushed nor deprived of the good life.

Migennes is a busy little town; being properly known as Laroche Migennes - from the nearby Laroche railway station and its massive marshalling yard. For a long time, the electrified section of the south-east French railway system ended here and trains had to change engines at Migennes. All shops, including a supermarket, are within walking distance and there is an excellent cave close by. The church has a beautiful steeple - and the basin is visited by peddlers of diverse nationalities plying miscellaneous wares. After Migennes, the canal sides close in as it runs beside the railway for about 10 km, as far as Brienon sur Armancon. The next lock (Cheny 113) has actually been mechanised and automated, but like many of the recently upgraded locks along this stretch, it is in fact general practice for it to be operated by a keeper. Indeed, throughout the whole length of the Canal de Bourgogne, many of the locks have been modernised and automated; but only ninety per cent of the way, with the result that in spite of all the money that has been spent, for the want of a few thousand FF's more, most of them are still operated by keepers: some with modern cars - and some with bicycles that are not only old-fashioned but also extremely old and some that are in extremely poor repair. Somewhat in contrast, it is useful to know that many of the keepers use CB radio to contact one another - and are keen for all skippers to get geared up similarly.

The village of Brienon is extremely pretty and it is proudly possessed of its famous 17th century oval public wash-house; which, then and now, has to be a great improvement on modern launderettes. There is a good range of shops, but in spite of its claim to the official nomenclature of a port, it actually has no more than a basic mooring quayside. However, there are facilities to hand: water, rubbish bins, telephone and a supermarket. The local church, dedicated to one St Loup, an ancient Archbishop of Sens, has some goodly portions from the 13th and 16th centuries. It is just another 10km and 4 locks from Brienon to the next port of call, St Florentin. Its modern marina, which has full facilities (including basic repairs), is very pleasantly tucked away from the main canal and the staff are friendly and helpful - though not always obviously in attendance ... even when it comes to collecting harbour dues.

St Florentin has only 6,500 inhabitants, and they are known as Les Florentinois. It is an old but lively town and one of its most noticeable features is the near-superfluity of charcuteries and fromageries, affording a superb introduction to the well-known Burgundian obsession with good eating. In particular, the local cheeses should be sampled. The famous two are Soumaintrain and St Florentin, while Chaource originated nearby.

The eponymous St Florentin is a meltingly soft, washed rind cheese similar to Epoisses. It is supposed to be ripened for two months, by which time it has become a rich, ruddy colour with a strong smell and a really spicy tang. It is no longer easy to find true farm versions and the factory-made cheeses are often artificially orange-coloured rather than classically washed.

Soumaintrain is a very small village between St Florentin and Evry le Chitel, and the real thing is still made there. The 250g cheeses are washed in brine every other day for up to eight weeks. At that time, the crust has changed from a pale fawn to a deep reddish tint. According to the locals, it is pretty strong - and they have a high pong tolerance. This rinded cheese can also be eaten younger when it is still white and creamy. Artificial orange-coloured commercial versions are easily obtained.

Chaource is now primarily a cheese of Champagne, apparently named after a small village near Troyes; but the chances are that it began its life at Pontigny Abbey. It was especially preferred by Marguerite de Bourgogne, who was executed in 1315 at the age of 25 for flagrant indiscretions in the Bourgogne's town house in Paris. To make the cheese, the milk is allowed to ripen naturally before renneting, after which the curdling takes about 24 hours. After draining slowly through pierced wooden plates, it is removed and lightly salted, dried on wooden shelving in the airing room, then matured for at least fourteen days on rye straw. A thoroughly and evenly ripened Chaource is a rarity: it is a difficult cheese to mature evenly because of its deep drum shape. It ripens inwards from under its overcoat and it is supposed to be a milky-white, smooth-pasted cheese, but it can be very salt, hard and dry rather than creamy. However, it is the very depth of its soft pate that imbues the best of them with their special texture and flavour: although soft like Brie and Camembert, it is an entirely different experience. It has a thin covering of white rind tinged with gold and it is at its best in summer and autumn. It is worth noting that the monks cleared land not only for cheese-making but also to create the great Chablis wines.

Pontigny Abbey, no more than 10 km away, is an offshoot of the famous Citeaux. It was founded in 1114 on a site where three Episcopal Sees and three Comtes meet - and if the six superiors souls of those estates had ever met on the bridge, they could all have claimed to have been on their own land. On the banks of the Serein, the Abbey, which gave refuge to Thomas a Becket, is known as the second daughter of Citeaux. Different from the mother, Pontigny still possesses its church in good order.

Up the hill there is a 16th century church with absolutely splendid stained glass windows. The hill on which the town is built, dominating the confluence, is steep enough, but if you can face the extra haul up to the terrace, there is a panoramic view of the two lovely rivers, the Armance and the Armancon.

Take care shortly after leaving the marina, to avoid the wreck on the town side (north) of the canal.

There is no fully organised marina or mooring place for any craft with more than modest draught between St Florentin and Tonnerre, a matter of 26km and 10 locks The scenery gradually improves after Migennes, becoming increasingly picturesque as the canal runs closely alongside the Armancon river, a clear-water temptation to swimmers. Many of the locks and quayside moorings have notice boards promoting local canal and tourist attractions and information, but the lock-keepers' custom of selling wine, postcards and oddments starts to wane.

General provisions are available at Germigny. However, while mooring is possible it is very much a hit and miss affair: the quays are overgrown, the posts in poor repair and the depths variable. Percey is similarly placed. Flogny, with better shopping facilities, has a good quay and also bollards on the bankside, but mooring is only possible for craft under 1.0m. Water and rubbish bins are available between the bridge and the lock. Tronchoy has one unappealing stone verge for mooring and it is necessary to use land anchors on the banks. Happily however, the stretch is favoured with the presence of friendly cats, dogs and geese, and is particularly noted for its wild mushrooms.Tonnerre has an excellent basin in the short stretch between locks 96 and 95. Immediately after lock 96 is the local navigation office. According to the authorities, the staff keep a listening watch on VHF 22, but during the three weeks I was in the area I was quite unable to raise them. They also keep what are best described as eccentric office hours. However, the lock-keeper is perhaps better informed of all things local than they are so it is not a dire deprivation.

The basin is wide and deep, tying up easy at the quiet, well-shaded and well-equipped moorings, and the smart port office is regularly attended with a telephone next door. The town itself, which has a comprehensive range of shops and restaurants, is a good uphill walk away; but there is small general store not too far away, and a rousing horn heralds the early morning arrival of the bread van lady. The very ancient garlic town of Tonnerre, originally known as Tornodorum, occupied the plateau behind St Pierre until the 15th century. Built on a rock beside the Armancon, the 15th century church exploits the high ground, and from its rocky terrace there is a splendid panorama of the town and its environs. Its square tower, topped by a small lantern was originally a look-out over the Armancon valley. For protection, a network of high walls and gates divided the upper part of the town from the lower. One of Tonnerre's main attractions is the Fosse Dionne (or Fosse Divine), a Vauclusian spring that used to serve the ancient circular public 'lavoir' as well as providing the populace with its only supply of drinking-water. This source of never-ending clear water yields on average 100 litres per second. It has a 15m diameter basin, surrounded by an 18th century wash-house, which overflows into a small stream.

Perhaps the most austere, yet still beautiful, symbol of Tonnerre's past is its famous ancient Fontenilles hospital, built in 1293 by one Marguerite of Burgundy and endowed with great wealth which

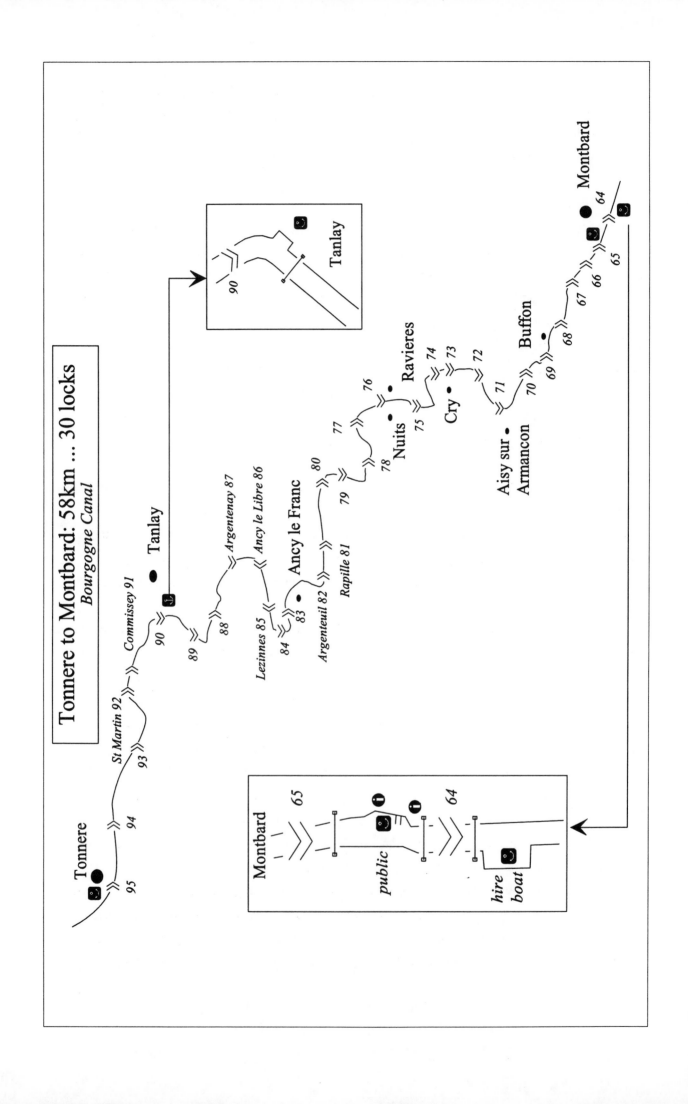

Tonnere to Montbard: 58km ... 30 locks
Bourgogne Canal

still partly exists. The dimensions of the sick-room are impressive at nearly 20m by 80m and 28m high. Its roof spread is a staggering 4,500 sq metres, supported by an impressive framework. In its prime, there were forty beds, each housed in a wooden alcove. Its Revestiere chapel, hidden away behind a small door, has a magnificent fabrication ('La Mise au tombeau' a sepulchre representing the placement of Christ in the tomb), an amazing tribute to Burgundy art, installed in 1454 by a rich merchant.

When it comes to fame however (and that must include infamy) pride of place must go to the strange case of Le Chevalier d'Eon. He was born in 1728 at the lovely Renaissance Hotel d'Uzes; and we can still gaze at it in awe, for it is now a Caisse d'Epargne bank. His christening marked him for an exceptional life with a singularly ambivalent appellation: Charles-Genevieve-Louise-Auguste-Andree-Thimotee Eon de Beaumont - an agglomeration he either lived up to or never quite overcame. During the course of a brilliant military and diplomatic career, he claimed it had been necessary for him to adopt women's clothes. So; later in life, he adopted such habits as habitual and became the focus of prurient attention. French good taste was so offended that he became exiled in England, where he also achieved notoriety. Indeed, such was the curiosity about 'his' genuine gender, that, after his death in 1810, an autopsy was held to determine the truth. In fact he had been a man all the time - if one of many parts.

The town is a good centre for wine; the local brew being Bourgogne-Epineuil (red and rose), taking its name from the village opposite. The home of the world-famous Chablis is only 16 km away.

TONNERE TO MONTBARD

It is 6 locks and just under 20 km to Tanlay. Just before it the small village and lock of Commissey have mooring posts on the bank, but they must be approached with caution, because of lack of depth. The previous lock, St Martin, must also be treated with respect, since it is impossible to see its traffic control lights from the radar post - and it is always wise to check that the mechanism has noted your passage before leaving the post behind.

Tanlay itself is an attractive market town with modest 'marina' facilities set in splendid surroundings. The town is famous for its moated Renaissance chateau. Built in 1550, it is one of the most beautiful in Yonne. After the first ditch there is a small castle, and then more ditches filled with running water. The chateau is set in an immense park, across which flows a magnificent strech of water called the Grand Canal. There are many rooms open to visitors, all with beautiful furniture and paintings. Amongst these many exquisite sights, the great trompe-l'oeuil gallery and the secret meeting room of the Huguenots, are pre-eminent. The latter possesses a renowned fresco ceiling depicting famous 16th century religious notables.

Just by the third lock after Tanlay, Argentenay 87 , there is an intriguing bar going under the name of Chez Meme - well worth visiting in spite of its difficulty of access. Still following the Armancon, the canal continues its way through the small villages of Ancy le Libre, Lezinnes and Argenteuil. They are all charming and worth walking around at leisure, especially Argenteuil with its 19th century public washing house.

Shortly after comes the attractive village of Ancy le Franc and the famous Renaissance chateau, one of the most beautiful in Burgundy. Built to the plans of the Italian Sebastien Serlio (started in 1546 and finished in 1622) it consists of four main buildings, with identical facades, linked by corner houses. Its apartments and galleries, 25 in all, were mainly decorated by Niccolo dell'Abbate and they all have fantastic 16th and 19th century furniture, much wood panelling and many paintings. The King's bed-room, the Roman Emperor's room, and Richelieu's bedroom are all open to public gaze.

In contrast with the above, specially designated outbuildings house the Car, Carriage & Harness museum which has ancient bicycles and veteran cars including fascinating examples of a 1900 Truffault, a 1903 Niclaux, and a 1905 Renault and a de Dion Bouton.

Unfortunately, the proclaimed halte nautique (only a couple of kilometres from the village) while having good depth at its open-river mooring, is a bleak spot with its facilities vandalised or completely absent. It is handy for a visit to the chateau but does not recommended itself for a much longer or indeed an overnight stay. In general, there are problems in the area: many bank-sides are in poor repair with troublesome access, and the quasi-automated locks 85-82 often have to be operated by a keeper. The last one is preceded by a very tight near/blind bend. Note that Rapille lock (81) is boater-operated by a button that looks like radar. Its control lights take an extremely long time to go through their routine so consider-al patience may need to be exercised. In fact, there is no proper resting place before Ravieres, which is also supposed to offer 'full facilities' but one arrives to discover there is no more than a bare quay and a dustbin (emptied at 0300)! The quayside is suitable for craft of 2m draught at its downstream stretch and 0.8m upstream. The appealing village and pretty church are a very good climb away, as is the nearest telephone. However, there is a small but well-stocked supermarket almost next the halte. On balance, Ravieres is well worth a short stay, being a classic of its kind - as yet hardly having come to terms with being on the brink of AD2000. Just across the river, lies the smaller but equally attractive village of Nuits sur Armancon with yet another Renaissance chateau.

Moving towards Montbard, the next major halt, the little village of Cry is just a few kilometres along. It is a pretty spot with an ancient bridge, and the nearby ruins of the Rochefort chateau. Next, Aisy sur Armancon is a small village with all traditional shops, and next again on the other side of the canal, Rougemont has a shop, a 13th century church and the remains of an old fort-cum-chateau.

Then comes the nearby village of Buffon. It is also a pretty little place; and while it has few amenities, there are unencumbered banksides with good mooring posts making it easy to stroll back to the forge from the boat. What forge? Well, perhaps the most intriguing individual curiosity in the whole area is the ironworks built by the famous naturalist Georges-Louis Leclerc (Comte de Buffon, Vicomte de Quincy, Vidame de Tonnerre, Marquis de Rougemont and Intendant du Jardin du Roi) in 1768. The blast-furnace, forge and foundry, which were powered by the Armancon, have now been restored and are open to the public. Although mooring facilities are good immediately next the industrial site they are fre-quently fully taken by hotel and trip boats.

The twin villages of Blaisy and St Remy face one another a few kilometres before Montbard, each with modest amenities and grassy banks - but mooring is not easy, so most will make for Montbard itself.

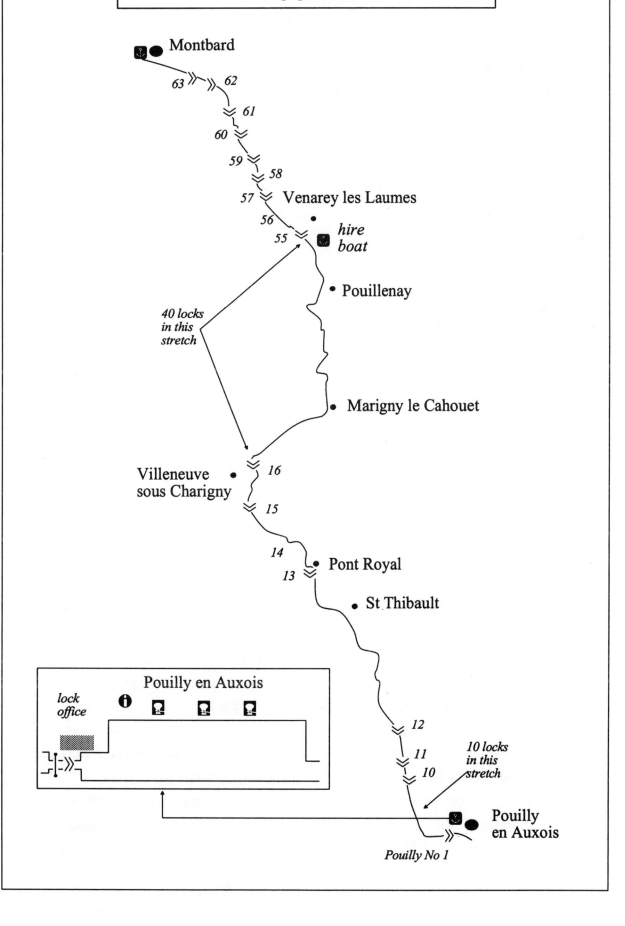

Montbard to Pouilly: 52 km ... 65 locks
Bourgogne Canal

Montbard

63 · 62

61

60

59 · 58

57 · Venarey les Laumes

56

55 · *hire boat*

· Pouillenay

40 locks in this stretch

· Marigny le Cahouet

Villeneuve sous Charigny · 16

15

14

13 · Pont Royal

· St Thibault

12

11

10 · *10 locks in this stretch*

Pouilly en Auxois

lock office

Pouilly en Auxois

Pouilly No 1

MONTBARD TO POUILLY

There are two marina facilities at Montbard: the first is municipal, on the left bank just after the first lock. The second, operated by a hire company, is just after the second lock on the right bank. The first is blessed with maximum depth and plenty of room to manoeuvre, while the second compensates for its shallowness and distance from the town centre by having accessible fuel pumps. The town has excellent shopping facilities and a first-rate tourist office. All these are close by the town marina.

It is impossible to get away from the man Buffon. This was his birthplace in 1707. He died at the age of 81, having become an internationally acclaimed naturalist who combined the sensitivity and artistry required of the Curator of the King's Garden in Paris with the hard-headed business and technical skills demanded of one who was to become one of France's first and most famous industrial giants. Without him, Montbard would never have achieved its metalworking provenance in the specialised manufacture of steel tubing.

Prime among Montbard's tourist attractions are the Fine Arts Museum, in the former chapel of the Buffon Park, the 40m tall Aubespin Tower and the St Louis Tower. This tower was the birthplace of the mother of the St Bernard who, in 1118, founded Fontenay Abbey, only 6km away. The abbey is a beautiful example of a 12th century Cistercian monastery. The Buffon Park, with the Buffon Institute and the office where Buffon worked, offers pleasant walks; while the Buffon Chapel where he is buried, and the Hotel Buffon all tell the same tale.

Fontenay Abbey, 6km away, is beautifully situated, in verdant, undulating country. Founded by St Bernard in 1118, it provides a perfect image of a Cistercian monastery in the 12th century. During the French Revolution, the abbey was sold and transformed into a paper mill, but in 1906, its new owners decided to restore it to its original state. Before Venarey les Laumes, the village immediately next lock 57, Les Granges sous Grignon is the family seat of the Buffon family, where there is an attractive 13th and 15th century church and an 11th and 15th century chateau. But the first proper stopping place is Venarey les Laumes itself, 9 locks and just over 12 km from Montbard. The lock here heralds the end of the relaxed regime that started at Laroches Migennes with boaters free to cruise and moor at will, and lock-keepers free to go the extra hour - as well as to disappear on a mini shopping spree during their morning stint.

After Venarey les Laumes things undergo a sea-change and the long haul to the summit at Pouilly en Auxois begins in earnest. From here on, boats move in organised convoys between locks 55Y at Venarey (the Y signifying Yonne) and 16Y at Charigny. Each of the 9 special convoy-assembling locks displays a board with the times of departure: e.g. 0900, 1330 and 1630 when moving upstream from 55Y to 50Y. Lock-keepers also distribute rather poor photo-copies of hand-drawn schedules. The regime is, in the main, strict and efficient, with two keepers, each with a car, keeping boaters constantly on the move. However, some stretches are single-manned, and when the distance is no more than one or two kilometres between locks, it takes the keeper far longer than the boater to get from point to point.

Venarey les Laumes has a new marina run by a hire-boat company. On the left bank, at the bridge between locks 56 and 55, it is equipped with all mod cons, but depth in the main is no better than 1.2m.

The quayside is in excellent order, and is consequently popular with berthing space at a premium. The small town of les Laumes and the smaller village of Venary are both a short walk from the locks and marina. Legend has it that the magnificent Laumes Plain is the site of the great Battle of Alesia, when Julius Caesar finally conquered the Gauls in 52 BC - while it is true that much blood was shed here by Romans and Gauls, it seems that the battle of Alesia actually took place far away - and the unvarnished truth is that the location is still a mystery. Nevertheless, it is still an awe-inspiring experience to view the spectacle of the Bourgogne Canal as it pursues its course round the Auxois hills before reaching its summit. What is real and uncontrovertible is the presence of Venarey's railway junction: justification alone for the town's 'position' of Auxois capital.

Not far away is the small community Alise Ste Reine: a portmanteau name conjuring memories of the 'Alesian' war and the martyrdom of a young Christian woman. Refusing to marry one Olibrius, the Roman governor, she was decapitated for her lack of discernment. You can weep by her fountain, which, legend dictates, sprang, poppy-like, from the blood-soaked ground where she lost her head. Many are the believers in the Lourdes-like qualities of her waters. Nearby is the chapel, a pilgrim venue, a 15th century statue of Reine, the St Leger 7/10th century church, the 1945 Roches theatre replica, and the museum, with exhibitions of statues, coins, ceramics and other objects with an evocation of the siege of Alesia.

Next in the convoy-cruising regime come the villages of Pouillenay, Marigny le Cahouet and Villeneuve sous Charigny. Pouillenay has a small basin with a decent quay and good shopping. Marigny has modest shops and a 15th century church and chateau, so a stop there is not a deprivation. However, mooring is not entirely problem free, since Marigny has only a collection of bollards - and both have depths little better than than 1.35m. Villeneuve is somewhat distant from the canal and without facilities - but it is noteworthy for marking the end of the long strictly-regulated haul and from here on up to Pouilly en Auxois the locks become further and further apart. After the nose-to-tail procession of the last cheek-by-jowl 40 locks, the two remaining before Pont Royal seem veritably isolated with all of 8km in their sole possession. Pont Royal is the last possible 'proper' stop before Pouilly en Auxois. It has a long narrow stretch of quayside on the open canal - and that is all. The water tap does not always function and the refuse bins are usually so full that they refuse refuse as it were. The deliberations of the parish council are publicly displayed on a wall by the roadside and they indicate that detailed improvements for boating and tourists have been discussed for quite some time - but so far it is all promises, promises. Pont Royal in no way lives up to any grandeur one might conjure up from its name. It is a tiny hamlet with no shops and one cafe/bar that operates in the front living rooms of one of the small cottages. The set-up is as eccentric as the proprietor and the clientele. Surprisingly, near the moorings there is a public phone that works.

There are two villages, St Thibault and Eguilly before Pouilly, but mooring is not easy at either. Apart from the unusual church in St Thibault with its 13/14th century basilica, there is little reason not to press on through the next ten locks (once again in close formation) to the summit at Pouilly where the port facilities are absolutely first-rate and comprehensive. You will be met at Pouilly lock No. 1 by friendly lock officials and the staff of Crown Blue Line who run the marina facility. They will check you out, sort you out if necessary, and send you on your legal way. More of this later, but first for the place itself, which is never seen from the boat since the famous tunnel runs right underneath it.

Pouilly en Auxois has an attractive 14/15th century church, but perhaps its most eye-catching feature is a quite amazingly old-fashioned hardware shop. It is so packed with goods, chattels, effects and equipment rarely seen away from museums that one wonders who would ever want what is on display - and what they would then do with it. One of the first attractions however, must be immediately across the road from the moorings where there is a lively little bar. Between the port and the town centre is a very good supermarket, with an excellent range of wines.

At Pouilly en Auxois, the summit tunnel and the approach cuttings are narrow. Overtaking or passing are impossible, so a rigorous one-way system is in operation. Your arrival at either end of the tunnel is carefully logged by the extremely friendly officials at the appropriate lock office, and it is they who will ensure that you are properly equipped for the trip through the tunnel. They also organise your departure. A permit to proceed is obtained at one end and handed in on arrival at the other end. This permit will not be issued unless the craft conforms to the local bye-laws, which are courteously but rigorously enforced. What the keepers mainly look for are working navigation lights, a good searchlight or a powerful torch, and a loud horn to sound in emergencies. You will also be provided with a small brochure to demonstrate how to pass through the many self-service locks that are to come - although in fact many of these actually have a peripatetic keeper in attendance.

POUILLY TO FLEUREY SUR OUCHE

Between Pouilly and Escommes you will cross the dividing pound. At the Pouilly lock the canal starts climbing down towards the Yonne and the Seine and at the Escommes lock it descends towards the Saone. Here the the summit reach is about 6km, with the canal going underground with a tunnel length magically measuring 3333 m. The tunnel first went into service in 1842 and in the beginning the navigators pulled their boats through by means of a chain attached to the wall of the tunnel. Six strong men were needed and the negotiation took 10 hours. In 1867 a chain tug was installed: a steam barge that worked by means of a chain laid on the bed of the waterway. So pestilential were the fumes generated by the boiler especially when trapped in the tunnel that many bargees fell ill and some died. In 1886 a more modern tug with a safer boiler was introduced. Seven years later, an electric boat, 15m by 3.2m wide, powered by generators situate at Pouilly and Escommes replaced the steam boat, reducing the time required for passage to 40 minutes. In the year 1903, 1300 barges and timber rafts were towed. It could tow up to 10 laden barges and left only twice a day at 0700 and 1300: the crossing cost 4 francs. The chain tug was finally put out of commission in 1987, and a diesel pusher took over in 1988. The ancient generator of electricity, "la Turbine" can be seen at lock No 1, while there are plans to restore the tug which is kept by the lock office at Pouilly.

The tunnel itself is quite beautiful: an apparent circle with the canal surface the diameter. Its sides are smooth and it is quite straight so that 'light at the end of the tunnel' can be seen as soon as you enter; the through journey being a memorable experience.

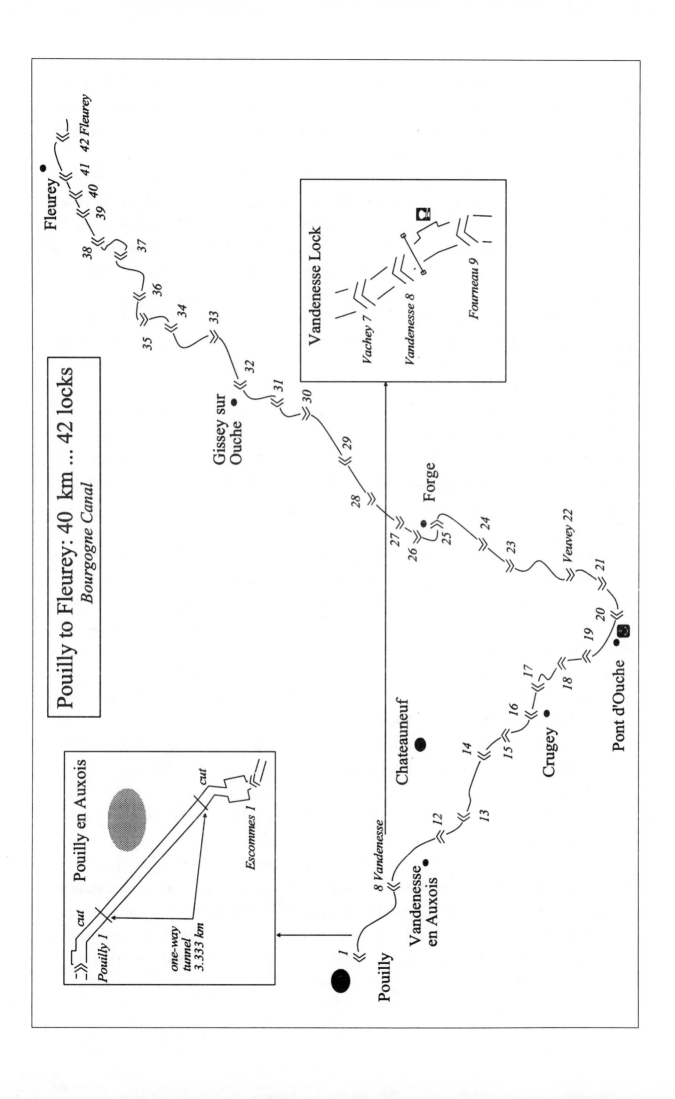

Pouilly to Fleurey: 40 km ... 42 locks
Bourgogne Canal

Fleurey

42 Fleurey
41
40
39
38
37
36
35
34
33
32
31
30
29
28
27
26
25
24
23
22 Veuvey
21
20
19
18
17
16
15
14
13
12

Gissey sur Ouche

Forge

Chateauneuf

Crugey

Pont d'Ouche

8 Vandenesse

Vandenesse en Auxois

Pouilly

1

Pouilly en Auxois

cut
cut
Pouilly 1

one-way tunnel
3.333 km

Escommes 1

Vandenesse Lock

Vachey 7
Vandenesse 8
Fourneau 9

On the practical side, headroom is restricted to craft of 3.1m in the centre, and 2.2m at the sides, and the restricting beam of the system is 5.0m. Long, strong ropes are required for the tow and a good distance must be maintained between craft. Happily, the tug operators are skilled at handling boats of all shapes and sizes and skippers of all levels of expertise.

Once through the tunnel, it is possible to moor in the Escommes basin, but the banks are not in the best of states and Vandenesse en Auxois summons most cruising folk with a clarion call. This is a healthy stretch, since the first dozen or so locks are all manual - and to be operated by ships' crews. They are all in good condition and the method of operation is clearly indicated by colour coded plates and handles. In addition, boaters are provided with sheets of instructions. Vandenesse is just under 10 km from Pouilly en Auxois and is the obvious next stopping-off place. It is so appealing that its well-equipped quayside facilities are in constant demand firstly by hotel barges and secondly by hire boats and chance passage-cruisers stand little chance of finding a decent unoccupied berth. The pretty village occupies both banks and has a good range of amenities.

Commarin, a tiny classic village of the Cote d'Or not too far away from the moorings at Vandenesse, is entirely dominated by the famous chateau. Parts of it date from the 14th century with some additions and improvements made through the 15th to 17th centuries, while the major building and reconstruction took place in the early 1700's. Much of what was done in the 1750's is still intact and it is well-known for its 16th century tapestries. Further down the canal, most easily accessible from locks 13 and 14, is the celebrated chateau at Chateauneuf. Dominating the picturesque valley for miles (almost from the tunnel exit at Escommes) this amazing and flamboyant edifice was started in the 12th century by the sire of Chaudenay for his, and the original keep still exists. Throughout the following centuries it grew and was furbished and refurbished, being 'finally' completed at the end of the 15th century. The last proprietor, le Comte G. de Vogues, made many restorations before giving it to the state in 1936. Its Round Room has a fantastic panoramic view of the plain of Morvan. The gastronomy of the Hostellerie du Chateau is famed - as are its prices. The chateau is separated from the village by a moat with an impressive drawbridge/gateway entrance. The village itself, a pleasantly hearty walk from any of locks 10-14, is also appealing, if not so dramatic as the chateau and its winding streets are a constant temptation to while away more than just a few hours.

In marked contrast, the new marina facility at Pont d'Ouche is 10 km away, with the little village of Crugey before it making a nice halfway stop for lunch. The marina with its obvious approach is well-equipped in attractive surroundings. It is the base of Force Three Boat Rental and is well used by hotel barges; as is the one bar/cafe/restaurant - run by an English couple who will warmly embrace you while tempting you to over indulge.

In the 15km between Pont d'Ouche and Gissey sur Ouche there are many small villages and hamlets affording a genuine welcome, especially Veuvey and Forge. The scenery gains in grandeur: the valley opens out ahead as the tree-lined canal is accompanied on its straightish route by the curves of the lovely Ouche. Gissey is an intriguing mixture of old and new with a superfluity of restaurants - the closest of which makes its own bread. The area is used by special units of the French Marines who both rush

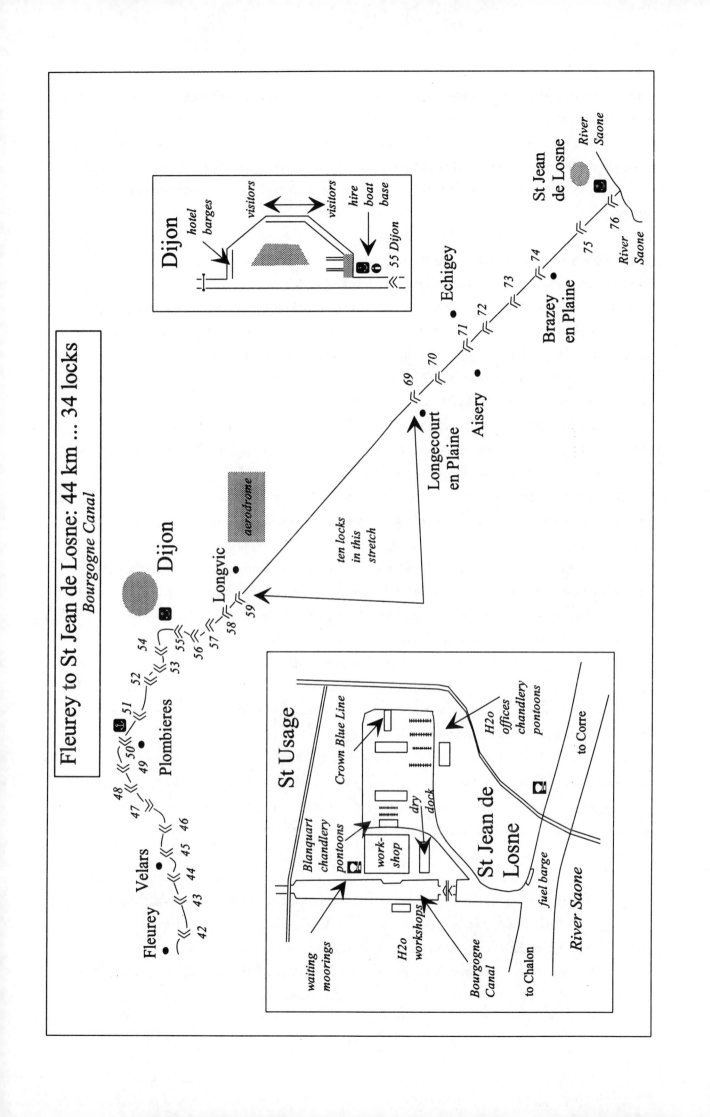

Fleurey to St Jean de Losne: 44 km ... 34 locks
Bourgogne Canal

Fleurey Velars

42 43 44 45 46 47 48 49 50 51 52 54 53 55 56 57 58 59

Plombieres

Dijon

Longvic

aerodrome

ten locks in this stretch

Longecourt en Plaine

Aisery

69 70 71 72 73 74 75 76

Echigey

Brazey en Plaine

St Jean de Losne

River Saone

River Saone

Dijon

hotel barges

visitors

visitors

hire boat base

55 Dijon

St Usage

Crown Blue Line

H2o offices chandlery pontoons

to Corre

Blanquart chandlery pontoons

work-shop

dry dock

St Jean de Losne

fuel barge

River Saone

waiting moorings

H2o workshops

Bourgogne Canal

to Chalon

and lurk without explanation. There is a small but very shallow basin just before the old bridge; but just after it there are plenty of bankside moorings with good depth.

For those who want to get on, Dijon is now within striking distance, but for those with time to linger there are quite a few possible resting places in the 25km before the capital itself. Ste Marie sur Ouche and Pont de Pany are close by: both enjoyable miniature experiences but neither with more than basics.

FLEUREY SUR OUCHE TO ST JEAN DE LOSNE

Fleurey sur Ouche and Velars sur Ouche are slightly larger villages, and the latter has the attraction of a supermarket immediately next the canal - where there are good depths, but also shoals and unexpected debris, so take care. Six kilometres on, at Plombieres les Dijon, there is a well-equipped marina facility (nearly 30km since the last) in the basin run by a hire-boat company. This is where change towards city life begins: attitudes are just that more sophisticated and the prices in the shops and the many restaurants reflect this shift.

Dijon, with its wide and open marina basin, is 5km away. It is a must as a stopover, the city being utterly fascinating; but the charges enforced at the marina make it one of the most expensive on the canals - even rivalling the coastal resorts of the Med. Its setting goes some way to mitigating these charges, being well laid out with attractive gardens and overlooked by a dramatic obelisk. Its 600 hextares of green space include a Lake Kir and Green Strip - both susceptible of ambiguous perceptions. The marina is efficient and all the services generally work well - but it is not always possible to find the staff. The charms of the city (which need a book of their own) are no more than a good walk away, but everyday needs can be met locally. Capital of Burgundy, Dijon used to reign supreme over a state that extended from the Frisian islands to Burgundy, and it is packed with standing relics of its fantastic past. In particular, the Palais des Duc et des Etats de Bourgogne with the Musee des Beaux Arts; the Quartier du Palais de Justice; the Chartreuse de Champmol and the Cathedrale St Benigne are arresting and time-consuming in their attributes. For gourmets, Dijon is a small paradise. The Maille mustard shop displays its famous command from Napoleon - but it is only one of hundreds of treats in store and in stores. Dijon has an absolutely splendid market - the pride of the area.

A speciality of the area not to be missed is the veritable Kir made from Bourgogne Aligote and Creme de Cassis. Both should be of superior quality with strengths of 12% and 15% respectively and extremely well-chilled. My preferred proportion for the classic 'straight' Kir is four-to-one wine to Cassis - but experiment is definitely to be recommended when near to a good champagne area for the heady Kir Royal.

By the time Dijon has been reached, the scenery has become less dramatic, the canal thereafter tending more to the straight and featureless; that is, except for the military airport on the outskirts. Its radar can cause eccentricities on echo-sounders, and the low-flying French airmen seem to adopt a regime adapted from their car-driving cousins. The din can be horrendous.

Between Dijon and St Jean de Losne the map indicates an absolute straight-line journey. At first glance, this might seem unprepossessing, but in fact the countryside is by no means unpleasing, and the trip can be an undemanding last leg to the Saone.

The standard halfway house stop on the way to St Jean de Losne is Longecourt en Plaine. It has a wide basin just after the lock with good depths in most places. The village which has good basic shops and services is a brisk walk away. An alternative halt before the end of all things rustic is the canalside near Brazey. This small town has many more shops, bars and restaurants but is very close to St Jean de Losne (just 2 locks and 5 km) where the Canal de Bourgogne ends its journey and meets the River Saone.

Here, you hand in your stamped card at the lock office. Once this minor piece of administration has been undertaken (and it can last half an hour) you are free to move on: straight ahead and out into the wide river, where it is just possible to moor against the banks, or turn to port under the bridge for the large Gare d'Eau. This houses a number of operations: Monsieur Joel Blanquart's Port Fluvial, the first collection of moorings to port; next, H2O to starboard, the Port de Plaisance run by the Anglo/French team of Robert Bond and Charles Gerard; and, last, in the far depths of the basin, is HQ of Crown Blue Line hire boats.

Monsieur B is an ex-barge skipper whose office and chandlery are on board a barge - so that everyone feels at home. He has been established for a long time and his reputation is sound right down the Saone. H2O is also reliable and is expanding year by year with well-found pontoons offering all mod cons; a comprehensive chandlery; friendly and efficient staff - with language no problem for English only speakers. Reasonable charges make it an attractive proposition for the many Brits who stop and then stay. In addition, the Tourist Office, laundrette and supermarket are immediately next door.

St Jean de Losne and Losne are two quite separate communities facing each other across the river, their connection being the wide road bridge. Originally they were one: known as Latona, then Laone, then Lone and finally Losne - and at that time St Jean was no more than a hamlet. Between them they provide enough amenities and places of interest for several days holiday, let alone a canal stopover. St Jean, in particular, has many old streets with delights around each corner. All in all, there are few needs, domestic or boating, that cannot be met in St Jean de Losne.

CHAPTER SIX

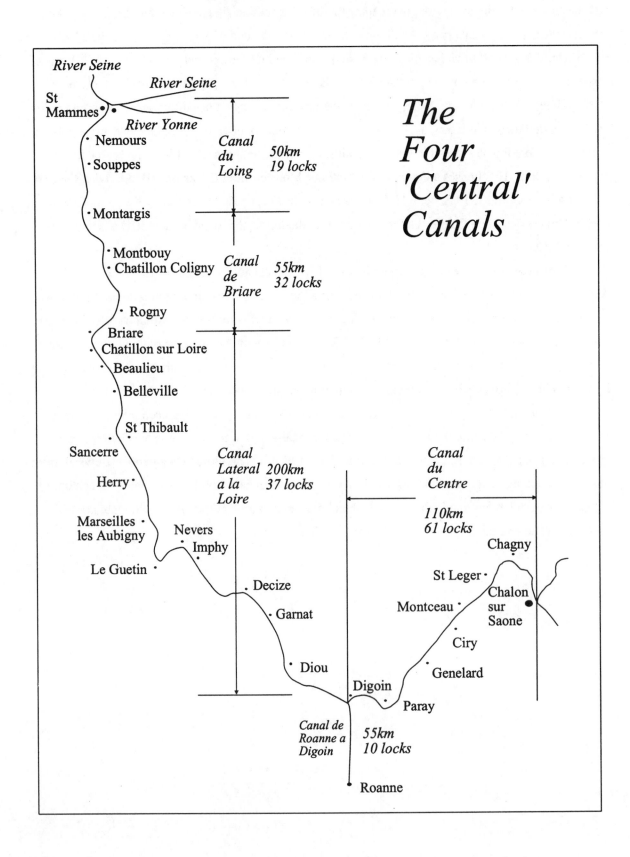

River Seine

River Seine

St Mammes

River Yonne

· Nemours

· Souppes

Canal du Loing   50km 19 locks

· Montargis

· Montbouy
· Chatillon Coligny   *Canal de Briare*   55km 32 locks

· Rogny

· Briare
· Chatillon sur Loire
· Beaulieu
· Belleville

· St Thibault

Sancerre

Herry ·

Marseilles les Aubigny

Nevers
· Imphy

Le Guetin ·

· Decize

· Garnat

· Diou

Canal Lateral a la Loire   200km 37 locks

The Four 'Central' Canals

Canal du Centre

110km 61 locks

Chagny

St Leger ·

Montceau   Chalon sur Saone

· Ciry

· Genelard

Digoin

· Paray

Canal de Roanne a Digoin   55km 10 locks

· Roanne

PART ONE: CANAL DU LOING - ST MAMMES TO CEPOY

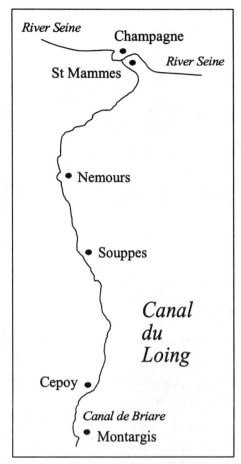

The junction of the Canal du Loing with the River Seine is a large and unmistakable one, more like a lake or inland water sport area than a mere confluence. At first glance both waterways seem to run straight ahead; while a second glance shows that the River Seine tends to starboard while the River Loing tends to port. The Loing route does not stay as a river for long: after no more than a couple of kilometres there comes the parting of the ways with the first lock leading, not into a canalised river, but a completely man-made canal: the Canal du Loing.

Immediately after the junction, to starboard on the left bank, there hoves into view what seems to be a small convocation of pleasure craft. With a sinister black buoy for sentinel, it has all the hallmarks and the air of an unwelcoming, unsalubrious society. For years, St Mammes has been filled with barges, most of them empty and somewhat hopelessly hoping for work. The apparently vacant spots along the bankside looked tempting, but many of them are reserved for trip boats. First choice and port of call for many visitors (especially Brits) has long been the boat station run by the friendly Englishman, John Faulkner, but there was not always room at the inn - although his shop was open almost all hours. Now, the good news is that there are well-laid and well-advanced plans for a new marina facility to open on the site in time for the begining of the 1995 season - all being well in the same capable hands.

There were, and still are, alternatives. If you are lucky, you might find a vacant berth on the public quaysides or happen upon a friendly barge. If even luckier, you might squeeze into a gap at the halte nautique. Other choices take you back into the River Seine, where, just round the corner, where the fairground and market are, it is occasionally possible to squeeze in or, once again, to hang on to a barge. The final option is further up the Seine where, on the left bank just upstream, is the Base Nautique and Sailing Club of St Mammes.

Back in the River Loing, there are black marker buoys in St Mammes before the first lock. They are to starboard towards the left bank, marking the parting of the ways with the river itself. Their intention is to ward skippers off, and their mere aspect does that really well.

Once through the first lock, Moret 19, and into the canal system there are two potential stopping places at the villages of Ecuelles and Episy. The latter, a very small and pleasant village has an intriguingly neat little restaurant situate most conveniently just by the lock. Its value was remarkable: their 59FF menu comprised an entree buffet, full main course, cheese, dessert and a pitcher of wine to choice. It is usefully also a bar/tabac.

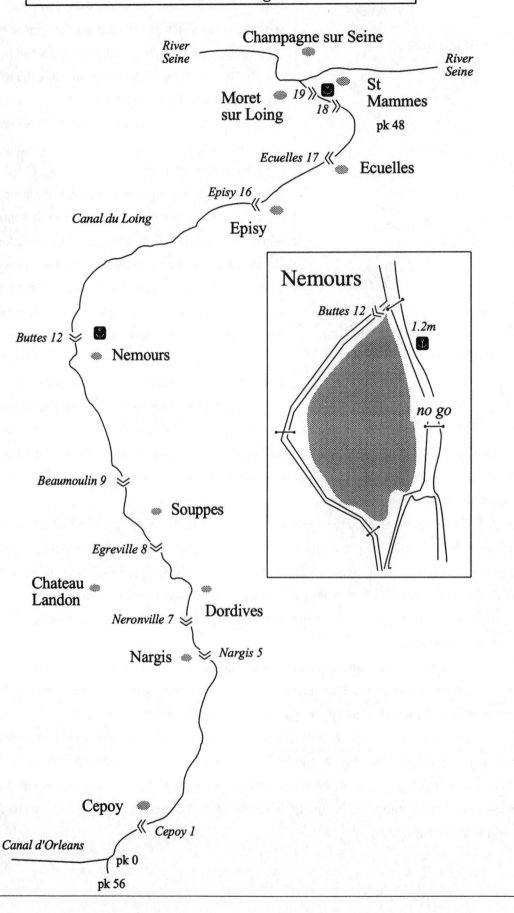

St Mammes to Cepoy: 50 km ... 18 locks
Canal du Loing

River Seine

Champagne sur Seine

River Seine

Moret sur Loing

19 St Mammes

18

pk 48

Ecuelles 17 Ecuelles

Episy 16

Canal du Loing

Episy

Nemours

Buttes 12

Nemours

Buttes 12

1.2m

no go

Nemours

Beaumoulin 9

Souppes

Egreville 8

Chateau Landon

Dordives

Neronville 7

Nargis *Nargis 5*

Cepoy *Cepoy 1*

Canal d'Orleans

pk 0

pk 56

The 15km or so to Nemours, during which the river rejoins the canal, are not among the most scenic and the canal itself suffers from shoal patches. These are not too grim depth-wise and the bottom is entirely soft. At the confluence of river and canal, there is a ghastly collection of broken poles and posts. Not only are they most unpleasant to look at, but they also represent a hazard if a careful watch has not been kept.

The approach to Nemours is wide and somewhat bleak. The river continues straight ahead under a bridge to the halte nautique which has a depth restricted to little over a metre. The canal is to starboard round a sharp bend and under another bridge. It is worth signalling with the ship's whistle. The lock office at Buttes 12 is a control point. Bearing in mind what a busy junction it is for Med-bound traffic, it is surprising that the operation is still run from a small wooden office that is pathetically equipped and inadequately staffed. The lock-keeper was as unskilled as the one I had first met six years before. In spite of my spelling out my details and actually showing him the real Lloyd's ship's papers, he still felt it necessary for me to write it all down for him in his scruffy log book. Wine was already being vastly consumed at 10 o'clock in the morning. When I asked him about lock-keepers closing for lunch, he said with a Gallic shrug of the shoulders and an equally Gallic raising of the eyebrow: "Some eat ... some don't. Some stop ... some don't".

While on the subject of the idiosyncracies of lock-keepers, I have always found it intriguing that, during the raise-and-fall lock cycle, many keepers make a habit of going into their house, cabin or office for perhaps no more than a minute or so and then wandering out again. More energy must be expended in getting to their seat to have a rest than in just standing still, if they did not bother to go.

There are many extensive lengths of quaysides in the town of Nemours. Most of them are unattractively undustrial and none has any facility for leisure craft. However, it is easy enough to find a place to tie up. The second bridge, in the centre of the town has a very bad blind corner, especially coming from upstream, and it is a good idea to use the whistle again.

The ancient settlement of Nemours is now an attractive town: its new buildings in near classical style, blend extremely well with the really old stuff and are set off beautifully by the tree-lined banks. After the last bridge, the tree-lined canal becomes even more attractive and the biefs now tend to be wider and deeper with many legs where there was as much as 2m under Valcon.

The next major port of call is Montargis, just over 30km distant and actually on the Canal de Briare, but there are smaller places of note en route. They are Souppes, Dordives and Nargis. Neronville 7 is the lock for both Dordives on the right bank and Chateau Landon further inland on the opposite side. The stretches just before and after the lock are positively beset with herons of noticeably slender stature: they are either young or a special breed. I asked around, but the locals were not aware of any local particulars. I felt there must be an ancient heronry in the district but could get neither confirmation nor information.

The halte nautique at Cepoy, in recent times has consisted of no more than a completely broken down mains power and water station, a big dustbin, and a rough quay with no bollard to be seen. Close by is a large quay with big bollards but with sloping sides that make access diffcult.

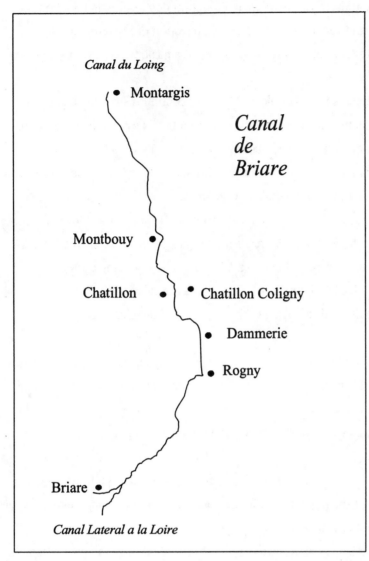

Canal du Loing

● Montargis

Canal de Briare

Montbouy ●

Chatillon ● ● Chatillon Coligny

● Dammerie

● Rogny

Briare ●

Canal Lateral a la Loire

After the disappointment of Cepoy, Montargis, the first port of call on the Canal de Briare, is a compensatory joy. The approach to the first lock bodes really well for the town that is to come. When seen from the soft under-belly of its canal, Montargis displays itself as a picturesque, flower-bedecked vision. In particular, the bridges are very prettily decorated, making the journey through the town especially enjoyable. There is plenty of wall space for mooring in the town, but no site to compare with the general sights of the town. The castle ruins, the church of la Ste Madeleine with its marvellous choir and the Girodet Museum exhibiting 'local' art allegedly going back into prehistoric times are well worth a day spent here.

There are spacious mooring quays on the left bank at the next, comparatively large, lock, la Marolle 33. While it is modest by comparison with those to come on the Saone and the Rhone, com-

pared with most on the Central route it is a substantial affair. Next comes a length of locks before the relief of Montbouy. The Montbouy 26 lock is very pleasingly found in a rural setting with the 9th century church standing tall behind the trees and shrubs; indeed, there are trees on all sides. The Montbouy halte consists of a small quay, modest bollards and mains power, water and showers. It is a charming spot. The small town has all basic shops as well as Roman ruins and relics of the Templars.

The stretch between Montbouy and Chatillon Coligny is marked in general by the rather strange absence of fishermen and the unhappy presence of many large, dead fish and assorted animals in various stages of putrefaction. There are also wooden stakes on the bank sides which, of course, are to be avoided - not always easy since some extend well into the waterway and are almost hidden under the surface. One bank side is usually more silted and encumbered than the other: you therefore need to thread your way through the channel to avoid causing too much disturbance on the 'wrong' side. In addition, if you read the banks and the water correctly you can navigate towards the 'right' side much faster than on the other.

The halte nautique at Chatillon Coligny was finished as recently as May 1994. It is about 100m

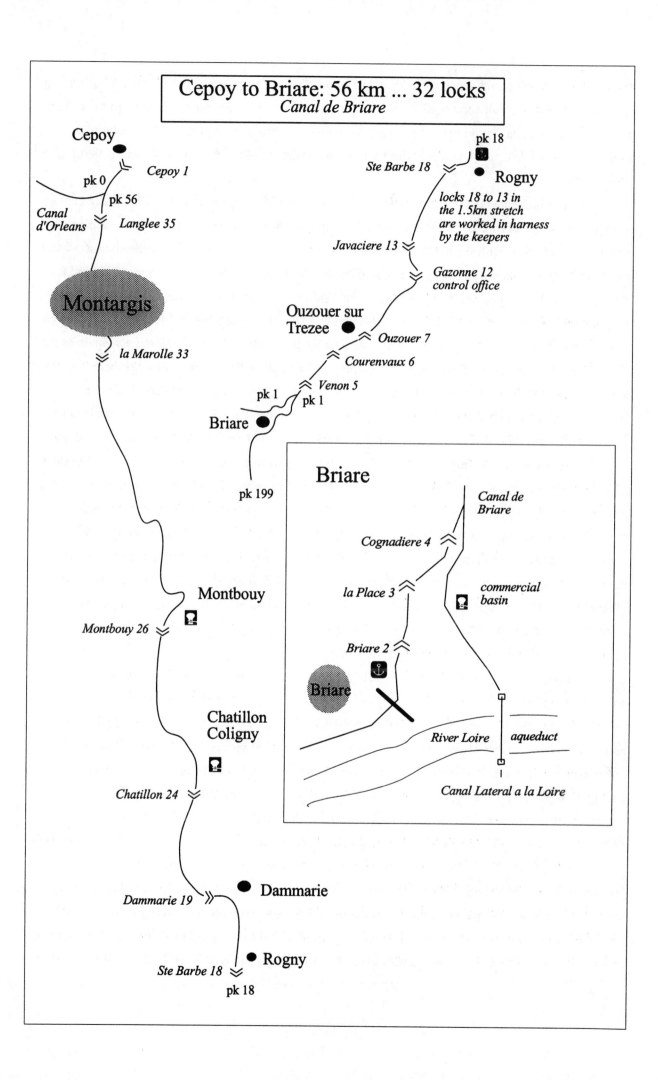

Cepoy to Briare: 56 km ... 32 locks
Canal de Briare

Cepoy

pk 0 — *Cepoy 1*

pk 56 — *Langlee 35*

Canal d'Orleans

Montargis

la Marolle 33

pk 18

Ste Barbe 18 — Rogny

locks 18 to 13 in the 1.5km stretch are worked in harness by the keepers

Javaciere 13

Gazonne 12 control office

Ouzouer sur Trezee

Ouzouer 7

Courenvaux 6

pk 1 — *Venon 5* — pk 1

Briare

pk 199

Montbouy

Montbouy 26

Chatillon Coligny

Chatillon 24

Dammarie 19 — Dammarie

Ste Barbe 18 — Rogny

pk 18

Briare

Canal de Briare

Cognadiere 4

la Place 3

commercial basin

Briare

Briare 2

⚓

River Loire — aqueduct

Canal Lateral a la Loire

long with mains power and water, showers and a sanitary station - quite unusual, this latter. The mooring is absolutely first rate: fully serviced, clean and tidy, with the gardener appearing all ready to sweep the path by Valcon's berth the moment I tied up. Shopping is easy and good; and there are two churches, a museum, the town hall and the ruins of the 12th century castle built by the Count of Sancerre all offering plenty to see.

Rogny is the next major halt, but the small community of Dammarie by lock 19 is a nice enough place to rest, and it has one of France's famous municipal wash-houses. The Port at Rogny has plenty of water in the entrance, but little more can be said in its favour. It somewhat ostentatiously advertises itself as a Paying Port, suggesting perhaps some space and services. In fact, there is little room inside and it is difficult for craft of more than 9m just to turn round: Valcon had to go astern to get out. The seven-lock staircase built at the direction of Heni IV is a masterpiece in both engineering and aesthetics. The design was efficient and the only real improvement is that the six present locks permit craft to pass, whereas the old staircase was 'impassable' and thus 'impossible'. Close by the village lock and bridge there is a clean quay with good bollards but no other facilities. All this is a pity, since Rogny is a place deserving just to be viewed as well as photographed and visited. There is also a plenitude of good shops and restaurants.

Different from all the other canals on the central circle, the Canal de Briare theoretically shuts down for the keepers to eat from 1200 to 1230 - whether they have already done so or not ... and in spite of perhaps not having passed a single boat before. Some of them apply the rule with a vengeance: closing ten minutes early and opening another ten minutes late. However, not all of them are so obstinately stubborn. The more intelligent and co-operative ones say "Well if I know I've two boats coming up and three going down, after which there will be nothing for an hour and a half I am very happy to pass them all through and eat later". Unfortunately, the Rogny sequence suffers from 'the enemy within'; and in spite of its efficient, electrically-operated locks, it is badly organised and much unnecessary time is lost. A point worth noting is that for craft waiting for the lock to be filled in order to descend there will be a strong pull towards the lock as it takes its water from the bief.

Gazonne 12 is the licensing control office here, and papers will be examined. The whole of the area is surrounded by lakes and pounds, many of which are resplendent with lilies and swans. Only one keeper on the Canal de Briare offered anything for sale; fruit, veg, poultry and wine. He was the personable guy at Gazon 23 and he brought on display a splendid array of pizzas and pear tarts. Now there is one potential stopping place before eponymous Briare and that is at Ouzouer sur Trezee. It is a pleasant enough village with good shopping, and reasonable arrangements for mooring.

There are two choices when it comes to stopping over at Briare, that is if your craft draws lees than 1.2m: first, the fully equipped marina right in the heart of the town and reached down the old branch line; second, the commercial basin in predictably semi-industrial surroundings where there are hire boats and trip boats as well as large barges. On many occasions, I have found it impossible to discover a mooring space in this basin which has a slipway at the far end. Briare marina is open from 0800 until 2100 from the beginning of June to the end of August. So; what with the hassle of having to negotiate the three locks to get to the marina (in what is a very lively and often noisy and bustly spot); and the difficulties of finding a vacant berth in the commercial basin, it seems hardly worthwhile when there are alternatives at Chatillon sur Loire (see below), Ouzouer sur Trezee and Rogny.

There is one matter that will bring most craft to a halt however, and that is the aqueduct or canal bridge over the River Loire. It is a staggering monument, 11.5m wide and some 662m long, the biggest of its kind in Europe. It was built in 1890 by Eiffel, he of the Paris Tower fame. Straight as a die, you can see from end to end - and a brilliant sight it is.

PART THREE: CANAL LATERAL A LA LOIRE - BRIARE TO NEVERS

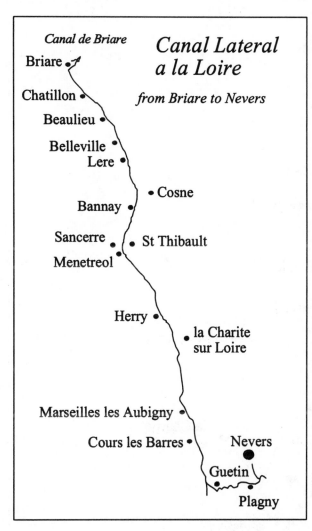

Canal de Briare

Canal Lateral a la Loire

from Briare to Nevers

Briare
Chatillon
Beaulieu
Belleville
Lere
Cosne
Bannay
Sancerre
Menetreol
St Thibault
Herry
la Charite sur Loire
Marseilles les Aubigny
Cours les Barres
Nevers
Guetin
Plagny

The very good news is that the lock-keepers on the Canal Lateral a la Loire and the Canal du Centre have got themselves very well accustomed to the antics of leisure craft and their crews. They now seem really pleased to serve them as efficiently and speedily as possible - and with lots of friendly help. I found this a noticeably happy change from my first visit six years before.

At Chatillon sur Loire, just a short distance from Briare, there are very good, really stable pontoons, with mains power (60 amps!) and water. The halte itself is attractively laid out as is the rural area just round the corner. This latter spot has lots and lots of shade from the afternoon sun. It is a complete transformation from when I first visited six years ago. Nearby, the bar has been smartened up but the clientele is as traditional as ever. Prices have changed: a glass of wine which was 3FF is now 10FF and the price of meals has quadrupled. All in all however, an excellent spot and much to be preferred to Briare.

Next comes the halte nautique at Beaulieu which is little more than a poor quay. The official notices advertising it suggests there is room for 6 boats and all services. In fact there is water and a dustbin. However, it is a pretty little spot; the quay does have a few mooring rings and the largish village has all good facilities. Unexpectedly, there is old-fashioned iron works nearby, undertaking all kinds of tasks in its various forges.

The next village, Belleville is very well named. Its banks are well planted with flowers and shrubs and tidily looked after. There are bollards at the quay by the bridge and the lock, where there is also a slipway with electricity and a decent depth adjacent. Some of the mooring points are a little short

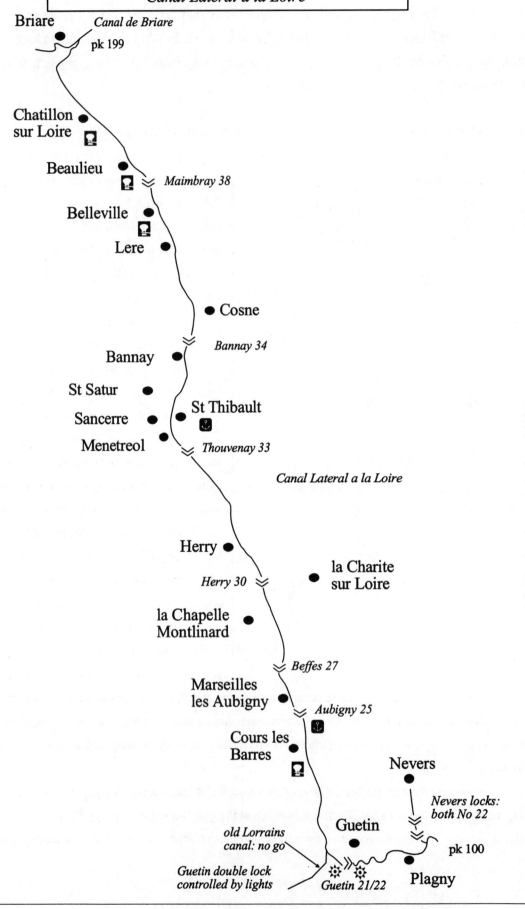

Briare to Nevers: 100 km ... 16 locks
Canal Lateral a la Loire

Briare — *Canal de Briare*

pk 199

Chatillon sur Loire

Beaulieu — *Maimbray 38*

Belleville

Lere

Cosne

Bannay 34

Bannay

St Satur

Sancerre — St Thibault

Menetreol — *Thouvenay 33*

Canal Lateral a la Loire

Herry

la Charite sur Loire

Herry 30

la Chapelle Montlinard

Beffes 27

Marseilles les Aubigny

Aubigny 25

Cours les Barres

Nevers

Nevers locks: both No 22

Guetin

old Lorrains canal: no go

pk 100

Guetin double lock controlled by lights

Guetin 21/22

Plagny

of water, but by the lock there is a stretch with a good 1.5m with mains and showers. Somewhat unexpectedly, Belleville has a nuclear power station.

At nearby Sury pres Lere, they bravely advertise their small community as possessing general shops and a telephone. Its quayside has small bollards and is fendered off with green and white tyres: a pleasant small village stop. It is much to be preferred to the next halte at Lere where there is nothing more than a quay with bollards. The only 'services' I could find consisted of a small hut with water. It is a desolate-looking spot with a commercial silo quay. The best place to take a break between Belleville and Menetreol (nearly 25km) is Bannay, a small but busy community with a renowned hotel/restaurant.

There are all facilities at St Satur, Sancerre and St Thibault, including an easily accessible large Intermarche. The water drops once inside the Relais Nautique St Thibault and quite a number of craft experience difficulty close to the side, with much of the mooring being no more than plain wooden stakes. If you can get in, it is a more than pleasant spot in a fascinating area - with the joys of Sancerre with its famous wines and cheeses.

It should be noted that 'Parking' for boats is restricted all the way from St Thibault to Menetreol, where there is a small halte just by the bridge. It has a few chairs, some very small bollards, and is lit. There are bars and shops close by but the mains supply is locked away behind a wire fence: not only inaccessible but also not working. Menetreol is a small self-contained community, presumably no longer able to compete with St Thibault and not bothering to try.

Many road bridges near villages in this area carry signs advertising their charms and services - in spite of the fact that it is extremely difficult if not frequently impossible to moor anywhere near. That is, of course, except for 20cm draught boats. For example at the Bridge of Ste Bouize by PK152, there is a notice offering everything that you can possibly need. It is situate by an apparently attractive basin. It is a snare and a shallow weed-infested delusion and any temptation to enter should be resisted. If you look astern at this point, the hills of Sancerre rise dramatically. Ponder it, for it is the last of the dramatically picturesque for some time. One of the highest hills is topped by huge radio/tv/satellite tower. In compensation, sunflowers and vineyards now abound.

The community of Herry, lock 30, has comprehensive services and there is a very pleasant tree-lined 100m with the possibility of mooring by the bankside. There is no properly organised mooring facility however, just a small quay with rough bollards to piling, degraded walls and areas of doubtful depth. Nearby is what seems to be a permanent home for an ex-floating hotel and a large working silo.

Good moorings can be found at la Chapelle Montlinard on both sides of the basin, once commercial traffic has settled down, and also on both sides of the bridge. There is not so much depth on the upstream basin side and the working quay has better water for deeper-draught craft. Cruisers tend to moor in the west corner where there is a small quay with small bollards. It is a charming small village very close to the canal; while a little further off, across the river is la Charite sur Loire, a most attractive and intriguing old town. It makes an overnight stop a most appealing proposition.

It is possible to moor at Beffes, lock 27, which has water, loos and shops, with just a few mooring posts. Rather oddly, it also advertises repair facilities for cars. There is a small inlet where it is possible to moor, but really it is best to move on to Marseilles les Aubigny.

At Marseilles there is a new halte nautique just after the lock and at the beginning of a large basin with many barges and a small barge boatyard. It is a well-planned and well-served facility and the village is most attractive. The church stands tall and high and there is a new cafeteria overlooking the River Loire. The church clock bell is erratic: firing at 1055 and 1205 - and similarly oddly throughout the day.

Generally, there tends to be a shortage of water in the canal in this area, so craft with the maximum permitted draught deviating at all from the centre of the channel will constantly be in danger of flirting with the bottom. The fault lies not in drought conditions, but is entirely due to silting and general disrepair. Also, it is easy to be confused by the old and the new PK numbers: the old ones have not been removed and it is not always evident which are the new.

The tiny hamlet of Le Poids d'Faire, PK122/3 advertises moorings for yachts up to 1.7m. Nearby, there is a 'bankside quay' with small posts overlooked by an amazingly ramshackle house. The legend above the door says, "The Watsons", and they offer a variety of 'goods' for sale: a very pleasant, quiet spot.

In contrast, mooring posts in the form of white crosses are to be found by the bridge at Cours les Barres. There is a new piled quay, a clean stretch, all neat and nicely laid out to the picnic area and water and electricity; indeed a pleasant spot.

There are goods banks for mooring on both sides of the large double lock at Guetin and the approaches are controlled by lights. The lock is now fully mechanised and you go through in two phases. Very long ropes are needed for it is nearly a 10m fall. It can be a daunting experience, but the short aqueduct affords a good view of the valley below. There is a small settlement at Guetin with a large hotel predictably named "Bridge Hotel". Just before the cut to Nevers comes the small marina at the Port de Plagny on the right bank. Take careful note and don't pass it by before reading about Nevers below. It is a modest but welcoming facility; a small hire-boat base, Loch 2000, with all facilities and no one to chase, hassle or hustle you - even for money. It is the kind of place that has a notice: 'If we're not here - try the bar across the road'. The pontoons are sound with very good depth on the outer ones and there is usually plenty of space for visitors.

Nevers, the capital of the Nivernais region, sits on the right bank of the River Loire and is known for its host of pointed church towers in the old part of the city; its nougatine, an iced chocolate cake filled with praline cream; and as the location for Hiroshima Mon Amour, made by Alain Resnais in 1954. There is a lot to see: the 16th century palace of the Dukes of Nevers; St Cyr Ste Juliette cathedral with 6th century baptistery and 12th century tombs; the Croux and the Paris gates; the Blandin pottery museum; the 11th century St Etienne church; and the Convent of St Gildard where the body of Bernadette Soubirous is held.

But no matter how luscious and tempting its shoresides appeal, Nevers has a marina that certainly does not deserve its self-appointed nemenclature, port de plaisance. The moorings are actually to a thoroughly weedy bankside. There are some mains and water points, but otherwise nothing. There is space for no more than seven boats at best and as is often the case, sitting tenants (many of them cheating on the system and exploiting the laxity of many of the navigation officials by being more or less permanent) who are unco-operative. Sadly, that comes at the end of a dead end to which access is made tedious by the probability of having to search out the lock-keeper who may be a couple of kilometres away. Since the lock is also frequently out of order, it is something of an unattractive proposition. So: never say Nevers again.

NEVERS TO DIGOIN

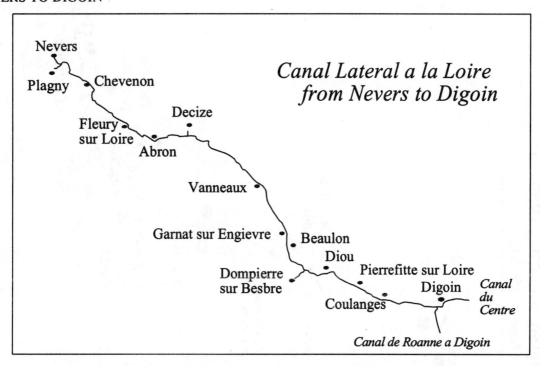

Fleury sur Loire is covered in fleury flowers. It is a small lock looked after by a big-hearted man. There is a small quay on the left bank before the bridge with a water point and a dustbin, where mooring is possible with caution since the area near the quay is, in places, badly silted. Indeed, many potentially attractive little basins have been left to silt up. They look appealing, quiet laybys - but there is no way of getting in. Some silted areas are designated by posts, some by danger signs indicating lack of depth, and some are not marked at all. Note that silt from these basins can spread into the actual canal channel with resultant general degeneration. The sides are frequently also in poor condition, but sometimes this has the bonus of bringing down to the water's edge the cattle of the area, and this is all big Charollais country.

The basic modern bridge at Avril sur Loire is quite disguised by its covering of flowers. Avril proclaims its halte nautique, but it is small with just a few black bollards and room for 2 boats, just. At lock Abron 17 there was a vacation keeper who was not only young and charming, but who actually ran round the lock to open the gates. Then comes a long stretch from Acourlan 16 to Decize with no attractive stopping place except for those who want complete isolation.

Apart from a very large television aerial, the approach to Decize can come right out of the blue. One minute it is complete countryside and the next the town. This is especially so when coming up from Gannay sur Loire. The Decize lock is automatic and there is a good stretch of quay immediately after but

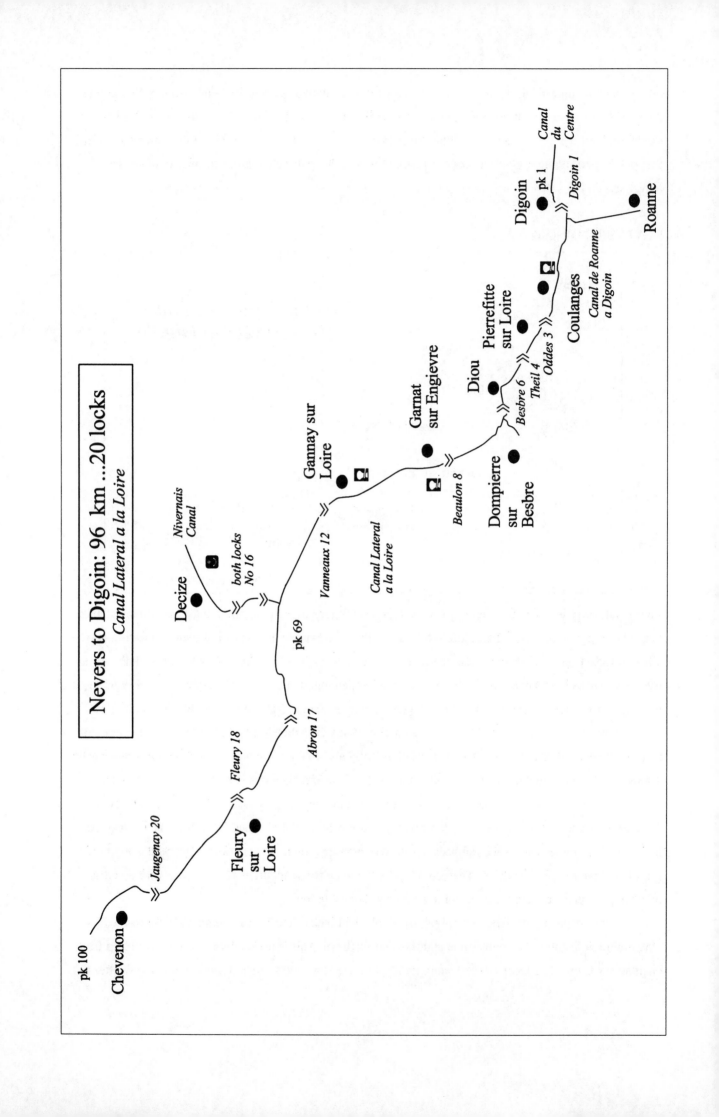

Nevers to Digoin: 96 km ...20 locks
Canal Lateral a la Loire

pk 100
Chevenon

Jaugenay 20

Fleury
sur
Loire

Fleury 18

Abron 17

pk 69

Decize

Nivernais
Canal

both locks
No 16

Vanneaux 12

Canal Lateral
a la Loire

Gannay sur
Loire

Garnat
sur Engievre

Beaulon 8

Dompierre
sur
Besbre

Diou

Pierrefitte
sur Loire

Besbre 6

Theil 4

Oddes 3

Coulanges

Canal de Roanne
a Digoin

Digoin

pk 1

Digoin 1

Canal
du
Centre

Roanne

without services. In spite of being the gateway to what is often referred to as the most beautiful canal in France, namely the Nivernais, the actual approach to Decize is quite unattractive. The town itself is attractive at a modest walk away, and locking into the basin and passing into the Nivernais syndrome is a time-consuming detour of doubtful depths. Best advice is to press on for another 15km.

To Gannay sur Loire in fact, where nearby there is a pontoon in a small basin. More significantly, Gannay is a tiny classic French village with a hire boat base where the quayside has been recently refurbished, and is now neat and clean with loos and showers, mains power and water: it is an absolutely excellent spot.

It is possible to find good moorings at Garnat sur Engievre. The local Hotel du Port is one of the reliable Logis du France. It has its own mooring posts where the river bank is piled. The large clean quay has water points and plenty of bollards. While without power, there is very good depth at the quay: a popular spot. Just over 2km along there is a very small quay for the village of Beaulon (lock 8). It is in a large basin, two-thirds of which is silted up and marked with small wooden posts. It has a sanitary station but nothing other.

Before the next main town of Diou comes the miniature deviation to Dompierre sur Besbre. The town is fascinating and a good centre for sight-seeing, but its first bridge carries navigational warnings for all but smaller craft. A few kilometres along, Diou is bigger than its nearby villages, but nevertheless has a relatively small quay with a depth no better than 1.1m. The moorings are attractively sited and are pleasantly backed by trees and well lit.

Between Theil 4 and Oddes 3, the Oujia Supermarket at Pierrefitte sur Loire goes out of its way to make its presence known in English and French and has even arranged a few mooring posts where the riverbank is well piled.

The quay at the small village of Coulanges has plenty of bollards, a loo of the old-fashioned type and a washbowl. On the small quay proudly stands the official notice board proclaiming the village's charms and the halte's facilities. Both mains power and water are advertised but none exists. There is good depth and a proper run of village shops. Like British Telecom, the PR department is ahead of the engineers.

The last stop before Digoin on the Canal du Centre is the small quay at Molinet, where I was able to find water but no power. Depths vary uncertainly along the quay. It is a pleasant, quiet spot - apart from the Route Nationale 69 that runs close by. Finally, before Digoin itself, is the junction with the Canal de Roanne a Digoin, known as "Peaceful One".

PART FOUR: CANAL DU CENTRE - DIGOIN TO BLANZY

The new port de plaisance of Digoin, known as "Paul Guichard Campionnet", is virtually at the beginning (or the end) of the Canal du Centre. After Digoin lock 1, there are four bridges before the new marina; but after the third, on the right bank, there are mooring places for craft up to 1.2m draught at what was the old marina. After the fourth bridge and the main body of the town, the new marina will be seen resplendent in its wide basin. The main part of the marina, with all facilities, which is also the HQ of a

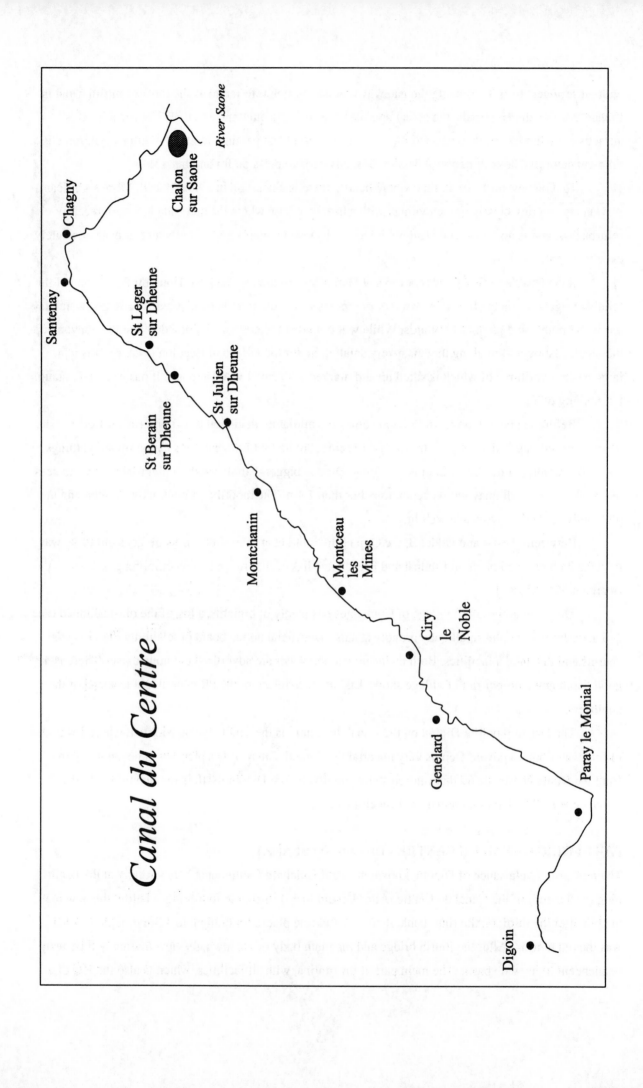

hire boat operation, is to port, while to starboard are more pontoons but without comprehensive facilities. The 24 hours' mooring is free; after that the charge depends on the boats' length plus 12FF per day for mains power and 5FF for each shower. It may be deemed expensive but it is efficient, well protected and very friendly. The town is itself a great joy and may well tempt travellers to desist from travelling a while; to rest and explore. Down the canal, just after the railway bridge, there is a bar/garage where you can order fuel. It will be delivered to the boat by tanker. The price is the cheapest I have come across in France.

The next stopping place is Paray le Monial, two locks and just over 12km after Digoin. It makes a special feature of its halte nautique from which there is a fantastic view of its 12th century church and other religious monuments and erections. It is a cult centre, devoted to the Holy Heart and Ste Marguerite Marie. There is a calm, quiet park on the north bank and a very busy road to the south. Part of the park is positively covered in season by tent after tent after tent: all devoted to the pilgrims who flock there. In general it is a quiet spot, but high-decibel chanting can go on for hours at a time. There is a very good, clean, public quay with mains power and water. In addition, it has really good depth. There is another un-serviced quay but with many bollards between the first and second bridge.

Palinges, six locks and 16km ahead has a Museum of Popular Arts - and in its turn has a small Quay of Popular Mooring. There are small bollards and a nearby picnic area and there is also a convenient car service station. The depth hereabouts is one of the lowest in the stretch, regularly dropping to substantially less than a metre below Valcon.

Between the lock and Genelard 16 and the road bridge going upstream there is a long deep cut with overgrown sloping stone walls and a massive tree verge. The attractive basin at Genelard is in fact completely silted up. There are bollards after it but you must make the big circuitous route right round the outside.

Just before Vernois 11, radar detects the passage of craft to prepare the lock. Once through the next lock, Chavannes 10, it is necessary to pull a mid-stream cord. This alerts the bridge operator who cannot see you. The two lifting bridges are worked in harness by this operator. In theory there are traffic control lights when heading upstream. There are good clean walls in the area, but with no facility for making off. However, this matters little since there is an excellent, very new and very smart port de plaisance in the heart of the busy town of Montceau les Mines. In 1994, sound floating pontoons and mains power and water points had been provided, but the services were not connected - they had been 'promised' of course. Moor well into the canal side of the basin if you can: there is a vivacious night club nearby. Once through the town, there is a Leclerc supermarket after lock Montceau les Mines 9. There is good piling here and the chances are there will be a dumb barge to hand.

Blanzy is a pleasant small town with decent quaysides but no bollards. Mooring is not implausible, but land anchors are needed. It is virtually the last possible quiet stopping place before Montchanin.

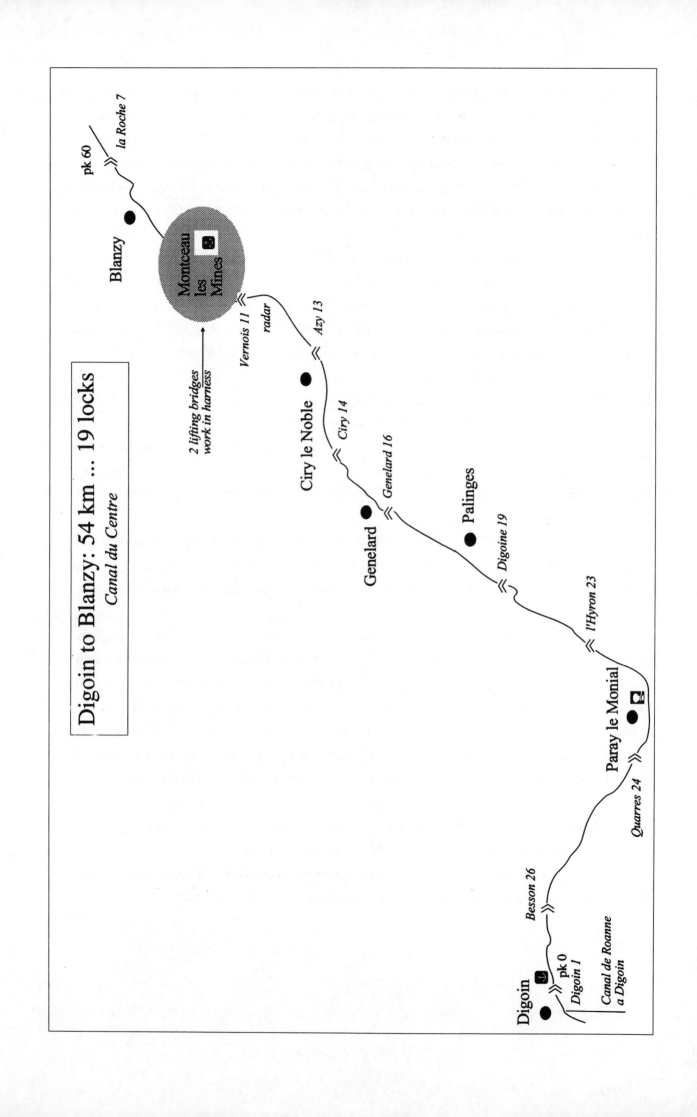

Digoin to Blanzy: 54 km ... 19 locks
Canal du Centre

la Roche 7

pk 60

Blanzy

Monteau les Mines

2 lifting bridges work in harness

Vernois 11
radar

Azy 13

Ciry le Noble

Ciry 14

Genelard 16

Genelard

Palinges

Digoine 19

l'Hyron 23

Paray le Monial

Quarres 24

Besson 26

Digoin

pk 0
Digoin 1

Canal de Roanne a Digoin

BLANZY TO CHALON SUR SAONE

Apart from the new hire-boat marina (with full facilities: for which much praise and many thanks!) the most appealing feature about Montchanin are the two locks marking the beginning and the end of the summit: Ocean 1 rising and Mediterranee 1 falling. From here on, your progress is guided and monitored by the chain operators, with much to-ing and fro-ing in the famous small white vans; and, being Gallic, many other bizarre means of travel. Unless there are special reasons to decide otherwise, the only three stopping places to be seriously considered between Montceau and Chalon sur Saone are Montchanin, where the town centre is a goodly distance from the canal, St Leger sur Dheune and Chagny.

In between, there are one or two points of note: just past Ravin 4, near the village of Ecuisse, there is a huge fruit and vegetable stall with all its goods open to the public at large. No one stands guard when the shops doors are closed for the long afternoon break - and honesty seems to work. Although there is a recently piled basin at l'Abbaye 8 there are no facilities, no restaurant and no bollards: nothing.

At St Leger sur Dheune there is a quite amazing cemetery just before lock 20. St Leger is a very popular stopping place. It has a sign for a low bridge which appears to be, if anything, slightly higher than average. There is a public quay with fuel on the south-east bank and a small inner port for craft of less than .95m. It is a good quay with water and electricity nicely situated and clean and well kept. Close by Dennevy with its flowered bridge, after lock 21, comes a very pretty area. There are small farms selling ducks, turkeys, pintades, lambs, regional products and wines. Sadly, it takes a little effort and engineering to moor, for there is nothing but overgrown banks.

Lock 23 at St Gille opened without any signal. I went in. After a minute or so, apparently with no one present, the gates closed, Valcon rose with the water level to the apparent surprise of the lock keeper who had been in ignorance of my presence.

At least two caves offer to deliver wine to the boat from Santenay. Fortunately their telephone numbers are advertised since it is a good half kilometre walk to the village. Shallow-draught boats can get in quite easily to the clean bank side with a small picnic area and waste basket. There is also a pleasant small quay where there are bollards but no other facilities.

It is now only 12 locks and about 25km to Chalon and the decent depths of the River Saone, and up to Chagny it is a very pretty stretch indeed with hills to the east and valleys and more hills further to the west. Before the last chain of eight locks and the town of Chagny, there is another chain of hoardings advertising the local wines: all the best - and all on offer. Chagny already has a good basin for mooring. It has good depth, is well lit and provided with water points. Promised for 1995 are pontoons, mains power and showers: that is, after the OAP's home has been built - the council is short of money! Comprehensive shopping is available after a briskish walk.

The main attraction must now be the vast lock, 34b, the last of the many; marking the end of the long haul from St Mammes to Chalon - a veritable Odyssey of a trip. For details of Chalon sur Saone please refer to pp.153 and 155 to 156.

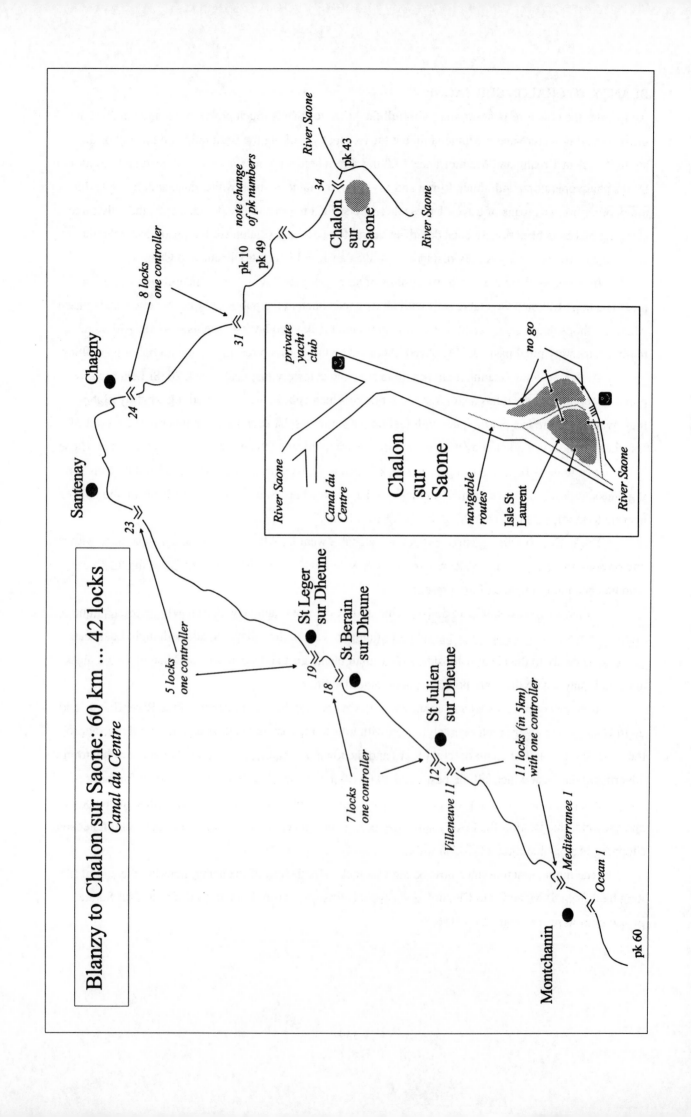

Blanzy to Chalon sur Saone: 60 km ... 42 locks
Canal du Centre

Santenay

Chagny

8 locks
one controller

note change
of pk numbers

pk 10
pk 49

pk 43
River Saone

34

River Saone

Chalon
sur
Saone

River Saone

31

24

23

private
yacht
club

no go

River Saone

Canal du
Centre

Chalon
sur
Saone

navigable
routes

Isle St
Laurent

River Saone

5 locks
one controller

St Leger
sur Dheune

St Berain
sur Dheune

19

18

7 locks
one controller

St Julien
sur Dheune

12

Villeneuve 11

11 locks (in 5km)
with one controller

Mediterranee 1

Ocean 1

Montchanin

pk 60

CHAPTER SEVEN

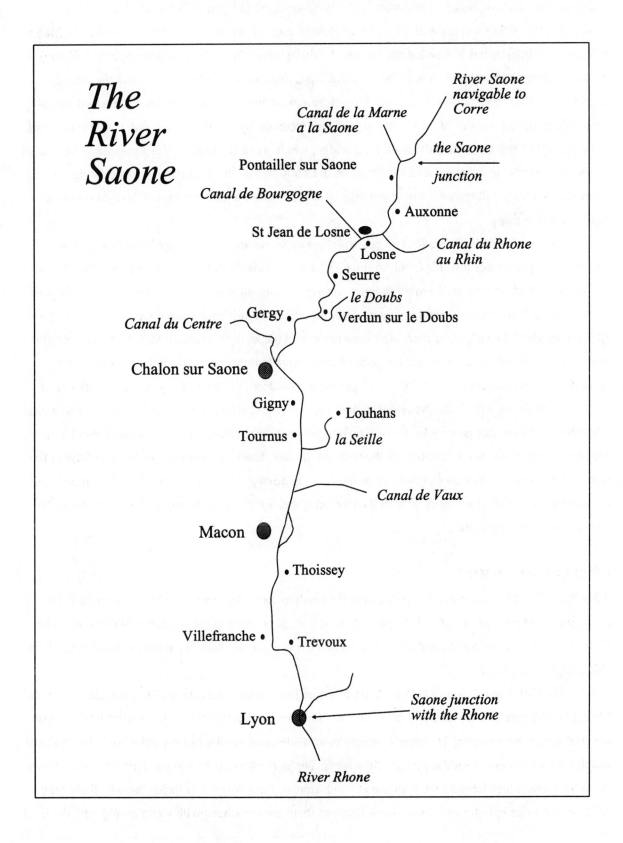

The River Saone

River Saone navigable to Corre

Canal de la Marne a la Saone

the Saone junction

Pontailler sur Saone

Canal de Bourgogne

Auxonne

St Jean de Losne

Losne

Canal du Rhone au Rhin

Seurre

le Doubs

Gergy

Verdun sur le Doubs

Canal du Centre

Chalon sur Saone

Gigny

Louhans

Tournus

la Seille

Canal de Vaux

Macon

Thoissey

Villefranche

Trevoux

Lyon

Saone junction with the Rhone

River Rhone

THE RIVER SAONE

The Saone, river-real or canalised, is navigable upstream as far as Corre where it meets the Canal de l'Est which goes on towards Nancy. The Saone is 365km from Corre to Lyon with a total of 24 locks. However, only 250km and eight of the locks are downstream of the junction with the Canal de la Marne and since our interest lies in moving towards the Mediterranean, we shall be looking only at that section. At the junction, there are two choices for mooring: first, you can stay in the canal, using the recently improved facilities near the last two locks. Or, you can move into the Saone, passing through the Heuilly lock to Pontailler, a couples of kilometres away. Here there are two opportunities: one is to use the marina on the right bank just before the main road bridge, where there is a bridge with a maximum headroom of 3m. The other is to use the public moorings on the same side of the river just below the bridge. Pontailler is a small village with a modest range of shops, while the larger centre of Vonges is only a short cycle ride away.

Once in the river, dramatic contrasts with the previous canal systems are immediately manifest. As the Saone progresses towards Lyon, so it widens and deepens. However, it does not deepen all over and it is necessary to keep to the main channel, always tending, if anything and commercial traffic permitting, towards the centre. In spite of much dredging, there are still banks and shoals to be avoided and on some bends and confluences there are sand/mud/gravel banks to be avoided. However, the over-all news is good, for all the hazards and important navigational features are well-marked: locks, weirs, bridges, one-way stretches, watersport areas and the like. Indeed, the buoyage system is excellent and provided you do not stray from the clearly-marked channels and always approach the banks with caution whether mooring or just passing by, there is no danger at all. Navigating well within the channel and keeping an eye on the depth sounder are the order of the day. There is, of course, the natural flow of the river also to be noted. In season, it will assist those going downstream to the tune of 2-3 km/hr and is of nothing but help. Out of season, and with the river in spate, a journey upstream for leisure craft can be difficult, slow and hazardous.

HEUILLEY TO TOURNUS

After Pontailler, the most natural port of call is the small town of Auxonne, one lock and about 20km away. But before it, and just after Pontailler, there is a small pontoon at the restaurant above Lamarche. Naturally, it is reserved for the use of clients and since it is a popular spot, it cannot be relied upon to provide a night's stop-over.

The lock that intervenes is Poncey 19, at the end of a small 'derivation'. This, the 'derivation de Poncey' is the first of many you will encounter and they are frequently laid out in exactly the same manner. The navigable waterway becomes a straight man-made canal stretch ironing out a big bend, many of which have ultimately created actual Ox-Bow lakes. The upstream entrance to the derivation is protected by guard gates, which have all the appearances and some of the attributes of locks, but which are only called into service in times of serious flood. Some of them are associated with weirs giving onto the river

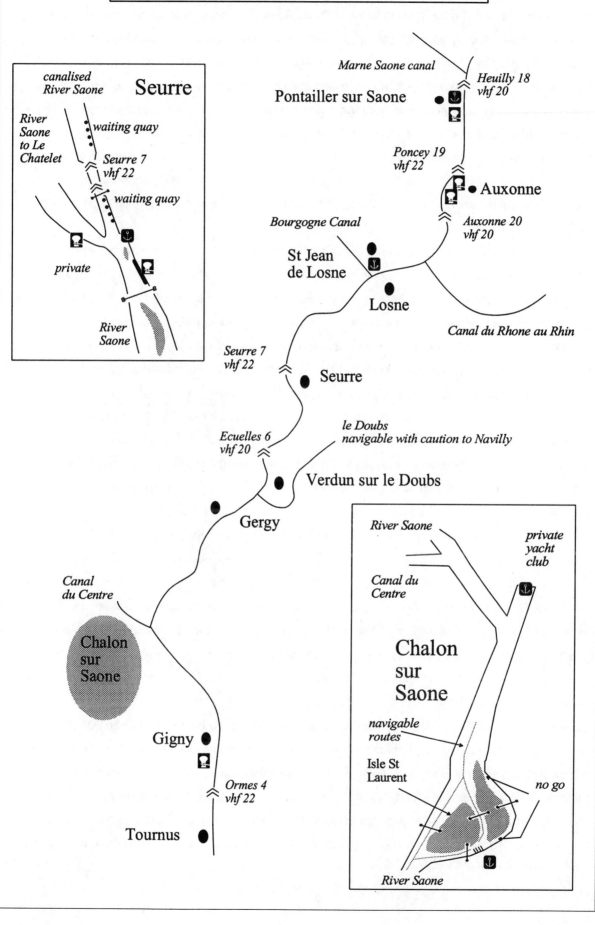

stretch, and these should, of course, be studiously avoided.

After a couple of unstraightened bends, Auxonne appears on the left. Before you reach the moorings, another feature of river life is to be seen: the markers of reserved watersport/ski areas. The buoys come in so many shapes, sizes and colours that their detailed meanings are by no means clear to the uninitiated passer-by. However, their over-all message is abundantly clear: Keep Clear. Within or close by these areas there is often a ski-jump ramp; sometimes extremely solid but occasionally quite rickety. I have never actually seen one in use, but I have seen and encountered the antics of the speedy jet-ski set. The chances are that you will not succeed in a navigation of the Saone or the Rhone without being buzzed by many a speed boat with skier in attendance - some of whom pay more attention to you than to their own business with the result that they come to a damp conclusion, perhaps immediately in your course. While many are really quite skilled and smooth customers, all such should be regarded with suspicion and avoided with care.

Auxonne has a good pontoon mooring on the left bank after the ski area and before the bridge. There is also the public town quay on the same bank just after the bridge. The town is an attractive resting spot, with a good range of shops and many more restaurants than the much larger twinned towns of Losne and St Jean de Losne farther downstream. When leaving the mooring, take care to keep to port and make for the derivation canal, leaving the island and the untouched river well to starboard. Once past the Auxonne 20 lock, it is just under 20km to St Jean de Losne, and the only other navigational item of note is the junction with the Canal du Rhone au Rhin, 4km above the town on the left bank.

It is not necessary to pass through a lock to reach the marinas in St Jean. You just turn right into the Canal de Bourgogne and then take the first turn to starboard under the bridge when after a short cut, the pontoons become apparent. For a map and full description of the facilities at St Jean de Losne please see pp. 129/131. In fact, it may not be necessary to leave the river to find a mooring for the night, for there are spaces upstream of the canal junction on the right bank. There are, in addition, barges often tied up both up and downstream of the road bridge and they are usually happy to accommodate a 'hanger-on'. Finally, an important amenity: there is a fuel barge immediately upstream of the canal entrance on the right bank. The proprietor and his wife are both fans of cruising folk and go out of their way to oblige.

A couple of kilometres downstream, in the old lock on the right bank, the marina company H2O at St Jean have established a mooring facility. It is mainly given over to residents, but is not unavailable as a haven. Just a little farther on comes the longer Pagny-Seurre derivation. For the last few kilometres before the Seurre 7 lock, the canal is provided with a plenitude of ladders - a most unusual amenity this - providing plenty of easy points of access to the quiet surrounding countryside. In spite of this, most people will want to press on to Seurre, where the public pontoons are to be found after the lock and opposite the confluence with the natural river that is navigable with caution up to Le Chatelet. The town fathers of this small town are to be congratulated on their provision for leisure craft. The pontoons are well maintained and the whole area is kept neat and tidy. In addition, there is an efficient supply of mains power and water, and you are under no pressure to move on - and it is all still free! The upstream moorings have the less water. The town itself is a delight, with plenty of choice shops and enough charm to occupy an average boatload for at least a couple of days. One morning I woke to the calls of a young lad with bread and croissants for sale, and the sounds of a saxophone being played, apparently to the birds, to the fish, to the river or just to himself by another lad on the pontoon - but a lad at least three generations on. Really cute.

For those want to move on, the next well-equipped stopping place at Verdun sur le Doubs could also pose a problem. It is one lock, Ecuelles 6, and 20km away. While it is just possible to moor by the tiny community of Chazelle and the small village of Ecuelles, tying up is a tricky affair and Verdun must be preferred. The central channel must be followed diligently, with no variation towards the shoal area on the left bank nor the disused old locks on the right. There is a backwater to port which must also be ignored: it goes round the Ile du Chateau which you also leave to port. In the end, it seems a really long way round the bend before the actual river navigation opens up on the left bank, just before the unmistakable road bridge. Once upon a time, there were plenty of free moorings at Verdun, but it has become so popular that a commercial undertaking has moved in.

The village itself has lots of charm and among its good eating places is one most excellent restaurant that overlooks the River Doubs, making for an evening's treat indeed. The river, which is utterly lovely, is navigable with caution up to the small village of Navilly; but while it is not a dead-end experience, it is a dead-end trip, and as such is a time-consuming digression from our main thrust.

A thrust which, in fact, takes us 25km downstream as far as Chalon sur Saone, where the other canal route, through the central canals, joins the main navigation. There is no lock between Verdun and Chalon, but there are two possible stopping points. The first is at the leisure centre of Gergy where there is a first-rate alongside pontoon and no problem of access or welcome, while the second is a small pontoon for the restaurant by Port d'Alleriot, where the welcome is just as warm. The woods nearby are also apparently attractive resting places, but there is insufficient depth to make it easy to approach either the restaurant or the banksides without great caution. No doubt many will choose the obvious option of making for Chalon sur Saone: the puissant and essential focus of the robust Burgundian domain.

Once past the junction with the Canal du Centre, Chalon becomes immediately discernible as the commercial and industrial town that it is, while the marina is no more than 3km distant. Before that, on the port hand you will pass what appears to have been at one time the beginning of a new canal cut to get rid of the bend. It is now no more than a short cut which houses at its head the marina HQ of the Chalon Yacht Club. There is no sign that actually spells out 'Keep Out', but there is very little spare space at any time in the year and I have found no one who has actually been made welcome. So, the plan is to move downstream a little to the proper marina that is situate behind the Isle St Laurent. The marina is accessible from both up and downstream routes round the island. It is important not to mistake the first channel to port once past the road bridge as this leads to a dangerous shoal area. The best approach from upstream is to tend just off centre to the left bank of the mainland, noting that the upstream point of the Isle St Laurent has a shoal that reaches well out into the river. There is no similar problem when negotiating the downstream approach to the marina.

The marina has comprehensive facilities, but many folk find its charges too high and look around for a barge or a wall to hang on to free of charge. Barges are, of course, OK once you have gained permission. The walls in Chalon are a different proposition. They are either fully occupied by barges; expected to be occupied by barges; private; devoid of any amenity to take a rope; foul just below the surface or prone to visits by 'owners' or 'officials' demanding money - sometimes with menaces. There are also vandals around the quays. Unless in extremis, best advice must be to use the marina: it has large visitors' pontoons which are fortunately obvious from both entries. In the season, particularly at week-ends, it can get very busy and they have been known to turn craft away. They also promote quite a few regattas, races and other special events throughout the season and they sometimes take over the marina lock, stock and barrel. It is possible however to phone ahead to try to arrange a booking, and the staff are generally amenable. (In contrast to many establishments, their telephone number has not changed for many years. I therefore risk giving it: 85.48.83.38.)

Chalon itself is a place of so many rich and varied experiences (especially, of course, food and drink) that it must suffice to say that a full week can be spent appreciating its many attractions - especially in the season when each week there is usually that little 'something extra' on which the French pride themselves. But for those who do not wish to be tempted by the whole Burgundian thing, the small Isle St Laurent just across the water (or the footbridge) will provide a sufficient and necessary taste to let you know have encountered the real thing.

The Saone is now into its stride as a major waterway, and barges can be frequently encountered in the main channel. Whichever exit you use from the marina, or even if you haven't stayed there at all, don't omit to look behind as you leave the Isle St Laurent for its small downstream headland is usually covered with a mass of flowers annually planted and dated in proud celebration of the one-time capital of all Burgundy. After this, you should keep well to the starboard hand. You will, of course, be navigating to the right in any case, but there is a nasty shoal and foul area in the vicinity of the Ile de la Brenne. Just over 2km further on, you pass the massive Port de Commerce. Its entrance is well-marked by red and black buoys but until you are close-to, it is not obvious exactly where the main channel is to be found. However, there is plenty of depth in the surrounding waters and seldom enough traffic to cause a problem - but it can still be a little confusing, if not off-putting for the over-anxious.

From here on, resting places need to be fairly carefully planned as some are close to one another, while others are well spread out. The first halt is at the old Gigny lock on the right bank, nearly 20km downstream from Chalon. Before it, there is a restaurant on the left bank, but the nearby quaysides are virtually impossible to use and its own pontoon is a very risky affair that I cannot recommend. The old lock-keeper's house at Gigny is now a bar/restaurant, with one of the best showers in the whole of floating France: that alone makes it worth a visit. The dangers are marked by buoys, keeping you away from underwater hazards and it is in fact straightforward to enter. Coming from upstream you pass the lock and then make a hairpin turn to enter it upstream, when the better facilities are on the port hand. Mains power and water are easily accessible, a member of the (local council) staff is usually ready to take your ropes, and the mooring fees are very modest. There are three communities nearby, none hardly bigger than a hamlet: l'Eperviere, Lampagny and the eponymous Gigny sur Saone. The closest is l'Eperviere which has a small grocery store and a camping establishment: the others offer just a little more. In the immediate vicinity it is possible to buy (real) fresh milk, butter, eggs and goats' cheese. There is no high life; but so much rural life that I try always to arrange my trips so that I can stay for at least a day or two.

Just 4km downstream is the lock Ormes 4, followed at a further 7km by one of the most charming small towns on the Saone: Tournus. There are two semi-public quays: the first downstream one is always available to leisure craft; that is, to those who get there first, for it is a popular spot. Water is available with a brilliantly long, strong new hose; but there is no mains power. The upstream quay is partly reserved for trip boats and hotel barges, all of which seem to operate erratic time-tables, so an overnight stop is not to be recommended unless you take up a berth late enough for the locks to have closed and traffic to have ceased on the stretch. Tournus has all the charms of the surrounding villages writ large, and the facilities of capital Chalon writ small. It is a positive delight of a place. What is more, all these goodies are within immediate striking distance of the moorings. These inlcude a superb cellar by an equally superb abbey and cloisters, with excellent if expensive hotels and restaurants nearby. I cannot find a single thing to say against it - as a town; but when it comes to mooring, there have been promises of improvements for years, but nothing has materialised. While it would be good to have electricity, that is not the crying need. The difficulty is that when the water level in the river is high, because of the low pitch of the stone quay, mooring can become extremely difficult and at worst impossible for some craft, dependent upon their draught and hull shape. It is also poosible to moor at the pontoon of the hotel on the opposite bank just downstream, but that is reserved for (deep-pocketed) clients.

TOURNUS TO LYON

After Tournus, it is really the 30km trek to Macon that most skippers will opt for. There are some choices en route: the River Seille is a possibility for shoal craft with no more than just over a metre draught. Developments are taking place near the Canal de Pont de Vaux which is to re-open for navigation in the near future, but in late 1994 no mooring was possible except for very small craft. There are also pontoons, each 10m long and without mains, at the small communities of Asnieres sur Saone and Vesines. There is a bar-type establishment at each, but little else. Care must be exercised when approaching the pontoons as the surrounding banksides are weed-encumbered. So the next main selection is likely to be the Big One at Macon.

Here there are two very contrasting choices for mooring. The first is the fully equipped marina just by PK83 on the right bank. When approaching, it is important to keep a central course (tending if anything, to starboard away from the headland which is silted and encumbered) into the narrow channel which leads to the marina. Facilities are comprehensive and security is good, but the town centre is a very long walk away. The marina is very busy and during the season there is a good chance that it will be full - and there is no possibility of booking ahead. Nor is there much likelihood that the marina master will come to offer you assistance. In general, you are left to find a place of your own - and if you get it wrong you may not find out until it is too late, when you will be left bereft for the night. The better fitted out berths are at the pontoons to port just after the fuel/crane quay. Those deeper into the marina are stern-to

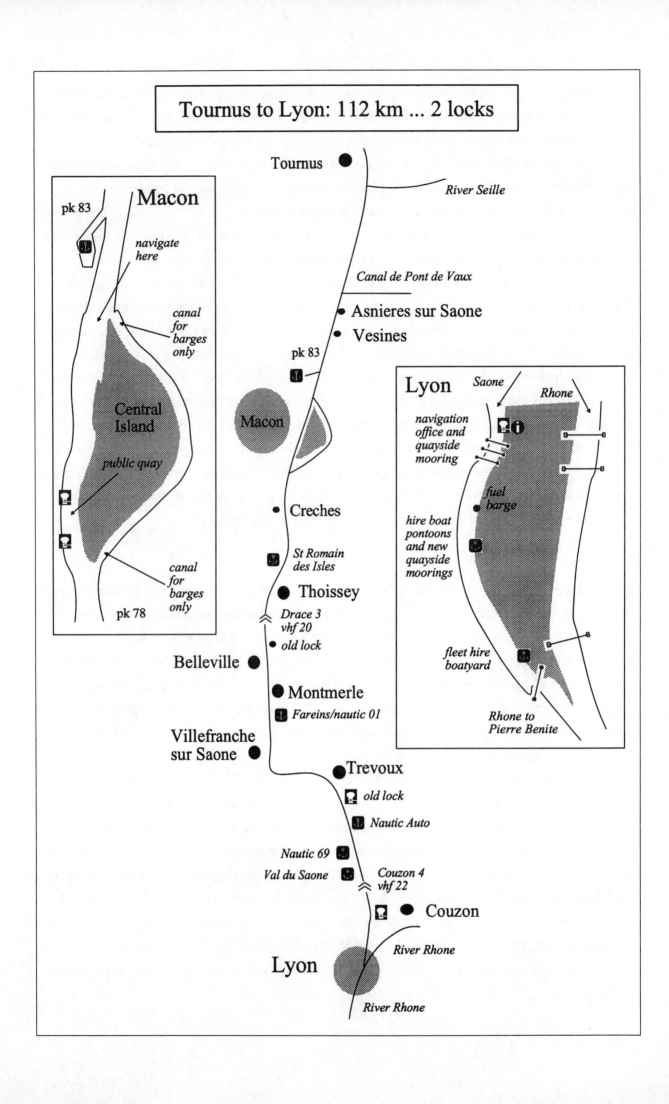

Tournus to Lyon: 112 km ... 2 locks

Tournus

River Seille

Canal de Pont de Vaux

Asnieres sur Saone

Vesines

pk 83

Macon

Creches

St Romain
des Isles

Thoissey

Drace 3
vhf 20

old lock

Belleville

Montmerle

Fareins/nautic 01

Villefranche
sur Saone

Trevoux

old lock

Nautic Auto

Nautic 69

Val du Saone

Couzon 4
vhf 22

Couzon

River Rhone

Lyon

River Rhone

Macon

pk 83

navigate
here

canal
for
barges
only

Central
Island

public quay

canal
for
barges
only

pk 78

Lyon

Saone

Rhone

navigation
office and
quayside
mooring

fuel
barge

hire boat
pontoons
and new
quayside
moorings

fleet hire
boatyard

Rhone to
Pierre Benite

and require extremely long cables and hoses if you are to connect to the mains. Prices are steep.

The second choice is the town quay. It is 3km downstream on the right bank of the main channel. Do not make the mistake of going to port at the junction with the new bypass canal. This is reserved for commercial traffic unless weather or river conditions are such that the authorities will display special traffic signals. (For example, it is not permitted to pass through Macon in fog or when the Saone is in spate.) The town quay is not well provided with mooring rings, but arrangements can be made. Neither is there power nor easy access to water, but the town centre is very close and the moorings are free. Legend has it that it is a noisy spot, prone to vandalisation and theft but this has never been my experience. In general, there is a small gathering of craft on their way to or from the Med and they act in concert to take watch while others go ashore. On balance, this mooring seems of more appeal: the sense of camaraderie is greater and the proximity of the town a bonus - especially bearing in mind not just the general excellence of the food (cooked or otherwise) but the wine and cheeses of the district.

It is 80km from Macon to Lyon, with two locks to negotiate. Stopping places present something of a dilemma, since there are quite a few small and unreliable ones but nothing of any substance until close to Lyon. The first possibility comes at a small quay known as Port Arciat, near the village of Creche sur Saone but mooring is not easy and the walls and steps are not appealing. There are red buoys to indicate the safe demarkation zones. Even if this does not deter you, the place is no more than 7km from Macon and thus of little use. A further 7km downstream is the small marina at St Romain des Iles. The few outer berths have good depth, but this decreases once inside, although some of the others can be approached with caution - and some craft are prepared to accept rafting. A drawback is that the village, which is a pleasing little spot, is accessible only at week-ends: safety precautions keep the gates securely locked.

Just over 2km down again is the Pont de Thoissey, where there are good depths at the mooring walls, but they themselves are not very inviting - and the town of Thoissey is at a good distance. Lock Drace 3 is fine when descending, but when rising the flow can become a real surge. It is wise to stay well to the rear and be prepared with stout ropes and fenders. An alternative halt to Thoissey comes immediately after Drace 3, in the old lock on the left bank. The usual problem obtains with this kind of well-protected, deep-water, free mooring: it is impossibly crowded. Occasionally here, you may be able to finagle your way through the other boats and gain permission to rest outside another: beacons mark the safe passage through the remains in the river. Six and nine kilometres further down are Belleville and Montmerle, both largish towns with old stone walls. Prohibitions against leisure craft are sometimes enforced, but at the same time improvement and refurbishment are promised. Belleville has only a very small pontoon, but the latter is reported as having a substantial one newly installed - although without services.

So it is nearly 10km to the next real possibility which has been known variously as Fareins, Nautic 01 and Villefranche Yacht Club. It is reasonably well equipped, but is not really suitable for craft with a draught in excess of 0.90m. Less than 1km down, you will come across a sign for a restaurant that advertises moorings. I have tried to get in on more than one occasion and have always encountered encumbered ground or lack of depth: it is very risky. Next, in Villefranche sur Saone itself, there are commercial quays on both sides, and usually a proliferation of out-of-work dumb barges. These make good mooring stations, but shops and other facilities are not close and the area cannot be said to have a really wholesome atmosphere. It is also possible to moor just upstream of the St Bernard bridge only 5km ahead. On again to Trevoux, where for years there is supposed to have been a very good marina and an equally good boatyard. There is a small boatyard on the right bank, with equally small and rickety pontoons just before the big bridge. Under this bridge, on the left bank, is an excellent wall with good rings - but it sports a legend requiring it to be kept vacant for trip boats. Slightly upstream of the bridge is a long stretch of quay in a fetchingly verdant spot. Depths vary greatly and it must be approached with caution, but once installed you will find it very convenient for the good range of shops in Trevoux itself.

After Trevoux, the next 8km apparently contain a great variety of mooring places but in truth, some turn out to be chances, some mischances and some just chancy. The first comes after no more than 3km and is a small pontoon on the left bank marked 'Prive/Paying'. For such legend and strange device it is indeed a youth: a very insubstantial affair. After two more kilometres is another old lock, which proclaims itself as the Port de Plaisance de l'Ecluse; once again inflated ideas are to the fore. It is true it is an old lock, but any traces of a marina facility in the normal sense of the word are vestigial, except that there is a power point. In addition, it is usually filled with barges and used by back-packers and campers of dubious aspect and demeanour. Notices saying Keep Out appear from time to time. Just near the end of the Ile Beyne (which is to starboard) is a new single pontoon, which is extremely difficult to access due to lack of depth. At one time intended for public use, it is now restricted and clearly denoted Private.

After a further kilometre, Nautic Auto will be seen on the left bank. While apparently a well-got-together enterprise, close inspection shows it to have restrictions: access, depth, room to manoeuvre, berthing space and facilities being just a few. In 1994, there was a large barge/restaurant immediately to starboard, making entrance difficult for any but the smallest craft. The proprietors claim their minimum depth to be 2.0m, but such a figure is unsupportable. After another kilometre, Nautic 69 will be seen on the right bank. Whereas Nautic Auto might have its serious drawbacks, at least the way in was clear and plain. For this establishment, the entry to whatever few pontoons may be available (namely unoccupied or unbroken) is by no means straightforward - although there are marker buoys to keep you away from most of the shoal ground. Here, they specialise in selling and servicing very fast, very swish plastic speed cruisers; and such craft get complete precedence at the well-equipped boatyard. In general, there is no shortage of water in the area surrounding the engineering shops and its own quays, but the mooring amenities at what was once the eminent and celebrated Yacht Club du Rhone are a disgrance.

The lock Couzon 4 comes after another 5km. To approach you keep to the left bank, leaving the conspicuous islands to starboard. There are good mooring possibilities in this area. If you sweet-talk the lock-keeper, he may just let you stay overnight at one of his walls. This is a very acceptable proposition, especially if you can do so downstream, thus facilitating an early get away in the morning and doing away with any need to stay in Lyon, if you have no wish to do so. There are two other choices: one before the lock on the right bank and one just after the lock on the left bank. The first is a relatively new marina that suffers from only one catch, and that is the common one of lack of depth for craft over 1.5m.

Many improvements and additions are promised - including the cleaning up of some of the (1994) rubbish tips and poor paths. The second is a public pontoon that is almost hidden by overhanging trees. There are two sections to this halt. The outer (river) and larger one is reserved for trip boats and similar, while the inner is set aside for leisure craft. It is not the most appealing or scenic of spots, but it is convenient for a good start for an early morning passage straight through Lyon.

The city of Lyon is now only about 8km away. Two features to be noted en route are the fabulous restaurant run by the master chef Paul Bocuse. It has a private pontoon that will just take two boats, but that is for paying guests - and PB runs one of the most expensive restaurants in France! The exterior colour scheme has to be seen to be believed; it could have come straight from Breughel. You will see it on the right bank just before the double bridges after the large Ile de Roy, which has traffic separation about 4km downstream. The second is yet another old lock. It is on the left bank and comes just after the next island, Ile Barbe, just another couple of kilometres along. It suffers, like many of the others, from being packed to bursting point with live-aboards, and being apparently surrounded by unsavoury folk of No Fixed Abode. Best advice is to stay back at Couzon or press on to the heart of Lyon.

After the Il Barbe, it is perhaps a bridge too far to the mooring in the heart of Lyon, but it is in fact only ten. It just seems more as you count them off in their different sizes, colours and shapes. Many have splendid names: Masaryk, Clemencau, Koenig and Bonaparte; but not all the paintwork lives up to them. The public mooring that is favoured by most Brits is just before the Navigation Office (Bureau d'Affretement) on the left bank. Neither the offices nor the quay draw attention to themselves, but they can easily be identified by the three big bridges that are sited immediately after them. There are plenty of small shops and bars close by, while the larger shopping centres are not too far away. Many skippers deem it necessary to leave a watch on board because of the terrible tales they have heard about Thieves and Vandals Lyonnaise. Some even go to the lengths of searching out a barge with a friendly owner and an unfriendly guard dog and ask permission to stay alongside overnight. I have not personally met or heard directly of any unpleasant incident.

Downstream, the fuel barge is easy to spot. It is worth investing in fuel here, not only for the obvious purpose of filling up before tackling the Rhone, but also to chat to the proprietor who is knowledgeable on most things to do with the Saone and the Rhone. Close by, on the same bank are the pontoons of the hire boat company and the recently installed length of public quay. The first are not the most approachable (literally and metaphorically) since some are frequently roped off and members of staff often quickly appear with finger-wagging gestures indicating your need to depart swiftly. The public stretch is usually pretty full. The last chance to find a mooring on the Saone comes just before the bridge known as La Mulatiere, almost on the point of confluence with the River Rhone. On the left bank again, there is a small boatyard which also has a hire boat business. When approached in the right manner and spirit, and when there is a vacancy, the owner and his doughty assistant will try to squeeze you in.

Since the first possible stop down the Rhone is Vienne, at nearly 30km distant, and the mighty works of the Pierre Benite lock must be negotiated even before that trek can begin, it is worth preparing well in advance not just your first choice or even your best preference but also your contingency plans.

CHAPTER EIGHT

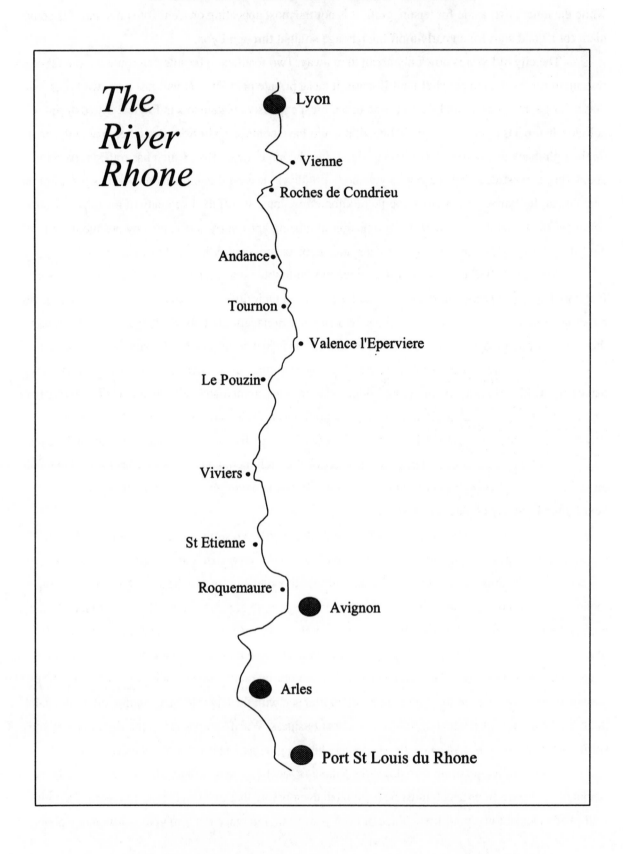

*The
River
Rhone*

Lyon

Vienne

Roches de Condrieu

Andance

Tournon

Valence l'Eperviere

Le Pouzin

Viviers

St Etienne

Roquemaure

Avignon

Arles

Port St Louis du Rhone

THE RIVER RHONE

LYON TO MONTELIMAR

After the close quarters and confines of Lyon, it will still be a while before you reach the wide open spaces of the mighty Rhone, but an excellent introduction to the proportions, size and scope of what lies ahead is to be found in your encounter with the first lock on the River Rhone: Pierre Benite. Dependent upon which lock-keeper is on duty and what sort of day he has been having, you may be permitted to pass through almost immediately after he has merely checked your boat's name through his binoculars. You may, alternatively, be held up for ages while he interrogates you about almost everything to do with yourself, your crew and your boat. As if such an inquisition were not enough, he may suffer you to wait until a far-away slow barge coming upstream has negotiated the lock.

At first sight, the locks on the Rhone appear monstrous. However, it doesn't take long to come to love them as they work so sweetly and speedily and, most of the time, are ready to pass you through without let or hindrance. In general, all ideas of leisure craft being required to travel in convoy and/or to wait up to two hours or so have disappeared. What with the smoothness of the flow and the amenity of the easy-to-tackle floating bollards, the locks on the Rhone are nothing but a delight. Don't be put off by first impressions of Pierre Benite. The enormity of the construction belies the gentleness of its operation. In any case, its magnitude is as naught when compared with the mighty (and indeed awesome to view) Bollene much further down the river. But all that lies well ahead, while immediately after Pierre Benite come over 10km of dreary straight canal, surrounded by nothing but industry, both thriving and decaying. The canal is then rejoined by the river and the aspect begins to improve slightly over the next 14km to Vienne, the first plausible/possible stopping place after Lyon. Here is little of appeal at the quayside or indeed immediately shoresides other than at the most basic level of being able to tie up and to purchase necessities. The moorings at the public quay are frequently fully occupied, often by trip boats on a boozing expedition, and there is considerable noise from the nearby busy main roads. Nevertheless, Vienne is not to be dismissed lightly. It is free; and the next mooring station is the fairly expensive marina at les Roches de Condrieu, which does not appear for another 12km after the Vaugris lock.

From Vienne onwards, it is clear you are on a major waterway. From the skipper's point of view it is extremely reassuring to know that the further you progress downstream the better the navigational marks become. Since they start off at a high level, by the time Avignon has been reached they are indeed first class and more than plentiful - not prodigal but one might very well say prodigious. Let us thank the river authorities for it.

There are two communities at Condrieu: plain (but only in name) Condrieu on the right bank is the larger of the two, while les Roches de Condrieu on the opposite bank is the one with the marina. The way in is clear and plain, and spaces for visitors are usually easy to spot. In any case, there is usually a member of staff to help you find a berth and take your ropes. The over-all facilities at the marina are very good indeed. Ample scope for shopping exists in the small village that is just a few minutes walk away. But it is Condrieu, over the bridge, that you must not fail to visit if only to experience the excellence of

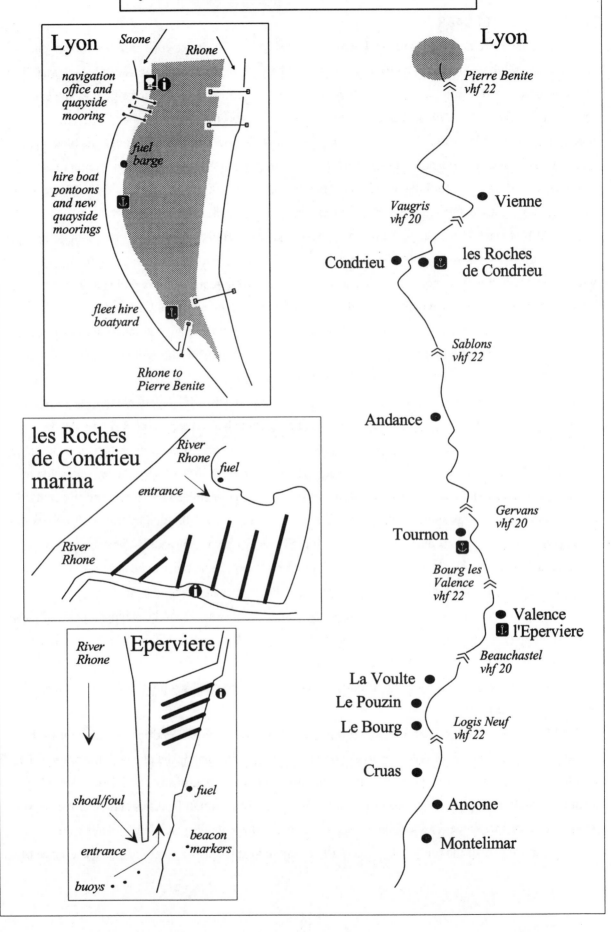

Lyon to Montelimar: 157 km ... 7 locks

Lyon

Saone
Rhone

navigation office and quayside mooring

fuel barge

hire boat pontoons and new quayside moorings

fleet hire boatyard

Rhone to Pierre Benite

les Roches de Condrieu marina

River Rhone

fuel

entrance

River Rhone

Eperviere

River Rhone

fuel

shoal/foul

entrance

beacon markers

buoys

Lyon

Pierre Benite
vhf 22

Vienne

Vaugris
vhf 20

Condrieu

les Roches
de Condrieu

Sablons
vhf 22

Andance

Gervans
vhf 20

Tournon

Bourg les
Valence
vhf 22

Valence
l'Eperviere

Beauchastel
vhf 20

La Voulte

Le Pouzin

Le Bourg

Logis Neuf
vhf 22

Cruas

Ancone

Montelimar

the local wine and cheese: both are world famous. The cheese is known as les Rigottes de Condrieu. It is made from a combination of cow's, ewe's and/or goat's milk and comes in various shapes and sizes (though mainly very small) having been steeped (or not) in white wine or oil and are to be eaten very fresh when they are soft or not so fresh when they are hard. The white wine of Condrieu is equally renowned. It is a fantastic soft and flowery wine with a great taste and a grand price tag. There is also St Joseph, a very good local red. Pay your money; take your choice - but don't miss out.

After Condrieu, while there is a possible mooring at Andance, about 7km after the Sablons lock, it is not a very attractive proposition, and it is best to consider pushing on the next 50km to Tournon, 4km after the Gervans lock. The small marina facility here is not in the same class as Condrieu (nor Valence not far downstream) and manoeuvering can be quite tricky once inside. On the plus side, the quay is well-lit at night, with the town immediately accessible with good shopping and great character. Mains power and water are laid on but the electricity supply is not completely reliable. You pay at the nearby caravan park; if 'pay' is the right word for the modest charges that are levied. That is, if they are levied at all, for more often than not, you will have to search out the manager's wife and almost demand to give her the money.

There is another reason why Tournon is a more attractive idea than Andance, since on the opposite bank are to be seen the vineyards and twin villages of Tain l'Hermitage and Crozes Hermitages. Happily there are plenty of cellars that permit liberal tasting - otherwise coffers could empty at great speed. Their wines are superb and the names Chapoutier and Jaboulet demand attention and respect all over the world.

After two such heady stays, it may come as a relief to find the marina at l'Eperviere to be a less exotic location. The well-laid out and equipped marina is just past Valence; one lock, Bourg les Valence, and just over 20km from Tournon. There are some walls and mooring posts on the way, but they are neither safe nor sound: some are also very isolated. Entry into the marina is via a buoyed channel with leading marks on shore. Not all the buoys are always on station, but I have deviated from the channel and the line of the leading marks more than somewhat without finding trouble or the bottom. Sometimes the deviation was the result of carelessness due to preoccupation with camera work when single-handed; but twice it was because I had not given enough thought to the power of the stream. Cruising merrily downstream with its assistance, I had completely under-estimated how strong it actually was. There is a shoal patch coming out from the mini-headland at the end of the jetty. Once you are close to the leading marks the actual entrance to port is plain to see and the visitors pontoons are at the far end of the marina and clearly marked. There are comprehensive facilities and the friendly and efficient staff like to practise speaking English. An excellent marina, with a swimming pool nearby and a vast supermarket not a long walk away.

The next is quite a different affair: just a small quay with large bollards very far apart. It is by the small community known as le Bourg which is immediately next to le Pouzin. You moor to a huge earthwork platform, very much like the spy-laybys used by the police on UK motorways. A modest range is to be found in le Pouzin, which is only a short walk away; but of more interest perhaps is the small bar/restaurant just across the main road. For an isolated, really small eating place, they offer a truly enlightened menu at quite light prices. A quiet, nearly rural spot where you can relax free of charge and recuperate if necessary.

After le Pouzin, the next best base comes after 33km and the two locks of Logis Neuf and Chateauneuf: it is Viviers. In between are various possible stopping places if exhaustion or accident should strike. The main ones are the small isolated quay at Cruas (where the whole area is dominated by the almost unbelievable edifice of the nuclear power station - quite sentimentally decorated); the equally isolated double mooring posts at Ancone and the public quay just past Montelimar. I must confess I was highly undelighted to find that it was quite impossible to moor in secure comfort at this last spot, since an indulgence in the famed nougat seemed not only to be an obligatory part of research, but also an enjoyable treat. I do know of real people whose craft have been burgled and vandalised here, not only when left unattended, but also when they were asleep on board. Once again, the other place, this time Viviers, has all the attractions and no serious drawback.

MONTELIMAR TO PORT ST LOUIS

The entrance to Viviers is on the 'real' Rhone on the right bank very soon after Chateauneuf lock. There is a small interior 'port' but it can be accessed only by small shoal craft. General practice is to tie up to the quay: there is a harbour master, and although he is very relaxed in his attitude to his office he will not let you moor where you will have to be moved after a couple of hours or so. Water can be obtained, but not with instant ease and there is no electricity; but there is good depth at the wall and improvements are being made all the time - if slowly. There are often large barges here, and it is understood that visitors have rights of hanging-on without quibble. Mooring is free of charge. The small town is only a short walk away and is prepossessing enough to detain even the most ardent movers-on. Since it is well-known to land travellers as an attractive resort it has a tourist office much larger than would be expected in a town of its size. Viviers is almost exactly half-way from Lyon to Port St Louis du Rhone.

The next leg is the quite amazing 22km of the Canal de Donzere Mondragon, the first (in time, fame and size) of all the river-taming schemes on the Rhone. Take care to watch out for strong cross winds which tend to gust from time to time; also for those huge barges that navigate on the 'wrong' side of the waterway without displaying their blue flag - expecting leisure craft to intuit their intentions and get out of the way. While perhaps not being able to do the former, we all instantly do the latter. This brings us to the massive lock of Bollene, with its staggering drop of 23m. It starts slowly and is always smooth but at its fastest it is fast indeed. On one occasion I logged a drop of more than a metre in 20 seconds. This is truly a place to be thankful for the excellence of the engineering and the brilliant facility of floating bollards.

There could hardly be a greater contrast between the massive contemporary works of Bollene and the miniature, old-fashioned community of our next port of call 14km on, St Etienne des Sorts. In the past, the mooring has had little to offer; with no more than a bare wall, but the last time I passed, a new pontoon was being installed. Nevertheless, it is still the village itself, with its wine co-operative and cel-

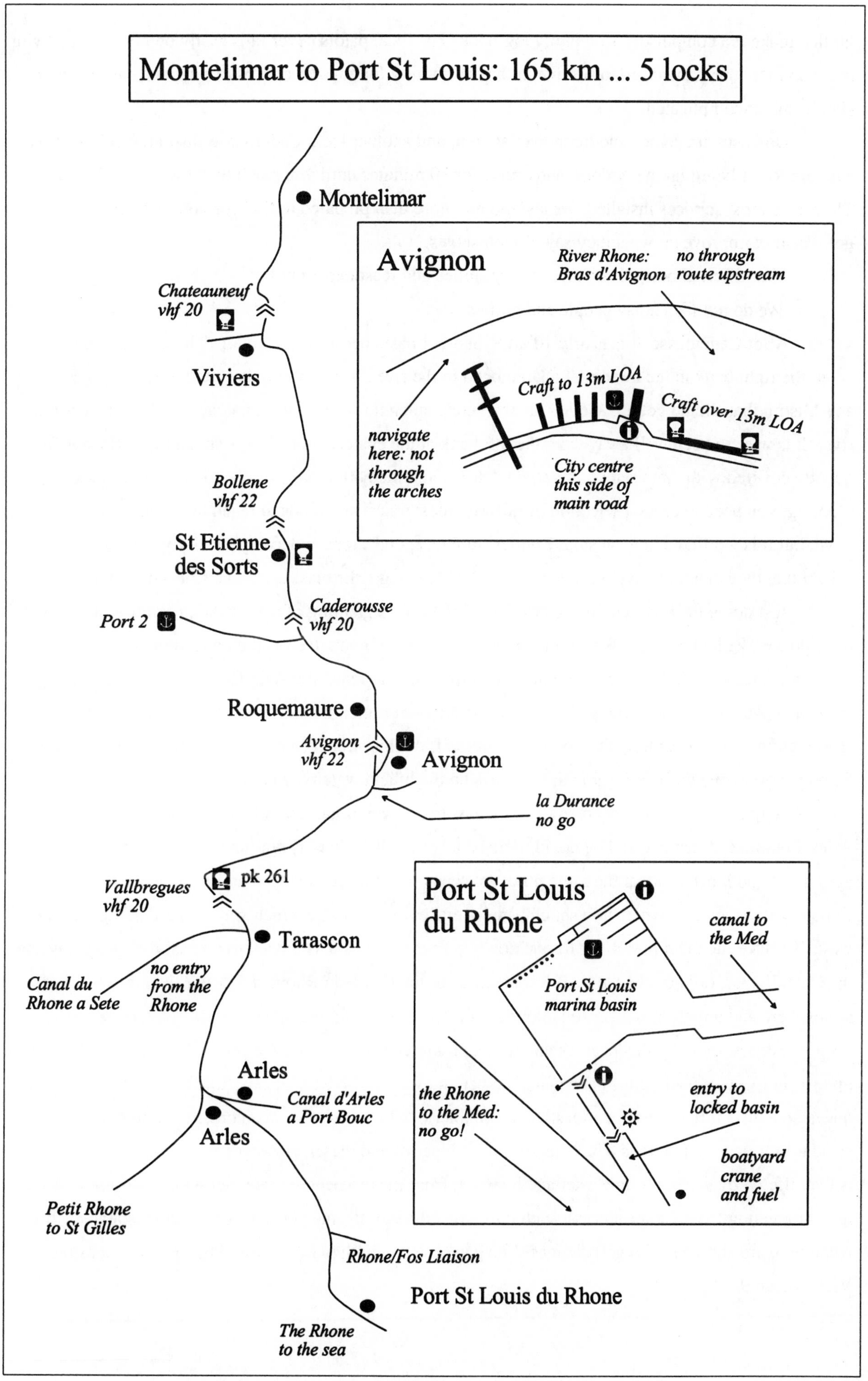

Montelimar to Port St Louis: 165 km ... 5 locks

● Montelimar

Chateauneuf vhf 20

● Viviers

Bollene vhf 22

St Etienne des Sorts ●

Caderousse vhf 20

Port 2

Roquemaure ●

Avignon vhf 22

Avignon

la Durance no go

Valbregues vhf 20 pk 261

● Tarascon

Canal du Rhone a Sete

no entry from the Rhone

Arles ●

Canal d'Arles a Port Bouc

Arles ●

Petit Rhone to St Gilles

Rhone/Fos Liaison

● Port St Louis du Rhone

The Rhone to the sea

Avignon

River Rhone: Bras d'Avignon

no through route upstream

Craft to 13m LOA

Craft over 13m LOA

navigate here: not through the arches

City centre this side of main road

Port St Louis du Rhone

canal to the Med

Port St Louis marina basin

the Rhone to the Med: no go!

entry to locked basin

boatyard crane and fuel

lar that make it a compulsory stop in my log book. The local patois never falls easily on my ears, but with perseverance I have managed to survive in the community for days on end. Shopping and eating out are simple and uncomplicated.

Downstream comes another power station, and another lock, Caderousse. Just after this lock, you can turn to starboard up the Ardoise and cruise for 30 minutes until you reach the new marina Port 2. They have most services installed already and are more than prepared to find for you what they have not got. I cannot improve on what they say of themselves:

"Our offer: almost all services, happy smiles and reasonable rates

We do not like: noisy people and parties."

After Caderousse, it is nearly 10km to another basic berth: Roquemaure. This one is really isolated on the right bank in the middle of a large bend in the river. The mooring is sound, if too exposed to any Mistral that should get up, and has an absolutely splendid view of the Chateau de l'Hers across the river. It is wise to keep well away from the left bank at the chateau's bend: it is shoal, the surface is frequently covered with large semi-submerged detritus and the bottom is severely encumbered. Back at the mooring, you need to cross a selection of railway lines, tracks and roads to reach the small mediaeval town; but it is worth the longish slog. Roquemaure has good shops and exceptionally good cellars, for it is here that they claim to have originated, over 300 years ago, the classic vintage Cotes du Rhone.

Just down the road a bit is the next lock, Avignon, signalling of course the proximity of the magnetic place. The lock is just 10km from Roquemaure and Avignon itself is then a further 7km, 2.5km of which have to be taken back upstream after a hairpin bend to reach the Avignon branch that is unnavigable at its upstream reaches. You pass a real eye-catcher en route: the old tower of Philippe le Bel. However, there is no berthing facility for leisure craft on this stretch so it is not easy to stand and stare. So on we go to one of the most popular marinas on the inland waterway circuit.

Avignon is generally deemed to be the last really well organised inland port of call (true, there is Arles, but more of that anon). Nor could there be a better place than its marina to recover from the ravages of 300 odd locks and, at the same time, get accustomed to life a la Camargue and a la Provencal. Certainly it is the place where you should finally make up your mind which way you are going: east or west. You take the main line River Rhone down to Port St Louis if you want to go east for balmy days on the Cote d'Azur; or you take the Petit Rhone down to the Canal du Rhone a Sete for the more bracing atmosphere and atmospherics of Rousillon/Languedoc. For the moment, let's rest at Avignon.

Purpose-built by the local Chamber of Commerce and Industry, Avignon's marina can take craft up to 13m LOA, and all berths have mains power and water. There are also berths for larger boats at the quayside a little further upstream, past the Capitainerie, which is situate in a converted barge. It offers all standard services and there is a fuel station for both petrol and diesel. However, the most special service is that offered by the Harbour Master and his staff, from the moment you are met with a smiling multi-lingual greeting from the reception launch until you come to pay the not low but not unreasonable (for where you are and what you get) charges. You can now pay with plastic cards. The marina listens on VHF 16 and 9.

"Sur le pont ... d'Avignon ... l'on y danse ... l'on y danse." Thus went many a classroom sing-song in my pathetic schoolboy French so many years ago. Now I know it should never have been 'sur' at all, Bien Sur; it should have been 'sous'. This little nugget came from the marina where their catchphrase is "Jetez l'ancre ... sous le pont d'Avignon." A few minutes walk from the centre, it is picturesquely situated by the Saint-Benezet bridge and blessedly so, as it were, at the foot of the Rocher des Doms and in the shade, as it were, of the everlasting arms of the Popes' Palace. There is so much in Avignon, especially in the summer, that the sounds of fairs and fetes must be likened to a siren lure - and not all of them have the character, the wiles or the wherewithal of a Ulysses ... no matter on how much of an odyssey we think we have embarked.

However, let us move on down the Rhone, giving a wide berth in every way to the well-nigh inaccessible/decrepit so-called marina at Courtine on the River (!) Durance. At PK261, just above the Vallbregues lock, there is a recently installed sound pontoon, but without services. After the lock, the ancient settlement of Tarascon takes the eye but offers no resting place. In fact, there can be heavy turbulence near the bridges where in 1994 big works were taking place. Across the river on the right bank is Beaucaire and the Canal du Rhone a Sete, but at the moment there is still no access from the river. It is promised that in a 'year or two at the most' the navigation will once again connect with the river - mainly for the convenience of leisure craft. And what a relief, nay luxury, that will be, saving the present round-the-houses route down the Petit Rhone which leaves the main river just over 10km downstream from Tarascon: we shall look at that route in the next chapter.

The great and ancient cultural centre of Arles is only 4km down from the junction, after which it will be full speed ahead (well if not quite, then at least non-stop since there is no choice) to Port St Louis. In theory, there is a sound resting place to be found in Arles at the public pontoons. In practice, the pontoons, which do house a goodly number of craft, are much occupied by live-aboards who are only too often 'unco-operative' about sharing 'their' amenities. The authorities do little to read them the riot act and even less to move them on, so they continue unrestrained in their monopoly of the best berths and the mains supplies. Never have I seen so many curtains twitched and heads ducked down as when a passing craft approaches as if in need of a berth. Sad, since this gets 'residents' (many of whom are Brits) a not necessarily deserved bad name. Additionally sad, since such remains as the Roman arena and the residual, brooding presence of Van Gogh are an irresistible magnet to many.

From here on, the Rhone is straightforward all the way down to St Louis. All you need to watch out for is the traffic at the junction of the Rhone/Fos Liaison: this canal, which is marked by tall cranes, is forbidden to leisure craft. The major traffic does not emanate from there, but from the two large and busy ferries that regularly and frequently ply across the river. They are unmistakable and in the hands of thorough professionals who will always respond to any ship's whistle signal you may employ. After the junction it is only 5km to the end ... or to the beginning, dependent upon how you want to perceive it.

The tower of St Louis on the left bank is a good mark for the port, which is hidden from view until you have opened it up. The entry is not particularly wide but causes no problem. Once you have turned in you will see the small boatyard straight ahead and to port the last short stretch of river-muddy water before the Mediterranean which takes you to the port office, the lock and the bridge.

By tradition and habit, Port St Louis, in a central position on France's Mediterranean coast, has been one of the favourite exits for those who have descended through the inland waterways of France in search of sun, blue water and even bluer skies. For many decades, that romantically named port never lived up to its namesake's magnificence, and was a place to get in and out of as quickly as possible. Its tiny basin was known to thousands as the HQ of Chantier Bayle where masts would be craned and tyre fenders jettisoned, and for many years it proffered a pretty disappointing welcome.

In addition the main section of the port was inhospitable because of the lack of decent mooring facilities, even simple posts and rings being in short supply. The 'visitors' quay was completely exposed to the worst excesses of the infamous French Mistral - an experience to be compared to that of the famous revolution and the lifting bridge that permitted access to all this glory was frequently prone to failure - for hours and days on end.

Now everything has changed. There is a new bridge, resplendent in the colours of the Med, immediately next the offices of the capitainerie and the inland waterways (VNF). In the street behind the boatyard are some shops; some market-type stalls and one small chandlery shop. But what the shop may lack in size is fully compensated for by the know-how, wisdom and friendly willingness of its proprietor. The bridge gives access to the main harbour, where, in the old Port des Pecheurs in the north east corner, there is a first-rate up-to-date marina. True, in the old days, the moorings were free, and now the marina charges standard Mediterranean rates; but that is a small price to pay for the services, security and civility that are now on offer. The bridge works on VHF Ch 12 and will open for yachts at (Gallic approximate times) 0900, 1115, 1415, 1630 and 1815. Although it may open at other times for commercial ships, yachts are not allowed through on those occasions - so don't get steamed up and cast off just because a tug is going through.

So, be it the end of the beginning or the beginning of the end, Port St Louis now welcomes visitors with open arms and a full set of amenities. The town consists in the main of one long street where shops and bars do not exactly proliferate, but where there is little in the way of everyday needs that cannot be met. Now it is an excellent Point of Departure for all parts of the East Med.

CHAPTER NINE

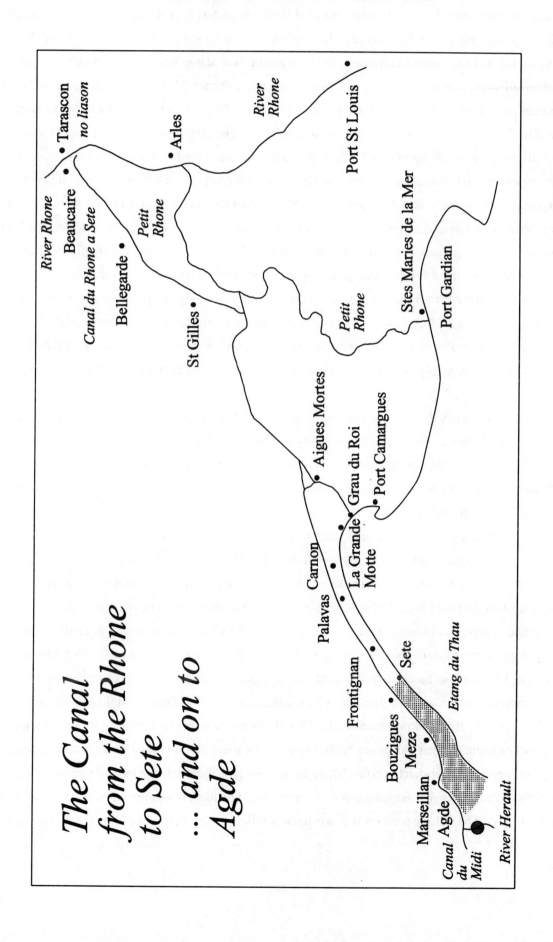

The Canal
from the Rhone
to Sete
... and on to
Agde

THE CANAL DU RHONE A SETE

ARLES TO AIGUES MORTES

Arles is the place where you must make your final choice to go east or west: the main line for Port St Louis or the Petit Rhone for the Canal du Rhone a Sete. To reach the easterly outlets, you leave the Rhone for the well-sign posted entrance to the Petit Rhone 4km above Arles. You turn gently to starboard, avoiding the headland which is silted well out into the stream. This has been the route since the closure of the exit of the Canal du Rhone a Sete at Beaucaire 20 years ago. The channel has a current of up to three knots and is well-marked by beacons and buoys. The 20 kilometres down to the Ecluse de St Gilles afford some insight into the wildlife of the Camargue although the famed black bulls, the classic white horses, the pink flamingoes, ospreys and beavers are not yet very much in evidence. It is not staggering in its scenery, but it is a closer kind of experience than has been the big river for many a long kilometre. Most of the navigation marks are pillars or posts, with only the occasional buoy to be seen. There is nowhere to moor, nor any cause to do so, but for those who are so inclined there are plenty of opportunities to anchor out of the channel: the habit of quite a few locals at week-ends in the season.

Although the Petit Rhone runs down to the sea, it has no navigable outlet. It can be cruised for a goodly part of its length, but in the end the end is dead so we must finally part company with the Rhone. In any case, the Petit Rhone from here onwards must be used only with extreme caution, and in some of its stretches is neither easily navigable nor particularly safe, particularly since it is neither beaconed nor buoyed.

Most skippers will want to make headway to the lock at St Gilles: very much a modest affair after those of the Rhone. With a rise/fall of hardly a metre, it is easy and efficient. The lock-keepers take no break for lunch and their watch-keeping on VHF is very good. If you do have to wait because of other traffic, there are well-maintained waiting posts on both sides of the lock. In no time you are once more in the quieter waters of a modest canal.

Once through the lock, it is only just over a kilometre to the junction with the actual Canal du Rhone a Sete. Straight ahead leads to Aigues Mortes while the turn to starboard goes up to Beaucaire, where the canal used to connect with the Rhone opposite Tarascon. All being well, that amenity will be opened again in the near future. We will make just a short excursion up this closed section. The first of the two main ports of call comes at the town of St Gilles, where there are now well-organised moorings, mainly stern-to immediately after the railway bridge, but with a few chances to berth alongside a little further on. The hire-boat base is improving its facilities greatly. The town has an exceptionally interesting Sunday morning market and two first-rate cellars within easy walking distance of the moorings.

Upstream, about 10km from St Gilles, there is a small community called Bellegarde. Its appellation raises expectations that it does not fulfil. There is little more than a broken down mooring surrounded by old barges and near-derelict boats. There are shopping facilities nearby, but not special enough to make this unattractive halt a stopping place. A further 5km upstream is another piece of eccentricity: the lock Nourrigier. The waiting pontoon is downstream a little way just before the bridge. It all seems very

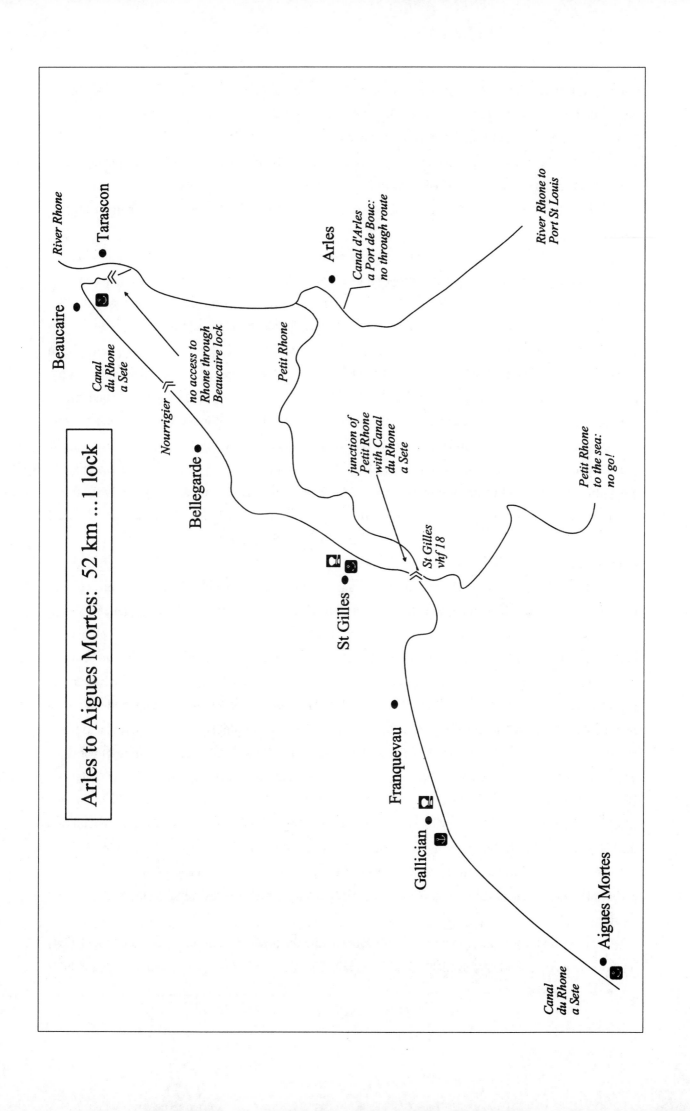

Arles to Aigues Mortes: 52 km ...1 lock

River Rhone

Tarascon

Beaucaire

Canal
du Rhone
a Sete

Nourrigier

no access to
Rhone through
Beaucaire lock

Bellegarde

Petit Rhone

Arles

Canal d'Arles
a Port de Bouc:
no through route

River Rhone to
Port St Louis

junction of
Petit Rhone
with Canal
du Rhone
a Sete

St Gilles
vhf 18

Petit Rhone
to the sea:
no go!

St Gilles

Franquevau

Gallician

Aigues Mortes

Canal
du Rhone
a Sete

much a hit and miss affair. There is a large legend that informs all prospective users that they operate the lock at their own risk. There is no choice, since there is no keeper to call except in an emergency. Instructions are laid out in full, but refer only to opening the gates. The actual process, once started, (of, course) closes the gates as well - but one is so used to closing any open set of gates before opening any other that it seems strange for it not to be mentioned. However, it works smoothly, in spite of its unexpected rise/fall of approx. 4m. You are required to enter your full details in a log book - coming and going.

From the lock it is less than 7km to Beaucaire. The canal is mainly straight and uninteresting. That is, until it closes the town, when it moves into a broken-down over-hung mode. There are two bridges before the town and there is a small boatyard (also in some disrepair) just after the first one. The main drag into Beaucaire is a long one, with a quite confusing array of quays and pontoons. In order, going upstream, they are: Connoisseur Cruisers; rowboat pontoon; boatyard; bridge; floating pontoons to starboard - fixed to port; very low bridge; stern-to buoys both sides and penultimately some quays with alongside moorings and a turning basin. After a sharp turn to starboard, you reach the bridges and the presently unused lock at the effective head of navigation. There is plenty of interest here, especially with Tarascon just across the river bridge. Shopping is easy and there are good travel connections by road and rail. The main attraction for the many full-time berth-holders is the extremely low tariff. For example, in 1994, the fees for a 9m LOA boat were something like £5 per night and £10 per week, yet only £250 for a year. Similar non-escalating rates apply at St Gilles. Low-level electricity and mains water are included, as are the services of the port staff. These last, I was told by others, are not as security conscious as they might be and winter break-ins are not uncommon.

Thus Beaucaire and St Gilles require a detour, but one that is undemanding and both offer pleasing rewards. Back on the working stretch of the Canal du Rhone a Sete, the first stopping place is near the small village of Franquevaux, where there are peaceful banks beside the bridge and a crumbling cottage. Crumbling is also the word for the banksides and mooring on the right bank, which should be used only with caution. Some food and really good wine is obtainable in the village. There is a much better fitted out mooring at Gallician, 4km along. There are two places where you can try to tie up, both on the right bank, before and after the bridge. The first mooring places are insalubrious in themselves and frequently occupied by owners of a similar disposition. The second are well-laid out, consisting of buoys and bankside stern-to arrangements and there is a good stretch of fully made up quay. There are snags: it is not possible to use all of the first buoys because of silting near the bank; and the quayside is often filled by a large converted live-aboard barge that is tied up illegally alongside, thus taking up several of the buoyed positions. Although there is a marina master, this state of affairs seems to cause him to become neither anxious nor active - perhaps because there is no charge. The upshot is that the most accessible, convenient and appealing berths are to be found at Aigues Mortes, which is just over 10km away.

The canal trip is likely to be uneventful. Just before the town, there is a by-pass canal (deviation) on the right bank, but it is not available to leisure craft. The final leg into Aigues is somewhat cluttered and there is a broken bridge to starboard to be avoided. Many craft are moored here, and some of the banksides look tempting, but they are temptations that should be resisted - or, if you are compelled, approached with extreme caution. Better to move on to the dog-leg junction which takes you first to the right (after which, straight ahead is the Canal du Rhone a Sete) and then to the left which finally exits to the sea at Grau du Roi. But first, just after the bridge, on the left bank are the public moorings. They are run by the Port Camargues authority and charges are made, but I have always found them reasonable, bearing in mind the excellence of their position and the generous provision of mains power and water points. The first moorings are stern-to with buoys, while the later ones permit alongside berthing. In addition, there is a hire boat base with pontoons at the end of the basin; and, on the opposite bank, a small boatyard whose proprietor will do almost anything to ensure a decent berth for anyone who is courageous enough to approach what looks like a dicey proposition. In fact, it is nothing of the sort: it is a first-rate small boatyard where small repairs (boat and engine) can be undertaken, but more importantly perhaps, masts can be craned.

The left-bank moorings save a long walk round the basin to get into the town, and there is a large cellar very conveniently to hand. It is just a short hop across the main road (busy) and railway lines (not busy). Aigues Mortes is a place that just asks to be explored. The ancient ambience of the old walled town, the City of Dead Waters, is everywhere: the famous Tour de Constance with its ramparts dating back to 1272 stands sentinel over all, including a splendid carousel; a very good tourist office; an excellent cellar and the pleasant old square called, predictably, the Place St Louis - where his statue stands, much danced upon and photographed.

The famous Constance Tower, was built from 1740-49 by Louis to protect those of his subjects he had managed to lure to the bleak spot by promises of tax exemption. Aigues Mortes, its name saturated with melancholy, was the scene of so many wars that they are not all commemorated. It was taken, lost and taken again by the king's troops and his opponents during the old adversarial wars between the Armagnacs and the Burgundians; the 100 years war and all the religious wars. It was the point of departure for the crusades of Louis IXth in 1248 and 1270; from which latter he never returned, succumbing to the plague in Tunis. It was also the meeting place, in 1538, of those powerful rulers, Francois the First and Charles the Fifth.

AIGUES MORTES TO FRONTIGNAN

Sooner or later it is time to quit Aigues so it is decision time again: to sea or not to sea? The Chenal Maritime, of which the mooring basin is a part, runs down to the Mediterranean at Grau du Roi. There is now a very good choice of public pontoons on the upstream side of Grau du Roi. In season they are very busy and fees are collected daily but out of season, it is much more relaxed. But in any case they provide a useful resting place from which it is easy to arrange to pass through the opening bridges to the sea. Leisure craft are permitted to moor on the downstream side only while waiting for the bridge to open. At these berths, where the fishing and ferry boats moor, up to two and three deep on both sides, there can be quite a strong current flowing out of the canal. There is often heavy traffic of trip boats, leisure ferries

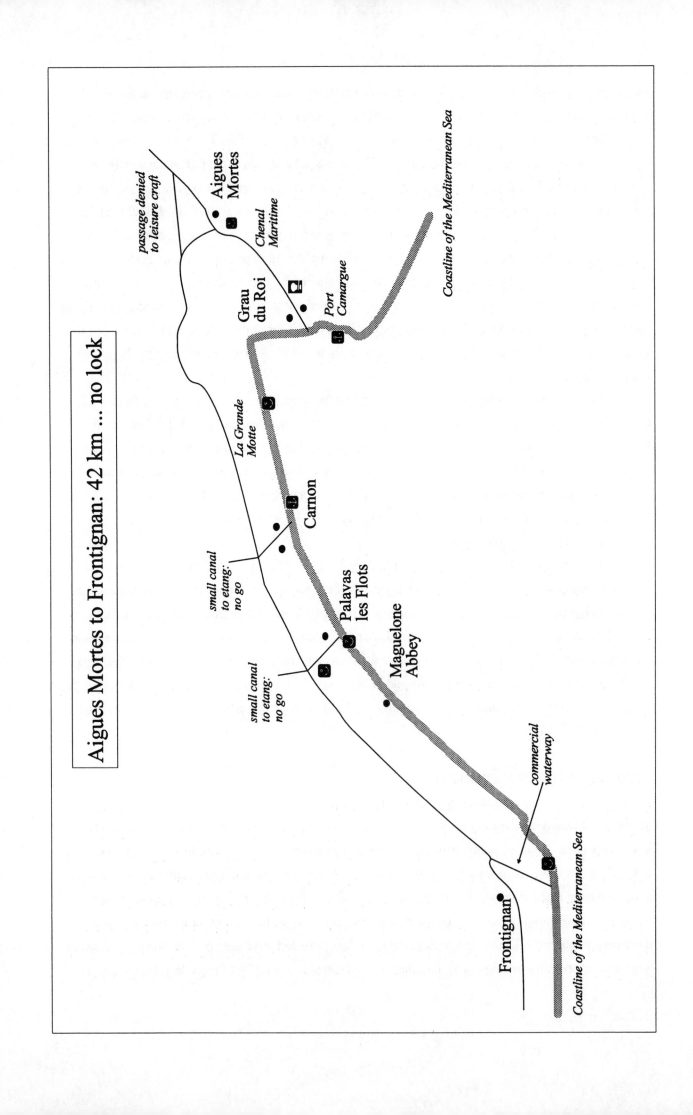

Aigues Mortes to Frontignan: 42 km ... no lock

passage denied to leisure craft

Aigues Mortes

Chenal Maritime

Grau du Roi

Port Camargue

La Grande Motte

Carnon

small canal to etang: no go

small canal to etang: no go

Palavas les Flots

Maguelone Abbey

commercial waterway

Frontignan

Coastline of the Mediterranean Sea

and fishing vessels in the 40m narrow entrance, not infrequently causing confusion and congestion. The bridge works on VHFch 73.

The word Grau is Provencal for estuary or river, and Grau du Roi has been known variously as Grau le Pelletier and Grau Napoleon. In 1806, there were only simple fishermen's cabins, but since the lighthouse was built in 1822, the place has never looked back. It is an unique fishing port rooted in the past, but not without modern services nor an eye to making a fast, albeit deserved, buck. Shopping is good here in traditional style and local manner. So is the food: a special curiosity being boiled octopus and potatoes with hot garlic mayonnaise. In addition, the Listel wines, which you pass coming down the canal, are most welcome during their boasted 300 days of sunshine a year.

Once in the open sea and away from the jetties and the prominent old lighthouse and towers, the huge buildings of La Grande Motte and Port Camargue can be seen as they stand sentinel each side of Grau du Roi. While free of all major hazards, the coast shelves and shoals hereabouts, so it can be risky trying to navigate too close in when not actually approaching the jetties. Port Camargue is swish and La Grande Motte is possessed of and by its amazing Corbusier-like architecture, the butt of many a snide remark, but both offer excellent facilities and give good value for money. It is impossible to visit La Grande Motte without viewing and then forming a view of its outstanding pyramidal form, which the inhabitants claim is unique on the coast. The project was conceived, designed and constructed all of a piece. The main buildings, decisively, perhaps even obstinately and aggressively modern in their ziggu-rat-like traps, were designed to provide maximum exposure to the sun. Critics condemn it as tawdry and heartless in human terms and cheap and 'contemporary brutish' in its architecture, calling it La Grande Grotte.

To get back to the Canal du Rhone a Sete, you turn your back on the route to the sea, return under the main bridge and then take the immediate left turn into the main canal. After a short while you will pass the new by-pass to starboard and then it is a straight run along a narrow strip between the Etang de Maugio and the sea. This continues for 10km until we reach Carnon. Halfway en route you pass La Grande Motte: it is less than a 2km walk to see the place, but the facilities for mooring here are poor, being in the main broken stakes and insubstantial pontoons. There is one small wall and the banks are in a reasonable state if you can get close enough to them. It is very quiet and pleasant, but not a guaranteed spot to find a mooring.

It is possible for craft with no more than 1m in either water or air draught to get to the sea via Carnon Plage. While there are full facilities for all kinds of craft in the marina at Carnon Plage, there is little of real assistance on the canal. In spite of legends of marina-style facilities and a nomenclature that speaks of Port de Perols and Port de Carnon, the most descriptive word for the few services and pontoons must be 'feeble'.

There is little to say about Carnon, other than that it is a popular lido for many folk from nearby Montpellier. It is one of those beach and marina resorts that exist for no other purpose than tempting crowds down to the sea in ships, and down to the beach in (or out of) bikinis. This is where La Jeunesse Doree pursue La Dolce Vita, and it has been dubbed the French Florida. It is purposeful and it works; but this particular venue has little to offer other than convenience for the sea, the sun, and the miles of sand, sand, sand.

Five kilometres on, after navigating between two etangs, de Perols/Mejean to landward and du Grec to seaward, there is another first-rate coastal marina at Palavas les Flots. Once again, however, there is little or nothing on the canal itself. However, help is at hand, on the port hand actually: by taking the seaward arm, the now dredged river/canal Lez, at the canal cross-roads known as les Quatre Canaux, you will find an absolutely splendid marina called Paul Riquet. If you have a boat with air draught not much more than 2.2m (this is dependent upon pressure and local weather conditions) and water draught of no more than 1.0m you can actually reach the sea.

There is no need to do so to gain really first-rate marina facilities. Paul Riquet is outstandingly impressive in an area where marinas are big business. For example, by the end of the 1995 season, the marina at Palavas les Flots will have been doubled in size and facilities. By many standards, it was already large: it will become huge, and the authorities claim that they have in mind it shall be the biggest and best marina in the Mediterranean.

At Paul Riquet, not only are the excellent and comprehensive amenities modern and well-cared for, but also the staff are efficient and friendly. Nothing is too much trouble; nothing is too difficult, except for some who speak little English but try very hard. It is a sophisticated set-up, with all facilities and a method of berthing at 45 degrees to the bank that makes tying up a painless process. The wooden stages are buffered by a clever scheme of tyres that afford protection to all craft, no matter what size nor from whatever angle they approach. One of the special services offered by the staff is to deliver fresh bread and croissants to your boat early in the morning, if ordered before 18.00 the day before.

The resorts and marinas at Carnon to the east and Frontignan to the west were created from nothing, while Palavas was already something decades ago. This difference is manifest not only in the architecture but also in the general flavour/savour of the places. Palavas has not yet surrendered its old, provincial character. Basically, it was a small fishing port, and like many in the area, much given to tuna sport. It became news in 1872 as the resort for the rich of Montpellier when the minor miracle, the Little Train Shuttle was opened. For many years it was the only 'civilised' beach in Languedoc Roussillon.

It retained that unique position until the massive development scheme of the 1960's, when before any kind of tourist/leisure area could even be thought of as plausible, it was necessary to drain the stagnant lagoons that had been mosquito hotbeds for centuries. After this, and much conservationist controversy about spraying, the area was rendered if not free, then less troubled by the little pests. But even now, although the area is much improved, many of us still find it essential to be well-prepared with creams and lotions for both before and after.

Palavas has a particularly eye-catching feature: the cable car that plies its trade above the river at its seaward end, thus saving folk the hike up the main street to the road bridge. On both sides of this river lie the characterful halves of the old town, which the Lez successfully divides. All the worthwhile shops are in the back streets; many of then behind closed dark doors, but which open to disclose choice goods, bits and pieces.

Palavas is one among many centres in this region that are fanatical about their Joutes Nautiques. These water jousts are famous in Languedoc Roussillon. Born of the embarkation of the St Louis crusades, they represent local folklore. Special Catalan-type craft, one in classic blue and the other in classic red, are fitted with a kind of elongated bowsprit, a for'ard out-station, on which stands a 'knight' with shield and lance. The boats are rowed ferociously towards one another by a crew of eight, and each forward lance/spear-holder attempts to shaft the other into the water. Loud and proud are the salutes: the noise of bands accompanying the cheering and jeering of the quayside crowds. Les Joutes Nautiques symbolise the spirit of this ancient port de peche in an unique and unforgettable manner.

If a quieter life is more your style, you will find an ideal spot just a couple of kilometres down the now thoroughly coastal stretch of the canal. Situate among the etangs and sandbars is the legendary Abbey/Cathedral of Maguelone, now bereft on its strange inland island. In the Middle Ages it was the port of Montpellier and is supposed to have a history going back to the 2nd Century. Certainly it is the site of a long list of religious wars. Its fortunes rose and fell with Catholics and Protestants alike, until Louis XIII lost patience entirely with the Protestant inhabitants of that time and in 1633 destroyed the defences and houses in one fell swoop. Maguelone used to be an islet, but is now permanently joined to the mainland. Today, there is only the Romanesque Cathedral, restored in the 19th Century by the family who owned the estate in which it stood. More a fortress than a church, its thick walls with only narrow openings for windows; its vast single-arched nave and housings for nearly a hundred cannon are all there is to speak of the glory that once was paramount here. Fame and fortune have returned by courtesy of the tourists to whom it is open throughout the year.

A quite different eye-catcher is the unexpected floating pedestrian bridge by the Maguelone. The operator 'drives' it from on board, looking most precarious as he swings across the canal with great panache. Usually there is no need to alert him; he is at it all the time. The inland 'port' of Frontignan is 12km from these two attractions and is itself one of the most well-known attractions in Languedoc Roussillon. The old town of Frontignan is reached by passing through more etangs on each side.

To seaward of the canal, on the Etang d'Ingril, you will observe, no doubt with interest as well as amusement the comings and goings of the unusual local fishing craft; each one is usually powered by a massive outboard - or two or three. Clearly, they are more at home in the etangs than in the open sea, but there is little in the way of Mediterranean weather that keeps these hardy souls and their small craft from venturing seaward. They leave the amateurs to go after the tuna; their own catch being almost exclusively shellfish. When they go out in the small hours in their peculiar craft and strange clothes, it is difficult to know whether they are Musselmen or Mussulmen.

It is presently a classic old small town, leaving the tourist industry for the nearby marina. Its famous Muscat makes a stop here obligatory; as do the bridge opening hours, unless you plan carefully. There are good waiting pontoons on both sides of the bridge, and the town's amenities are close by so no wait need be really tedious. The public quay is beyond the bridge: it is popular and very busy, so do not count on automatically being able to gain a place to stay, particularly at the height of the season. Perhaps the city fathers will consider improving the facilities for there is both space and demand. Shortage of good berths is not the only drawback here: the darker side of Frontignan for many is the presence of the massive refinery project of Mobil Oil Francaise. When the wind is wrong, you get a mild-to-powerful taste of the sweet-to-sickly odours from the chimneys. No perfumery this.

On the bright side is Frontignan town itself. It is an old town, on the Etang d'Ingril and the Canal du Rhone a Sete. There is very good shopping here, but nothing will lift the spirits as much as a visit to Co-operative du Muscat for a taste of the golden/amber liquid known as the Muscat de Frontignan. It is a delicious wine, deliciously strong to be taken as an aperitif or with/and/or after dessert. There is more however: you must not leave without marking (as in mark, learn and inwardly digest) the local variety of their Marcs, the powerful near-stunning brandy, also known as Grappa. A visit is a life-enhancing experience, and well worth the risk of a touch of the Mobils. After savouring the Muscat, you may feel up to scrutinising yet another church fortified against the world, with a cannon platform masquerading as a clock tower.

The new quayside and facilities at Frontignan sea marina have made a great difference. No more a small portacabin for the harbour master either and the harbour staff are among the most helpful and efficient along this stretch of coast. For those who fancy night life, there is the Cythere night club, next the loos and showers. Another improvement in the area is the new connection between the canal and the sea just before Frontignan. This removes all the previous tedium and aggravation surrounding an exit or entrance through Sete and will also tempt folk to stay longer on the canal side in old Frontignan, secure in the knowledge that the worst is all behind them - and Sete is no longer a threat.

FRONTIGNAN TO SETE

The old port of Sete is only 5 uninspiring kilometres away. At the very end and terminus of the Canal du Rhone a Sete lies the Etang du Thau; and it is decision time again. This time to Sete or not to Sete? The choices are the town itself or the various ports of call on the Etang. We'll take the port hand turn to the old settlement of Sete, one of the biggest harbours in France.

Most charts of the area, including those promulgated by the British Admiralty, show the channel to Sete marked by numerous buoys and beacons. In fact, there are just one or two poorly maintained beacons, which in any but the best weather conditions are not easy to spot. However, there is no real hazard or shortage of water in the area and the few residual beacons take you to the stone-walled entrance.

Since the Etang is a vast and exposed stretch of water, very different from the narrow enclosed canals on each side, it is much affected by winds and weather. When the mistral strikes, the short sharp waves that are generated can appear menacing. Not only that, they can become near-violent and dangerous. In addition, the spray is a combination of salt, mud, grit and sand and is difficult for standard wipers to cope with. The Etang du Thau is not a place to be cruising in inclement weather. There is another hazard: the many divers near the main channel (indeed, divers of diverse divers). Their general presence is marked by an unoccupied dinghy or small inflatable. Their particular diving patch is marked by a red buoy that is often so small that it is difficult to spot - especially in bright early morning sunlight.

Once past the end of the stone jetties at the entrance to the port, the chances are that you will

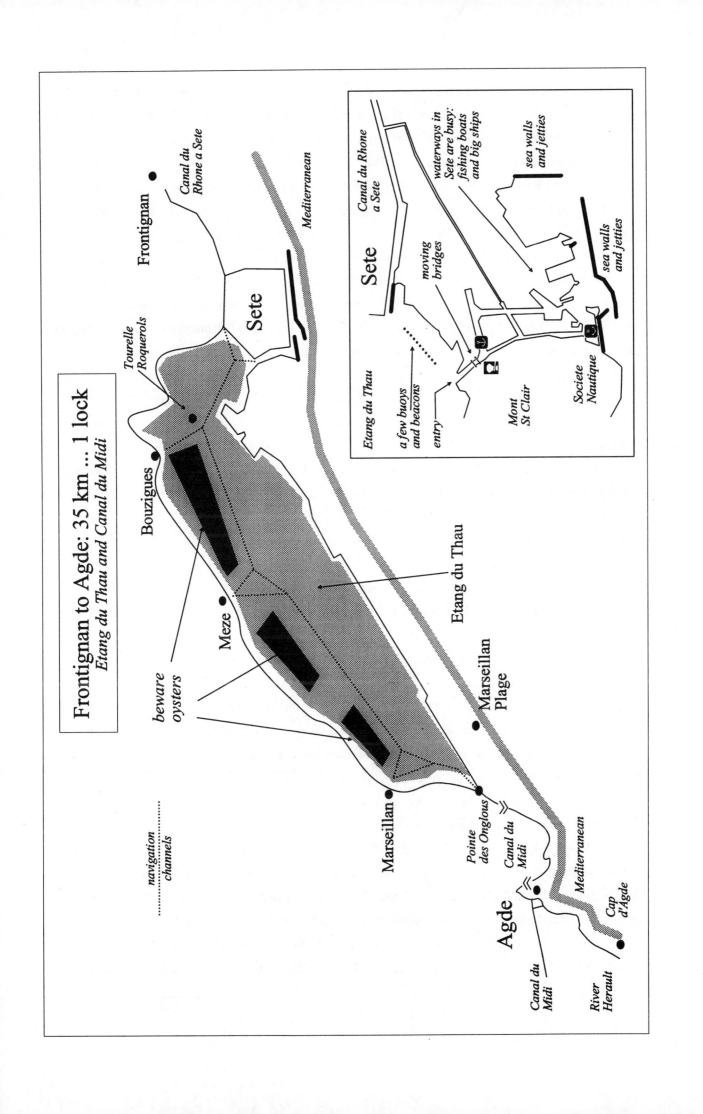

Frontignan to Agde: 35 km ... 1 lock
Etang du Thau and Canal du Midi

beware oysters

navigation channels

Frontignan

Canal du Rhone a Sete

Mediterranean

Sete

Tourelle Roquerols

Bouzigues

Meze

Marseillan

Etang du Thau

Marseillan Plage

Pointe des Onglous

Canal du Midi

Agde

Canal du Midi

River Herault

Mediterranean

Cap d'Agde

Sete inset:

Canal du Rhone a Sete

Sete

waterways in Sete are busy: fishing boats and big ships

moving bridges

sea walls and jetties

sea walls and jetties

Etang du Thau

a few buoys and beacons

entry

Mont St Clair

Societe Nautique

have to wait for the bridges to open, although craft with little air draught can move straight in. The place for this is on the port hand against the rough and tough old stone walls. There is a bar and plenty of well-informed hands (some involved with the trip boats) who will keep you instantly informed of what you may and may not do. In general, there is no problem in waiting at the quay for the bridges. It is also possible to moor there for as long as you like free of charge - provided you do so on the Etang end of the channel. There is nothing but a wall to hang on to, and the situation is exposed to funnelled weather. It is also a goodly hike into the town - but it is free and bread and grocery vans appear at irregular intervals.

After the bridges, there is a public wall to starboard and a newly installed marina ahead, just to port. The former offers a wall, fendered by huge tyres, while the latter has modern pontoons. Both give easy access to Sete and all its features/creature comforts. If you wish to proceed further into the port or on to the Yacht Club by the outer entrance there are five mobile bridges to be negotiated, and their operators suffer neither fools nor yachtsmen gladly. If you are to get through safely, you must be prompt to the minute and very fast.

Other than the Societe Nautique in the old port, there are few berths of any kind; and even fewer that have services or are secure. Most are alongside the noisiest parts of the port. Some may be gratis, but you pay a high price for that gratuity.

Fishing boats demand right of way at all times. As they say, "The Captain of the Port is not the Captain of the Port: the Fishing Mafia is king." They make life well-nigh intolerable at the Societe Nautique moorings from 0300 to 0600 and 1500 to 1800, storming in and out at full speed creating near havoc for the tied-up leisure craft. The yacht club will make you welcome and does what it can to help. Masts can be easily craned and they will advise about bridge exits and entrances.

The guide book to Sete (or as of old, Cette, Bains de Mer, Reine des Plages de la Mediterranee) gets off to a flourishing start: "Between the blue shades of the sky and the sea, Sete embroiders its lace with the streets and canals, coiling up round the Mont Saint Clair."

There are three excellent markets. The covered market in the centre of the town is open every weekday morning; on Wednesdays there is a great open-air market and on Fridays there is a quite bizarre street market near the railway station and the canals. To this, the local traders descend, as if another race from the mountains, to sell their personally tended small crops of veg; their home made breads and cheeses; their hand-raised eggs and poultry and their strange looking and stranger tasting biscuits, cakes and buns. When it comes to eating out, there is an even greater choice: hundreds of restaurants, many specialising in the regional dishes of Languedoc. Gorgeous fish dishes proliferate and Bouillabaisse can be ordered here for one - not always easy.

However, it is perhaps to wine that the final accolade and bouquet should go. Red wines abound and can be drunk abundantly, if the mood should call, at less than FF10 for a litre. However, they are at their best when chosen from the many varieties of Cotes du Roussillon and Coteaux du Languedoc. Very special indeed is the Picpoul de Pinet white wine from grapes grown by the Etang du Thau.

If you can find a peaceful mooring, Sete will no doubt delay you for days on end; but if your eyes are on the last easily accessible exit into the Mediterranean at Agde then you will avoid Sete and straightway cross the 24 square miles of the salt water lagoon, the Etang du Thau. The channel is central and the main navigational marks are the Tourelle Roquerols to the east and the white lighthouse tower at the Pointe des Onglous to the west. There is plenty of depth all around the central channels. The only areas to be avoided are the oyster beds, and these are well-marked and obvious from afar.

If you are not pressed for time, there are several pleasant stopping places in the Etang. The first is Bouzigues, straight across the water from Sete. It is a small old port devoted to shellfish with a modest space for visitors, but not for large or deep-water craft. It is a quite charming spot, and the new buildings have not destroyed its addiction to its glorious past. Meze and Marseillan, also on the inland side of the Etang, can accommodate any craft that can negotiate the canal system. Meze has at best only eight visitors' moorings, all stern-to between piles; while Marseillan has more moorings and they are alongside, but without electricity. Both harbours are welcoming and easy of access and have good facilities for visitors. Both are miniature experiences offering everything needed for a couple of days relaxation. All three harbours are up to date with their charges.

For those continuing inland to Agde, les Onglous marks the beginning of the Canal du Midi. The yacht club moorings just manage to make a feasible stopping place, but it is mainly featureless and with minimal facilities.

Once past les Onglous and actually negotiating the Canal du Midi, the shortage of depth in the channel becomes immediately apparent - a drawback that has hindered many a sea-going craft from using it for years. Although improvements to the banks and a full dredging programme have been promised for ages, the old problems of silting and decay still prevail. However a boat drawing 1.5m can make careful, cautious progress: at all times keeping to the centre of the channel; avoiding the inners of bends and approaching the banks only with doubt and suspicion.

There are two locks between the Etang and the well-known round pound at Agde. The first is 4km from les Onglous; a small lock with a rise/fall of about 1.5m. You may need to resort to firm use of the ship's whistle to gain the keeper's attention and services. The next is just over 2km and gives on to a short stretch of the River Herault, where the current can be quite strong. You stay on the river for no more than half a kilometre, after which the navigation divides: the canal goes to starboard, while the river (unnavigable at this point) is straight ahead. We are now arrived at Agde - and the virtual end of the line or the tale.

You will never need to attract the keeper's attention at Agde's round lock, for it is an extremely busy junction, with its three gates that permit access to and from the Canal du Midi for the Garonne and the Gironde, and the River Herault for the sea. You may, however, have to wait both inside and out, for the machinations take a long time and the banksides are quite shallow in places. You may also need to take prompt action once inside: the lock can get very full and you may need to fend off other craft, for the lock is often used by those enjoying their first days aboard.

For the Canal du Midi you take the exit straight ahead, but we leave by the gates on the port hand to use the short unnamed canal stretch to the River Herault and then the sea. There is usually plenty of depth in this short leg which soon opens out into the main river. There are plenty of small spaces at the walls and a number of pontoons where, after discriminating selection and delicate negotiation a mooring can be arranged. There is little officialdom or formality on the town stretch of the river and there are good facilities for repairs and craning masts.

Agde, pronounced as in Magdalene, was founded by the Greeks as far back as 2,500 BC. It was among the first of their colonies and is one of the oldest towns in France. Its name was originally, Agathe, meaning the Good Place. This was an unlikely concept since it is dominated by Mont St Loup, a volcanic mountain from which black basilic lava came, eventually being used for many of the town's buildings.

This ancient church of St Etienne is yet another example of the fortified variety that resembles a military fort almost as much as a place of religious worship. With walls over two metres thick, it was built in the 12th century, to replace the previous church which was probably first laid down in the 9th century. It was much refurbished in the 17th and 19th centuries. Its darkly sombre walls are crowned with crenallations and machicoulis: these enabled enemies of the town to be bombarded from above and so routed in the name of God, always a staunch ally. Supporting the warlike image is the huge edifice, built like the defensive keep of a warlord's castle, and purporting to be a simple clock tower. Back from the river's edge, near the Rue de la Republique, is the Musee Agathois, based in a Renaissance hotel in the old quarter. Founded privately, it houses a vast collection devoted to local archaeology, history, culture and Agde's life at large.

Town life is now almost entirely based on the seasonal tourist industry. Not only does it attract by regular and regularly packed bus services, crowds of folk from Cap d'Agde, but even more crowds from the nearby naturist resort of Port Ambonne. The town is extremely pleasant by the river, and there are some intriguing back streets. While some of the market stalls and shops still sell straight goods, you will find it difficult to avoid the all-pervading displays of tourist trappery.

There are now two choices: to moor on the Herault in Agde, or to move downstream to the Grau d'Agde where the river meets the Mediterranean, and where the marina at Cap d'Agde is just 4km to the east. It is a vast leisure enterprise with all facilities - including the bonus of a large avant port where many folk anchor for free. Cap d'Agde marina is one of the largest on the Med, but it manages to keep itself within decent physical and social bounds. It has all the services and facilities you expect of a well-run, modern marina, with an excellent variety of shops and restaurants. Choice is no problem. Extras are the underwater museum for those wanting a quiet introspective break and the merry acres of Aqualand, for those with excess energy and a penchant for water sports.

Between them, the River Herault and the town of Agde, and the sea-fresh marina at Cap d'Agde offer such contrasting experiences that it is difficult to think of a happier end or a better beginning for a cruise between The English Channel and the French Mediterranean.

INDEX